THE BUTCHER'S TALE

North Sea

Norwich
1150

ENGLAND

LONDON

GERMA

Xanten
1891

Neuenhoven
1834

Dormagen
1819

Weissensee
1303

Fulda
1235

Oberwesel
1287

Mainz
1283

PARIS

Weissenburg
1270

Pforzheim
1267

Regensburg
1476

Endingen
1470

Überlingen
1331

Munich
1285

FRANCE

Ravensburg
1429

Bern
1294

Judenstein
Chapel
1670

SWITZERLAND

Trent
1475

ITALY

Valréas
1237

Chazaud

Ritual-murder accusations throughout history

THE BUTCHER'S TALE

Murder and Anti-Semitism in a German Town

Helmut Walser Smith

W. W. NORTON & COMPANY

New York and London

Title page art: Postcard of Konitz, circa 1900

For information about permission to reproduce selections from this book, write to
Permissions, W. W. Norton & Company, Inc., 500 Fifth Avenue, New York, NY 10110

The text of this book is composed in Horley Oldstyle MT Light
with the display set in Fairfield LH Swash Italic and Copperplate
Composition by Gina Webster
Manufacturing by the Haddon Craftsmen, Inc.
Book design by Mary A. Wirth
Production manager: Julia Druskin

LIBRARY OF CONGRESS CATALOGING-IN-PUBLICATION DATA
Smith, Helmut Walser, 1962–
    The butcher's tale : murder and anti-semitism in a German town / Helmut Walser
Smith.
      p. ; cm.
    Includes bibliographical references (p.) and index.
    ISBN 0-393-05098-X
    1. Antisemitism—Germany—Konitz. 2. Blood accusation—Germany—Konitz.
3. Trials (Murder)—Germany—Konitz. 4. Konitz (Germany)—Ethnic relations.
I. Title.

DS146.G4 S57 2002
305.892'404382—dc21   2002022883

W. W. Norton & Company, Inc., 500 Fifth Avenue, New York, N.Y. 10110
www.wwnorton.com

W. W. Norton & Company Ltd., Castle House, 75/76 Wells Street, London W1T 3QT

1   2   3   4   5   6   7   8   9   0

For Meike

"Not until the hills are all flat . . ."

Contents

Acknowledgments

When you write, it's a good idea to have a map of where you're going. When I started this project, I had such a map. But somewhere along the line its bearings and markers ceased to make sense; that's when the fun began, and that's when I came to depend, more than ever, on the advice, help, and counsel of friends and colleagues.

Christhard Hoffmann first suggested that I pursue the story and convinced me to stay with it when prudence would have suggested otherwise. If it were not for him, this story would still be in my desk drawer. Christoph Nonn, who has written an important article on the Konitz case, offered valuable criticism at an early stage as well as insight and encouragement. Christoph is also writing a larger work on Konitz, and readers who are interested in how differently two historians can approach the same topic should consult his work as well.

In the initial stages of writing, the searching questions and criticisms of three friends—Margaret Lavinia Anderson, Michael Bess, and James Epstein—forced me to reconsider my assumptions and, in a sense, to start all over again, for which I am grateful. In the course of subsequent writing, I benefited enormously from the discussions about the case with friends and colleagues on both sides of the Atlantic, including Werner Bergmann, Chris Clark, Paul Freedman, Peter and Ruth Gay, Pieter Judson (and his wonderful students at Swarthmore), Christian Jansen (who organized a forum at the Deutsche Historikertag in Aachen to present the work), Thomas Mergel, Jim Retallack, Marianne Sedlmeier (who more than feigned interest), Henry A. Turner, Siegfried Weichlein (who explained to me why Aristotle is important to the story), and Mieczyslaw Wojciechowski.

Discussions with friends at Vanderbilt, including Frank Wicslo, Margo Todd, Matt Ramsey, Rebecca Plant, Jose Medina (who saved me from a philosophical blunder), Jane Landers, Adrienne Lerner, Cheryl Hudson, Joel Harrington, Ed Harcourt, Katie Crawford, Beth Conklin, and Tycho de Boer, also shaped the manuscript. Bill Caffero, our medieval historian, patiently read, and reread, the chapter on the historical origins of ritual murder. Collectively, their suggestions have helped me a great deal.

I shamelessly assigned an early draft of this book to my undergraduate students in a class on the Holocaust and to my graduate students in a class on historical methods. Fortunately, my students did not shy from suggesting to their professor how he ought to improve his manuscript; one of them, Emily White, even took a red pen to my stylistic infelicities. At Vanderbilt, I have also received help in other ways. Mona Fredrick, the executive director of the Robert Penn Warren Center for the Humanities, and her assistant, Sheri Willis, got me through the tribulations of a different book, thus allowing me time to work on this one. Lori Cohen, our administrative assistant in the history department, read chapters, charted graphs, and helped me in many other ways; as always, she has been wonderful to work with.

In the course of my research, I have also come to depend on the generosity of friends. In Berlin, Ulrike Baureithel and Christian Jansen have always helped me find a roof for short stays, and I am grateful to them for this and for our wonderful conversations. In the Polish city of Torun, Natalia Mielczarek, Lydia Smentek, and Andy Hess opened their home to me, and with their effusive hospitality helped me through the logistical difficulties of my research stay in Poland. In Chojnice (Konitz) itself, I was fortunate to have met Tomasz Myszka, who talked with me about the history of his hometown, showed me around, and eagerly read early drafts of the manuscript.

I am also grateful for the help of archivists and librarians in the United States, Germany, and Poland. The main holdings concerning the case are in the Geheimes Staatsarchiv Preussischer Kulturbesitz in Berlin-Dahlem, and I would like to thank Peter Letkemann and the staff of that archive for their help. I also found valuable documents in the Archiv Panstwowe in Bydgoszcz, in the Museum of Local History and Ethnography in Chojnice, the Brandenburgisches Landeshauptarchiv in Potsdam, and in the Family History Library of the Church of Jesus Christ of Latter-Day Saints. The staffs of a number of libraries, including the University Library of NCU (Nicholas Copernicus University in Torun), the Staatsbibliothek Berlin, the Klau Library of the Hebrew Union College in Cincinnati, and the Jean and Alexander Heard Library at Vanderbilt, were immensely helpful. Special thanks to Jim Toplon and Marilyn Pilley, of Vanderbilt's interlibrary loan office, who went out of their way to track down obscure pamphlets for me.

I am also happy to thank my friends at the Kim Dayani Center at Vanderbilt. Writing in the tenth century, the scribe Brother Leo of Novara complained that while three fingers write, the back is bent, the ribs sink into the stomach, and the whole body suffers. These days we have it easier, but the business of writing still requires long hours, in my case standing, before our keyboards. Moreover, poor brother Leo did not have Carmen Arab, Cassaundra Huskey, and Karen Dyer (and Karen's smiling seniors and hugely funny Tuesday afternoon sculpting class), who watched out for me, joked with me, listened to my odd stories, endured my music, and in the course of things kept me, and my back, from coming further undone.

The book underwent substantial transformations in the hands of Bob Weil and his assistant, Jason Baskin, two wonderful editors at W. W. Norton. Bob suggested substantial revisions, the kind that change the whole tone of books, while Jason poured his prodigious intelligence into my sentences and taught me, all over again, a lot about writing.

Finally, I thank my wife, Meike Werner, partner in all things that matter. For the past three years, she has listened to the stories of *The Butcher's Tale* and read drafts of chapters; she has told me when it was not good enough and when it was, and she has shared her life, patience, and love with me.

THE BUTCHER'S TALE

*Alleyway between the houses of Adolph Lewy and
Gustav Hoffmann. The white cross on the left marks
the door through which the Lewys allegedly emerged
from their cellar with the torso of Ernst Winter.*

Prologue

The greater part of historical and natural phenomena
are not simple, or not simple in the way we would like.
—PRIMO LEVI

When all is said and done, a single word,
"understanding," is the beacon light of our studies
—MARC BLOCH

A murder occurred on a Sunday night, March 11, 1900, in Konitz, a small town on the eastern reaches of the German Empire in what is now Poland. At first no one noticed that something was amiss. But then, two days later, the first body parts began to surface. They had been severed with a saw and sliced with a knife and then wrapped in packing paper and distributed, the upper torso here, the left arm there, throughout the town. The details of the murder unsettled the local population, but so too did the growing clamor of anti-Semitic accusations. A deafening chorus of voices charged the Jews with the murder.

> The Jews slaughtered a Christian
> Not far from the temple of Moses.
> They sowed him in a sack
> And brought him to the lake.
> For them it was a blameless deed.[1]

The accusations, hurled by neighbor against neighbor, centered on an elaborate story, the butcher's tale, which drew from the ancient blood libel: that every year at Passover, Jews ritually slaughter Christian children and use their blood to bake matzo. The Jews had planned the ritual murder long in advance, ran the refrain; the Jews needed Christian blood, the people repeated. Many years later the expressionist writer Ernst Toller still remembered the shrill reverberation in his own hometown some fifty miles away. "The Jews in Konitz have slaughtered a Christian boy," his schoolmates called after him, "and have baked the Matzo in blood."[2]

Charges of ritual murder quickly led to violence, at first sporadic, then increasing in intensity, finally culminating in a series of major anti-Semitic riots. For the Jews of Konitz, their peaceful hometown had suddenly became a perilous place, "a war zone" where they "hardly dared leave their house."[3] Local officials were alarmed as well. Fearing that they could not control the riots, they called in the Prussian army to restore order and protect the Jews, who numbered just over three hundred men, women, and children in a town of ten thousand. As the army arrived in the region, the otherwise obedient West Prussian citizens stoned the troops, denouncing the men in spiked helmets as a "Jewish defense force." "Had the soldiers not arrived," a Jewish denizen recalled, "they would have torn us from our bed at night."[4]

The anti-Semitic violence of Konitz in 1900, we now know, augured a calamity of altogether different proportions, in which the state, far from protecting Jews, pursued and nearly achieved their annihilation. Forty years after the rioters in Konitz shouted, "Beat the Jews to death," a modern government, supported by a cast of willing executioners and ordinary men, did precisely that: first during the state-ordered, nationwide pogrom, *Kristallnacht* of November 9, 1938, in which shop windows were smashed, synagogues burned, and Jews beaten or killed; then with special killing units, the *Einsatzgruppen* and the police units, which during the war descended with unheard-of savagery on Jewish towns and villages in eastern Europe; and then, almost finally, with the industrial methods, at first primitive, later increasingly sophisticated, that made the extermination camps—Chelmno, Belzec, Sobibor, Treblinka, Majdanek, and Auschwitz—into factories of death.

For the Germans of 1900, however, Auschwitz was literally unthinkable. The claim that within half a century their country would start two world wars and attempt to annihilate a people, some of whom were their neighbors, would surely have stretched their credulity and aroused their indignation. Their present, like ours, was contradictory and contingent—marked as much by the possibilities of hopeful development as by the portentous signs of calamity. As Peter Gay reminds us about Jews and other Germans of this time, their future seemed "anything but a chamber of potential horrors."[5]

By 1900, Germans had already left behind the stern authoritarianism of Otto von Bismarck, though they still venerated the Iron Chancellor, who had stepped down from the helm in 1890, and had passed away on his Pomeranian estate in 1898. Bismarck's departure opened the way for the more ambitious and unpredictable rule of Kaiser Wilhelm II, whom Bismarck once likened to a helium balloon that one constantly had to rein in. Flanked by his aristocratic entourage, the young kaiser increasingly overshadowed the mediocre chancellors who succeeded Bismarck. In the Wilhelmine era, as the period since 1890 came to be called, the kaiser watched over a system of "monarchical constitutionalism," which gave modern form to Immanuel Kant's famous characterization of Prussian politics: "Argue as much as you like and about whatever you like, but obey!" The crown controlled the army and foreign policy and safeguarded law and order at home. The chancellor answered to the kaiser, not to the German parliament, the Reichstag. Yet the Reichstag, elected by universal manhood suffrage, determined taxes and tariffs, and this meant that chancellors could not easily govern without it. Even though Germany was not a beacon of democracy, the existence of the Reichstag nevertheless ensured that Germans, and their politicians, practiced democracy, and, as the historian Margaret Lavinia Anderson has convincingly argued, they were getting better at it.[6] The political party with the most delegates in the Reichstag, the Catholic Center, vigilantly guarded the constitution, while the most popular party, the Social Democrats, urged progressive reform, including women's suffrage.

The effect of this democratization, however tentative, was palpable. By 1900, the power of feudal lords and imperious employers seemed on the wane, and authoritarian solutions to political deadlock, such as outlawing political parties and repealing universal suffrage, were no longer self-evidently in the offing. Instead, a new and modern civil code cemented the rights of citizens, including Jews, and progressive measures, such as voting booths and ballot envelopes, would soon ensure secrecy in elections. In other areas, too, Germany hardly appeared destined for a malignant future. After intermittent bouts of depression between 1873 and 1896, the economy had recovered and by 1900 seemed robust. By the turn of the century, Germans were everywhere involved in civic organizations: life-reform movements, beneficent societies, patriotic leagues, and recreational clubs. Often boisterous, sometimes chauvinistic, at times exclusive, these organizations nevertheless attested to the pervasiveness of the public sphere. The general education of the population also gave cause for optimism. In 1900, Germans counted among the most literate people in the world, with literacy rates in the range of those found in the United States today. Their primary and secondary schools were widely admired—if also feared because of their discipline—and their universities attracted students from all over Europe, including Russia, as well as from the United States. W. E. B. Du Bois, for example, welcomed the German universities as havens from the racist constraints in the educational system of his native country. Finally, German scientists distinguished themselves with great discoveries, honored in the first two decades of the twentieth century with more Nobel Prizes than most other major countries combined.[7]

"Past is prologue," Antonio tells Sebastian in *The Tempest*: subsequent acts had yet to be written, and no one could know how events were to unfold.

Sensitive spirits, some historians rightly point out, already discerned something of an impending doom in those years. Admirers of the playwright Henrik Ibsen talked about "the demonic character of our age," and critics, the philosopher Friedrich Nietzsche most pointedly among them, saw anti-Semitism as dyed deep into the fabric of what it meant to be German. The problem of anti-Semitism, its origins and persistence, also haunted the imagination of men like Aby Warburg, the brilliant art historian and scion of a wealthy Jewish banking family in Hamburg. Of the events of the times, it was the ritual-murder case in Konitz that drew his particular attention and inspired his reflections on the plight of Jews in an enlightened society intermittently punctured by the pointed awls of the atavistic.[8]

Warburg framed the problem of anti-Semitism in a way that has resonance for us as well. How do we understand prejudice, hatred, and violence in the context of modern societies, like our own, among people much like ourselves, among men and women who lived, not in dark times, but in an era when the balance of opinion was against the all-too-open expression of hatred?

This is not the only, or even the most popular, way of seeing the problem. In his immensely successful book, *Hitler's Willing Executioners*, Daniel J. Goldhagen described Germans who lived in the Third Reich as belonging to "a radically different culture" and the study of them as "disembarking on unknown shores."[9] The anti-Semitism of the Third Reich, he argued, was already anchored in the Second Reich, a society permeated by "eliminationist anti-Semitism." Yet his critics rightly point out that in France during and after the Dreyfus affair, anti-Semitism was worse still; that in Russia murderous pogroms blotted the landscape with blood; and that in turn-of-the-century Germany, by contrast, political anti-Semitism had already ebbed, and other kinds of anti-Semitism were increasingly confined to the estuaries of social snobbery and the backwaters of the ideological fringe. World War I and the Weimar Republic changed things, to be sure. But in the final analysis Hitler came from the fringe, not the center, and it is from the ideas of this fringe, the radical nationalist milieu, that the coming disaster derived its ideological dynamic.

The Konitz case allows us to pursue a single, exemplary episode, cameo history, if you will: it neither tells us what all Christians in Germany thought about Jews nor explains whether Germany was already on a track to destruction. Yet the focus on the Konitz case reveals something that both Goldhagen and his critics overlook, and that something I would call here "process."

Process is what makes latent anti-Semitism manifest, transforming private enmity and neighborly disputes into the blood-stained canvases of persecutory landscapes. In one context, the whispers of rumor and the wages of private malice fall on heedless ears; in another, they unleash a murderous dynamic. The preexistence of anti-Semitism, nationalism, or racism influences outcomes, but the outcome cannot be fully understood by a static measure of attitudes, anti-Semitic or otherwise. Looking at the process, we see historical forces converging: how local enmities become potent symbols resonating with larger antagonisms; how spiteful stories and tavern tales are elevated to public spectacle; and how these tales conform to a preexisting pattern of political and religious beliefs. We can also see how the accusations shift relations of power and support political agendas, and how people caught up in the resulting dynamic come to believe in the objective truth of their own lies.

The uprising in Konitz, the most severe outbreak of anti-Semitic violence in Wilhelmine Germany, allows us to see historical process at work.[10] By training our sights on patterns of anti-Semitism at the local level, we can re-create, as Shulamit Volkov once put it, "the unique environment" in which anti-Semitism flourished.[11] Save for scholars who have analyzed anti-Semitism in the metropolitan centers, historians have tended to eschew small-scale, high-resolution investigations.[12] Instead, the vast and by now sophisticated scholarship on German anti-Semitism has typically focused either on the ideas of prominent anti-Semites, on the anti-Semitism of a particular group or institution, or on anti-Semitic politics.[13] But important as such studies are, they do not show us how, among myriad influences, anti-Semitism became part of the warp and woof of everyday life. At the local level, we can see these things with greater precision than is often possible in a general study.[14] And we can see the truth and the past, in the words of the Polish-American writer

Eva Hoffmann, as "more striated, textured, and many-sided."[15]

More than six decades after the events in Konitz occurred, I was born in a small town in Germany and grew up in a small town in the United States—both places roughly the same size as Konitz. I thought I understood something of how, within narrow confines, good men and women could become angry and vengeful and turn on their neighbors. Yet, despite having also studied for many years the long history of German anti-Semitism, I was not fully prepared for the extent of prejudice that pulsed through the Christian community of Konitz. I was able to trace the abundance of rumor and malice in this town because of the remarkable archival legacy of the unsolved murder. The notes of the district attorney, along with reports of the county official (*Landrat*) and the trial records of people charged with perjury, became pieces of old x-ray slides, which, when put back together, rendered transparent a more complete picture than even the people of the town themselves saw. Remarkably, we can re-create the various pressures operating in a small German town in the throes of a murder investigation and the tumult of anti-Semitic violence. We can see how stories were manufactured, who told them, and why. And we can analyze the violence, a ritual in its own right.

Now we can begin to see anti-Semitism at work. Sometimes, as we know, anti-Semitism remains abstract. In earlier eras, as well as today, people talked about "the Jews." In Konitz, however, anti-Semitism became painfully concrete, as Christians denounced the Jews they knew. In a way hitherto impossible, we can hear the voices, follow the denunciations, and re-create the relationships, one neighbor to the next. Soon, a pattern emerges, and with this a process: of a small-town Christian community redefining itself, breaking bonds, and turning neighbors into strangers.

Finally, the documents presented in the story of *The Butcher's Tale* allow us to consider the murder case anew and to discern how a gallery of prejudices—about Jews, class, sexuality, and the criminal mind—skewed the investigation, possibly blinding both the police and the people to the identity, and the whereabouts, of the real killer among them.

Portrait of Ernst Winter.

CHAPTER ONE

Murder and Retribution

. . . a population with a penchant for brutality.[1]

—BARON KARL VON HORN,
president of the district of Marienwerder,
on the people of Konitz

We're persecuted in the most civilized languages.

—THE CHARACTER JULIUS OSTROVSKY
in Bernard Malamud's The Fixer

I

It was a cold Tuesday afternoon in the second week of March; the birch trees that lined the Flatow Allee remained bare after a long winter, the grasses still frozen and brown, worn and without life.[2] Johannes Winter and his friend Hermann Lange, a baker, walked over to the basin of the lake, where the ice had melted. In the knee-deep frigid water, they saw a package, carefully sown shut and wrapped in strong packing paper. Lange fished out the package with a stick, and the two men tore off the paper and ripped open the sackcloth.

"My God, this is my son," Johannes Winter cried out.[3] It was, however, only an upper torso—naked, pale white, cut off at the bottom of the ribs. It released a sickening combination of water and blood as the two men heaved it to shore.[4]

News of this discovery flashed through the streets and taverns of Konitz, a somnolent West Prussian town where such grisly events were confined to works of fiction. Full of anticipation, the people gathered at the edge of the lake, the Mönchsee, and stared spellbound as Lange and Johannes Winter searched among the water grasses for more remains. The crowd did not have to wait for long. Almost immediately, the two men found another package. It was the lower torso—disemboweled, but with an intestinal sliver, the buttocks, and the penis still attached.

There could be no mistake, Johannes Winter insisted. His son—missing since Sunday, March 11—was a tall, strong, robust eighteen-year-old, a swimmer, a gymnast, a dancer, and a bicycle rider.[5] The police, the fire department, and a number of hunters with dogs now commenced a search for clues and body parts.[6] They combed the woods on the outskirts of town.[7] They made inquiries and investigated people's houses. But it was not until Thursday, March 15, that a limb was found. In the early morning hours, the full white moon faint on the horizon, a fourteen-year-old boy stumbled upon the right arm in back of the small door flanking the main portal of the Protestant cemetery. The arm rested on top of a light blanket of snow that had fallen just the night before, and leading up to the arm were footprints—small steps, a narrow gait.[8] Five days later—almost a week after Lange and Winter's original discovery—another person found a left thigh, again in the local lake.[9]

"The four body parts fit exactly together and come from one and the same human body," the chief prosecutor, Max Settegast, reported.[10] A comparison of the boy's last meal (soup, pork, potatoes, and sour cucumbers) with the vomit traces in the alimentary canal conclusively proved the father right. The body parts belonged to his son, Ernst Winter.[11]

Not much is known about Ernst Winter. Born in 1881 in Prechlau, a village about twelve miles northwest of Konitz, Winter was raised as the only son in a Protestant family with four sisters. His mother, whose name never appears in the town's records, was a tall woman with high cheekbones, piercing wide-open eyes, and stringent black hair parted in the middle. We do, however, know more about his father, Johannes, who worked in construction.[12] Sixty-three years old at the time of the murder, he was strong for his age and stocky and carried a full beard and mustache that rimmed his round face and inscrutable eyes. A simple man, he preferred his rough-shod, horse-drawn wagon to the comforts of the fast train.[13]

In the normal course of events in Wilhelmine Germany, Ernst Winter would have followed in his father's footsteps and learned a trade. Yet, at the age of twelve, he took the unusual step of entering the Konitz Gymnasium. A prestigious college preparatory school, the Gymnasium opened up a new middle-class world to the young boy and gave him a chance to live at a boardinghouse in the center of town, some fifteen miles away from his father, mother, and sisters.[14] From then on, we know only what his friends and teachers reported: that Ernst Winter was gregarious and handsome and of middling intelligence. He enjoyed sports and was already a lady's man, who liked to dress smartly and stroll up and down the street, from the Wilhelmsplatz down the Danzigerstrasse, then around the corner toward the marketplace, and back. This is where he was last seen, sporting a dark blue blazer with a velvet collar and a dark blue silk tie, and over that a lambskin coat and a blue silk scarf. He also wore a black felt hat, with gold buttons on its brim, and he carried a silver pocket watch.

The police could not say when Ernst Winter might have looked at his silver watch for the last time. They believed he had been killed sometime between the late afternoon and the early evening. The evidence, however, conflicted. The vomit traces found in his alimentary canal had hardly been digested, suggesting a time of death early in the afternoon, and no later than 4:00 P.M, though witnesses claimed to have seen Ernst Winter later in the day.[15] Anna Streuz, a store proprietor, saw him walking with a young man around 4:30 P.M; Hedwig Spohr saw him at the end of the Schlochauerstrasse an hour later; and Klara Spiegalski, who knew Winter from dance class, claims to have seen him twice, once at 4:30 P.M. on the Danzigerstrasse, and then just over an hour later on the street leading to the shooting club. Finally, two men, Max Meibauer, a dentist, and Albert Hofrichter, a schoolteacher, also claimed to have seen Winter later that evening. Hofrichter allegedly spotted Winter on the Danzigerstrasse as late as 6:30 P.M.

The autopsy promised to shed more light. Although Winter's head, left arm, right leg, and left shin and foot were still missing, two local doctors proceeded with the examination of the corpse. Forensic amateurs each, the county medical examiner, Dr. Müller, and the general practitioner, Dr. Bleske, concluded that "because of the nearly complete lack of blood . . . it is to be assumed that death occurred through loss of blood brought about by a cut throat."[16] A subsequent autopsy largely concurred with the conclusions of Müller and Bleske, but also noted the existence of petechiae, minute reddish spots, on the lung tissue, leaving open the possibility of suffocation.[17] The way in which the body had been cut also seemed remarkable: the spine had been neatly severed at the first lumbar vertebra, and the incisions seemed precise throughout. Even the muscles in the limbs, head, and neck appeared cleanly separated. Significantly, no sperm traces could be discerned.[18]

Further clues, however, were not quick to surface, and local investigators soon found themselves as bewildered as the crowd on the banks of the Mönchsee. The police could not fix the time of death. They could not conclusively show how the murder occurred. They had no obvious suspects, and no obvious motives. Moreover, major body parts were still missing, and, because of the crowds, the supposed scene of the crime—the edge of the lake—had been hopelessly contaminated from the start of the investigation. "Complete darkness still hovered over the deed," an investigating official lamented.[19]

Two long weeks had now passed with no additional leads. The days remained short and crisp, and the lake was still covered with a thin sheen of ice. With no solution at hand, the people became restless, and bewilderment soon gave way to suspicion. "Nearly the whole population of the town of Konitz as well as its hinterlands," Baron

Gottlieb von Zedlitz und Neukirch, the county official, wrote, "is convinced that Winter was a victim of a Jewish ritual murder."[20] In a letter to the Prussian minister of the interior, Zedlitz outlined the principal "facts" leading people to this belief: the body parts that had been found appeared bloodless; the murder had taken place a few weeks before Easter; credible witnesses had evidently heard a scream not far from the synagogue at 7:30 P.M. on the night of the murder; and still others claimed that a foul, burning smell had emanated an hour later from the same area.[21] These spurious "facts" animated the local imagination, making Konitz, to the chagrin of Baron von Zedlitz, prone to "a daily increasing amount of all possible rumors, partly of the most ridiculous kind."[22]

Konitz soon became the scene of nightly demonstrations; teenage boys from the evening school yelled insults and threats against the Jews and sometimes damaged shop windows and doors. The evening school ended just after dusk, and the students would then begin tearing through the streets in great numbers, smashing windows with stones, and calling "hep-hep" (a popular anti-Semitic catchword) whenever they spied a Jew.[23] By the end of March, the situation had already grown sufficiently disconcerting that Georg Deditius, the mayor of Konitz, issued a public warning: "It is not to be condoned," he admonished, "that a great number of people are, as a result [of the murder], being misguided into harassing Jewish citizens and their religious authorities."[24]

By now, the people of Konitz were no longer alone, as the outside press began to antagonize the population with a barrage of sensational stories. Starting on March 27, the Berlin-based anti-Semitic *Staatsbürgerzeitung* ran a series of major articles suggesting that the murder in Konitz was a ritual murder carried out by local Jews. The newspaper also reported a battery of vague sightings and suspicious circumstances: that a barber named Doehring had seen two strange men on the Danzigerstrasse; that Maschke, a gardener, had observed two dark figures near the Mönchsee; that the Jewish cantor Heymann had suddenly and inexplicably left town on a trip; and that a Jewish butcher named Adolph Lewy had sharpened his saw two days before the murder.[25]

As the Christian holidays approached, the din of rumor and denunciation became louder and more forceful. On Maundy Thursday, April 12, a local photographer, Max Heyn, began selling and distributing a picture of the deceased. In increasing numbers, people began to recall having seen Ernst Winter, typically in the company of Jews.[26] The din became a roar on Sunday, April 15, the first day of the Easter holiday, when two children suddenly stumbled upon Winter's decapitated head. Severed at the shoulder blades, the head lay covered in a ditch on the edge of a field lined by alder trees. Located just beyond the shooting club in the direction of Wilhelmshöhe, the ditch was near the border of the Dunkershagen farm, not far from the town park.[27]

Remarkably, the scalp buried in the dirt still seemed to remain intact, though the skin from the face had begun to peel, as beetles and other insects had already gone to work. The police could not say how long the head had been there. In the preceding month, temperatures in Konitz had rarely risen above freezing, and so it was conceivable, at least, that the head had been buried here all along. Perhaps, however, the killer had preserved the head in ice. There were other clues as well. Stuck to the remaining flesh on the cheek and at the crown of the head were pages of a Berlin newspaper, the April 29, 1896, edition of the liberal *Tägliche Rundschau*.[28] Not far from the ditch, the police also found a handkerchief torn into four pieces, one of which bore the letter *A*.

Then a witness suddenly materialized. Friedrich Fiedler, a provincial subaltern, came forward to testify that on Good Friday at 10:00 A.M. he had stood in front of the county courthouse and watched as Wolf Israelski, a skinner of animals, limped down the Rähmestrasse and, after passing him by, headed up the Schützenstrasse toward the Dunkershagen farm. Israelski, according to Fiedler, wore clean boots and carried on his back a sack with something round inside.[29] An hour later the skinner returned, his boots muddied and the sack empty.[30]

A fifty-two-year-old, down-and-out drunkard, Wolf Israelski was a bit deficient, a Jewish simpleton. When officials inquired about his whereabouts at ten o'clock that morning, he insisted that he had already returned home after going out for a shot of schnapps.[31] But Israelski's carping wife did not corroborate her husband's story. On the morning of Good Friday, she told police, her husband had been drinking and was muttering to himself.[32]

The police proceeded with the arrest and charged Israelski, who they believed had carried the head to the ditch, as an accomplice to murder. They incarcerated him in an isolated prison cell in the local jail, where behind double bars, and without kosher meals, he awaited trial.[33] For the excited crowds throughout the region looking for someone to punish, all of this—the rumors, the head, the news of Israelski's arrest—would suffice. They now took matters into their own hands and went after the Jews.[34]

I I

They went after Jews who, though residents of Konitz, also belonged to a venerable German-Jewish community, perhaps the most integrated Jewish minority in all of Europe. With the founding of the Second German Empire in 1871, the Jews of Germany had attained full emancipation, and, although discrimination did not thereafter cease, they nevertheless achieved striking successes in a country governed by the rule of law, "a safe harbor," as Raphael Kosch, a Jewish politician at the time, put it.[35] As especially prominent markers of these successes, celebrated scientists, artists, and scholars immediately come to mind: Paul Ehrlich, the pioneer of chemotherapy; the young physicist Albert Einstein, who published his revolutionary paper on special relativity in 1905; the impressionist painter Max Liebermann; the expressionist poet Else Lasker-Schüler; or the neo-Kantian philosopher Hermann Cohen.

Given these successes, it is no surprise that German patriotism permeated the Jewish community. The name of the largest Jewish organization in the country, the Central Association of German Citizens of the Jewish Faith, underscored this sense of belonging. The Central Verein, or CV, as it was usually called, far overshadowed the nascent Zionist organization, founded in 1897, just as the numbers of Jews who imagined themselves part of a German-Jewish symbiosis significantly outweighed those who believed this to be a mirage.

If Jews thought of themselves predominantly as Germans, they nevertheless constituted only one percent of the national population and were concentrated mainly in the cities: in 1900, half the Jews in Germany lived in urban centers with a population of over 100,000 people, and nearly a fifth of all German Jews lived in Berlin.[36] They worked mostly in commerce and trade, ranging from wealthy businessmen to humble store owners, in the free professions—among lawyers, doctors, writers, and journalists—and as artisans. In public life and in the world of business and trade, Jews and Christians interacted, though not always harmoniously. In private life, however, neighborliness was often less evident. As we know from Jewish memoirs, Christians rarely invited Jews into their homes.

In spite of these divisions, by 1900 separation was troubling Jewish leaders less than the accelerated pace of integration. Mixed marriages, for example, were already at roughly 10 percent among Jews, and the numbers were increasing; in large cities like Berlin and Hamburg, they approached 20 percent.[37] Conversion, while demographically not nearly as significant, was also on the rise, with an estimated 25,000 Jews baptized between 1880 and 1919.[38] Assimilation was partly a religious problem and partly a matter of concern for Jewish identity. In this context, the decline in religious observance proved alarming as well. Especially in urban centers, a significant number of Jews had either become indifferent to religion or become "three-days-a-year" Jews, who went to synagogue only on the High Holidays.[39]

As the twentieth century approached, though, old orthodoxies lingered, and there remained in Germany a vibrant religious community, especially in the towns and in the rural areas. Most Jews, roughly 80 percent, went to Reform (or liberal) services, which still included prayers recited in Hebrew and the separation of men and women. Regional pockets of Orthodoxy—especially in Alsace, Hessen, and Posen—also existed, but by 1900 the once sharp division between the two religious traditions had significantly softened, and many smaller Jewish communities, which could not afford religious divisiveness, had to work out a compromise.[40] Konitz, sandwiched between Reform bastions in Pomerania and Orthodox strongholds in Posen, very likely had such a Jewish community of compromise, where Jews struggled to maintain their religious identity and traditions in a rapidly changing, sometimes threatening environment.

In the spring of 1900, the Jewish communities of Konitz and the surrounding towns became the object of popular wrath. Between mid-April and mid-June 1900, three waves of some thirty separate anti-Semitic riots wracked these communities, instilling fear in the Jews and shattering their sense of belonging. The first incident occurred on Saturday evening, April 21. In the town of Baldenburg, in Schlochau County, anti-Semitic rioters prevented Jews from attending holy services and, in the course of the evening, damaged the synagogue. The president of the Central Association of Germans of the Jewish Faith complained to the Prussian minister of the interior that in Baldenburg "the small number of Jews living there see their lives in danger."[41] This was so not just in Baldenburg, however. The county official in Schlochau, Albrecht Mach, also received "complaints from the Jews about riots in Preussisch-Friedland, Stegers, and Hammerstein."[42] Not free of anti-Semitic prejudice himself, Mach reported that the complaints and the newspaper reports were "usually exaggerated," but the actions of the local police suggested otherwise.[43] In Hammerstein, where Ernst Winter's sister lived, anti-Semitic riots got so out of hand that the police were forced to call in the army for help, and the local commander sent eighty troops to restore order in a town of less than three thousand people and with a Jewish population of under one hundred.[44] Even before the troops arrived, vandals sacked the synagogue, rendering it an "appalling scene of havoc."[45] Similarly, in Konitz the anti-Semitic tumult on Saturday evening became so raucous that, according to the *Danziger Zeitung*, many people in Konitz "fear going out in the evening, and not only Jews, but also Christians, especially women."[46]

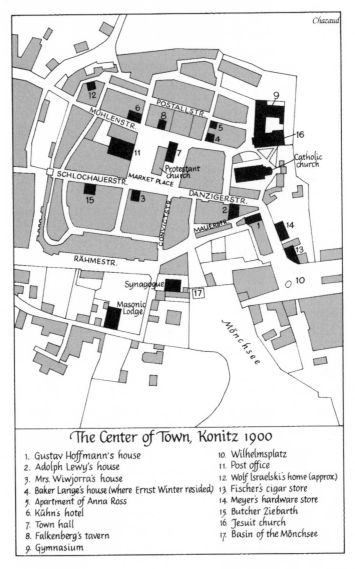

The Center of Town, Konitz 1900

1. Gustav Hoffmann's house
2. Adolph Lewy's house
3. Mrs. Wiwjorra's house
4. Baker Lange's house (where Ernst Winter resided)
5. Apartment of Anna Ross
6. Kühn's hotel
7. Town hall
8. Falkenberg's tavern
9. Gymnasium
10. Wilhelmsplatz
11. Post office
12. Wolf Israelski's home (approx.)
13. Fischer's cigar store
14. Meyer's hardware store
15. Butcher Ziebarth
16. Jesuit church
17. Basin of the Mönchsee

Word spread quickly, and the upheavals proved infectious. In Vandsburg, riots began late in the evening when "large crowds gathered and were reinforced by a significant influx of peasant sons and farmhands who swarmed in from the neighboring rural villages."[47] In Czersk, a German-Polish industrial town, the riots developed more spontaneously. Shortly before seven in the evening, a drunkard was thrown out of Jendryczka's pub, "a Polish-Catholic tavern." When he began smashing the tavern windows, someone yelled, "Let's go after the synagogue." One person tried to climb the fence around the synagogue and was arrested. As the police took him away, the crowd swelled "to a mob of several hundred." Stones flew from the crowd first at Jewish houses, then at the gendarmes as well; in the end, shots were fired. It was not until the gendarmes drew their pistols that the crowd was dispersed.[48] A similar scenario unfolded the next day in Neustettin, where nineteen years earlier severe anti-Semitic riots had followed a synagogue fire that local Christians blamed on the Jews. In Baldenburg, Hammerstein, and Czersk, the synagogue also constituted the symbolic focus of popular anger, and in these places, too, the crowd could not be scattered until the forces of order drew their weapons. While these remained the sites of greatest violence, minor incidents occurred elsewhere. In the villages of Bruss and Mrotschen, and in the towns of Bütow and Rummelsburg, synagogue windows were likewise demolished.[49]

A fter the riots, the Jews of Konitz and the surrounding area recognized the gravity of their situation. At first, they merely closed their shops early, but then they stopped frequenting public places and many no longer went out at night at all.[50] By this time, too, the town of Konitz was covered in anti-Semitic propaganda: fliers and leaflets littered the streets. "Nearly every day," a citizen complained, "fliers arrive here . . . that provoke the passions to the extreme."[51] The sluggish pace of the murder investigation did not help matters. Lacking new leads, the police increasingly compiled bits of evidence ground out by the local rumor mill. Invariably, these bits of evidence incriminated the Jews.

To gather this evidence, local anti-Semites formed an "unofficial" citizens committee. Organized in early May—nearly two months after the murder—under the aegis of two schoolteachers, Jürgen Thiel and Albert Hofrichter, and a dentist, Max Meibauer, the members of the citizens committee pressured the police to take the ritual-murder tale seriously and not to leave a Semitic stone unturned.[52] In search of evidence, they combed the pubs, stopped people on the streets, knocked on their neighbors' doors, and went into their houses. The members of the citizens committee "asked people all sorts of things," one official complained, and "suggested ridiculous stories to those hankering after a reward."[53]

For their part, the police and the district attorney also added grist to the rumor mill. Immediately after the murder, Settegast ordered that all Jewish cantors and butchers in the region be interrogated.[54] Under his direction, the police questioned the Christian maids of Jewish households in Konitz, asking them to comment on the whereabouts of their masters on the night of the murder and whether they saw or sensed anything suspicious. "Do you think the Rabbai could have committed murder?" an official asked Rabbi Kellermann's maid.[55] As one Jewish newspaper pointed out at the time: imagine the objections if the reverse were the case, and Jewish maids were asked to pronounce on the moral qualities of Christian ministers.[56] But the spurious investigation continued. Desperate for clues, Settegast entertained denunciations based on spectral evidence obtained through spiritual revelation. He even pursued the story of a four-year-old girl who bragged that her father, a Jewish merchant of herculean physical stature, had thrown Winter to the ground, killed him, and cut and carved him up; the family, the girl said, then sat around the dinner table and ate him.[57]

Amazingly, in this climate of rumor and gossip, of false sightings and bogus storytelling, the Prussian minister of justice increased the reward offered for clues leading directly to an arrest. Initially, the reward was set at 1,700 marks, already a handsome sum that exceeded what most workers took home in a year. The reward steadily increased: to 2,000 marks, to 6,700 marks—more money than the mayor earned—and then, on April 28, to 20,000 marks, a small fortune with which one could buy a nice bourgeois house. In the long history of the Prussian state, this was the largest reward ever offered in a murder case.[58] "For *this* money," a state official wrote, "I still have cautious optimism that among the Jews there will be a traitor."[59]

I I I

May was, for the most part, a quiet month, but the calm was no more than a respite before the coming storm. In the meanwhile, the anti-Semites in Berlin had begun to watch the events in Konitz. The murder of Ernst Winter and the violence that followed provided the struggling anti-Semitic parties with an opportunity to revitalize their movement. In this sense, the drama in Konitz must also be understood against the backdrop of the early rise of political anti-Semitism in Germany.

First circulated in September 1879, the term "anti-Semitism" stems from William Marr, who called his political organization the "Anti-Semitic league."[60] Frustrated and unsuccessful, Marr hoped to strike a new chord, different from previous attempts in the Christian tradition, in confronting the "Jewish question." Rather than demand the assimilation of Jews, he rejected them; and instead of trying to convert Jews, he declared them an implacable enemy, not of Christendom, but of Germandom. He thus turned anti-Semitism into hatred based on race, not religion. The term was then appropriated by the most famous historian of the day, Heinrich von Treitschke—a stunning orator, who championed Bismarck's unification of Germany by "blood and iron" in 1871. Throughout the 1870s, Treitschke had also supported Bismarck's subsequent attacks against the Catholics, but when the official "Kulturkampf" came to a close in 1879, Treitschke turned his polemical fire against the Jews. "The Jews are our misfortune," he proclaimed in an influential article in the *Preußische Jahrbücher*.[61]

Treitschke's article signaled a more general turn in German politics away from the liberalism of the 1870s. This reorientation, which some historians equate with a second foundation of the German Empire, ensured that henceforth anti-Semitism would be tied to conservative politics. In August 1880, a group of anti-Semites known as the Berlin Movement composed and circulated an "anti-Semitic petition" demanding that the immigration of foreign Jews be limited, that Jews be barred from positions of state authority, that the Christian character of elementary schools be restored, and that the government statistics office closely monitor the Jewish population. By April 1881, the anit-Semites had gathered 265,000 signatures, mostly among artisans and shopkeepers, classes hard hit by a deepening economic depression, but also among one out of every five university students.[62] Ceremoniously, the anti-Semites of the Berlin Movement presented the petition to Otto von Bismarck, who, rather unceremoniously, placed it *ad acta*.[63]

If Bismarck's silence suggested his reluctance to publicly engage with the populists of the anti-Semitic right, his policies bespoke a deeper ambivalence. In March 1885, Bismarck initiated the expulsion of Russian (and later Austro-Hungarian) subjects who had become residents, but not citizens, of imperial Germany, among them roughly thirty thousand Poles and nine thousand Jews, many of whom had since 1881 been driven out of Russia by vicious pogroms to seek refuge in the German Empire. These Jews would now be sent back to Russia to face an uncertain fate.[64] Without endorsing an anti-Semitic petition, Bismarck thus assented to, indeed went beyond, the suggestions of anti-Semitic politicians and expelled recent Jewish immigrants.

Even with Bismarck's tacit support in matters of policy, overtly anti-Semitic parties hardly made a dent during his reign; only one delegate, out of more than four hundred, being elected to the Reichstag in 1887. After Bismarck's departure in 1890, the anti-Semites met with more success, winning five delegates in the summer of 1890 and sixteen, or 3.5 percent of the total vote, in 1893. Hardly a breakthrough, the victory nevertheless alarmed authorities. Beginning in 1894, the

Berlin police closely monitored the trajectory of these anti-Semitic parties. In 1895, the police reported "complete stagnation," and in the following years "decline." They attributed this deterioration to improving economic indicators and to the deleterious effects of intraparty struggles.[65] By the general election of 1898, what had seemed like a rising tide of anti-Semitic politics had already begun to ebb. The anti-Semitic parties lost six of their sixteen districts and, though their vote total increased slightly, their lack of progress over the last five years boded ill for the future.[66]

With their parties in disarray by 1900, the anti-Semites considered how they could exploit the possibilities for sensation that Konitz presented. Political anti-Semitism was not a uniquely German phenomenon, and in France and Austria-Hungary the anti-Semites flourished in the late 1890s. France's Dreyfus affair provided one blueprint for revitalizing a sagging anti-Semitic movement in Germany, while a ritual-murder case in the Bohemian town of Polna suggested another.

As is widely known, the French army in 1894 accused Captain Alfred Dreyfus, a Jew from Alsace with a spotless military record, of selling secrets to the German embassy after offering expert testimony that Dreyfus's handwriting appeared on an incriminating list. It was a thin shred of evidence, yet in the swift trial later in the same year, a military court found Dreyfus guilty as charged and sentenced him to a life of exile on Devil's Island. Within two years of the sentence, it became apparent, as a result of the meticulous research of a persistent lawyer from Lyon, Bernard Lazare, that not Dreyfus but a Hungarian major named Walsin Esterhazy had leaked the information. Public voices demanding that the trial against Dreyfus be reopened became increasingly insistent and louder still after Esterhazy was acquitted by a military tribunal in January 1898 on the basis of forgeries generated within the army itself. In the wake of the tumult, Emile Zola published his famous statement "J'accuse," denouncing the army for its shameful cover-up and for betraying the ideals of the French Revolution. He also excoriated the Catholic right for conjuring the demon of anti-Semitism to serve its own selfish interests. The country divided into

two camps: the Dreyfusards and the anti-Dreyfusards, those who
fought for equal protection before the law as the bedrock of the republic and those who saw any diminution of the army's status as an ero-
sion of national glory. On one side stood the socialists, led by Jean
Jaurès, with the intellectuals and the anticlerical republicans. On the
other stood the forces of order: the church, the army, the conserva-
tives. Since the bloody repression of the Communards in 1870, no
other event had divided the Third Republic as dramatically. When,
following Zola, the Dreyfusards called for the army to repeal the false
conviction of Captain Dreyfus, anti-Dreyfusards rioted throughout
France: in some cities, such as Angers, Marseilles, Nantes, and
Rouen, thousands of people ran through the streets, smashing windows, pillaging shops, and shouting, "Death to the Jews."[67] Although
Dreyfus was pardoned by the president of France in 1899, and exonerated by the courts in 1906, a dynamic new nationalist and anti-
Semitic movement, the Action Française, had emerged from the
affair, and it would powerfully influence the politics of the Third
Republic until its fall in 1940. Germany's anti-Semites closely watched
these developments, and one of them later remarked that Konitz
would put Dreyfus in the shadows.[68]

As the smoke cleared from the Dreyfus affair, another anti-
Semitic cause célèbre erupted in the Austro-Hungarian Monarchy. On
April 1, 1899, the "bloodless" body of the seamstress Agnes Hruza was
found in a wood outside the small Bohemian town of Polna.
Convinced from the start that it was ritual murder, the people of Polna
immediately accused the Jews—in particular, Leopold Hilsner. A
twenty-two-year-old cobbler's apprentice, Hilsner was, like Wolf
Israelski, a social outcast. A poor worker given to drink and not particularly observant, he often took liberties with the truth. When accused,
he lied about his alibi, and when convicted, he incriminated two other
innocent Jewish men of being accomplices. Hilsner himself had been
accused of having "in association with others, murdered Hruza," and
of being "an accomplice in the murder." In September 1899 in the district court of Kuttenberg, the jury found Hilsner innocent of the first

charge (murder), but guilty of the second (accomplice to murder). The trial turned on the ritual-murder allegation, implicating as the real killers the Jews of Polna. "Hruza," the state prosecutor argued in his closing comments, "was murdered by a society that lives among us for the sole object of taking our blood from us."[69] The court sentenced Hilsner to death, but after the bold intervention of an audacious politician, Thomas Masaryk, the emperor stayed the execution and transmuted his sentence to life in prison, of which he served nineteen years until he was pardoned and set free, though not cleared.[70] In 1899, the events in Polna created a sensation and were reported in newspapers from Paris to St. Petersburg, whose readers had already been gripped by the Dreyfus case. The Polna case immediately preceded the Konitz affair, and aspects of the case were still pending when violence first erupted.[71] In mid-May 1900, Polna was the subject of a public debate in the parliament of the Austro-Hungarian Monarchy, and it was clearly in the minds of the men and women who mourned the death of Ernst Winter just over a week later.

W inter's funeral was to take place on Sunday, May 27. The event already worried local officials, who in the preceding week had attempted to convince both Winter's parents and Eduard Hammer, the pastor who was to perform the services, that it should take place on a Tuesday, Wednesday, or Thursday, when riots were less likely to occur. But the pastor, wishing to preserve the ceremony's religious aura, ignored their pleas. As local officials expected, the funeral, far from solemn, became a "stage piece for the many thousands of onlookers," who, as if attending a passion play, streamed into Konitz in their Sunday best from neighboring villages and towns.[72] According to the police, many of the onlookers were "anti-Semites," and more than a few accompanied the funeral procession by shouting anti-Semitic slogans while beating on the doors and windows of Jewish stores as they marched from the Protestant church on the marketplace, down the narrow Danzigerstrasse, and out to the Wilhelmsplatz. The towns-

people along the way crowded at their balconies and windows and
watched as every cobblestone of the street below became black with
mourners marching by. When the procession reached the Protestant
graveyard, Hammer delivered the funeral oration. A modest man, a
pastor in Konitz for more than two decades, Hammer did not mention
the Jews; he merely intimated that the murder must have been
planned.[73]

The funeral only deepened the public's desire for swift justice,
and the people of Konitz had reason to feel optimistic. On May 14, the
Prussian police had sent to Konitz a special investigator from Berlin,
Johann Braun, in order to solve the murder case posthaste.[74] Like others before him, Braun was impressed by the precision of the cuts and
believed that a trained hand, a surgeon's or a butcher's, must have
made them. In Konitz, there were no surgeons, but two butchers lived
near the scene of the crime, the backs of their properties abutting in a
dark alley, the Maurergasse. One of them, Adolph Lewy, was Jewish.
A quiet, even taciturn man, a fifty-seven-year-old father of two grown
sons, Lewy had moved to Konitz sometime between the Revolution of
1848 and the founding of the German Empire in 1871, most likely from
a neighboring town, like Flatow, Schlochau, or Schloppe, or from one
of the towns to the south of Konitz, like Krojanke, Cammin, Jastrow,
or Zempelburg.[75]

Over the course of the nineteenth century, such migrations had
become commonplace, as many of the Jews who lived in these small
towns moved to larger towns and cities. This process began with the edict
on the civil status of the Jews in the state of Prussia, issued by King
Frederick William on March 11, 1812. For German Jews, this marked
the beginning of their emancipation: with the stroke of a pen, it put an
end to the special taxes they had to pay, to discriminating trade laws,
and to the special permits required for marriage and residence. More
important, Jews had now became citizens of the Prussian state and
ostensibly enjoyed equal rights with Christians. But the edict was pred-
icated on an imperative: that Jews also change. They were to use the
German language and the Roman alphabet in their business dealings,

and they were to adopt permanent surnames, preferably ones that did not evoke the Old Testament. Salomon Abraham of Schlochau now became Salomon Abraham Lewy. Not only his addition of a new last name was important, but also the fact that he had kept the name of his father as a middle name, out of respect for his Jewish heritage. In Berlin, where more Jews wished to assimilate into German culture and to distance themselves from the old ways, more than a quarter of the Jewish men dropped the name of their fathers.[76] But in the villages around Konitz, nearly everyone kept his paternal name.[77]

In these villages, Jews carried on a life marked by the rhythms of religious orthodoxy and the grinding routine of hard work. The days began and ended with prayer, the weeks strung out from one Saturday to the next, and the years accumulated according to the calendar of Israel. Work, too, molded days and shaped people. In 1827, the local officers in charge of military conscription complained that the village Jews living near Konitz were "with few exceptions unfit for the military . . . since through their trade they are forced to carry heavy burdens and are overly strained, causing their chests to weaken."[78] For most of the nineteenth century, trade remained the primary occupation of Jewish men. In 1846, a Konitz county official wrote that little had changed, and that most Jews drew their livelihood from trading and peddling.[79]

The daily life of Jews had changed, however, especially as they moved in increasing numbers to the towns and cities, not least of all to Konitz. At the outset of the century, the Jews of Konitz, few in number, had gathered for holy services in a barn on a small side street. But by 1829 the Jewish community already comprised thirty-three families, enough to merit a synagogue of its own, and in the following year construction of a modest temple began. Coming from the surrounding area, these Jews were mainly traders, though the census of 1850 also lists two tanners, a cigar maker, a tailor, a rope maker, a butcher, a baker, and a soap maker.[80] In the second half of the nineteenth century, the population continued to grow, and by the 1880s the Jewish community in Konitz had increased to five hundred members.[81] It soon began to diminish, however, though not because of conversion or intermarriage, both of which often occurred in the big city but rarely ever in Konitz or Konitz County. Rather, the community in Konitz declined because Jews left for larger cities—for Danzig, Breslau, Stettin, sometimes for New York, most often for Berlin.[82] In those years, the largest part of Berlin's Jewish community had come from the small towns of the east. Certainly for young people of the time, Berlin was where so-called real life began.

By the turn of the twentieth century, the Jewish community of Konitz seemed tired and worn, and in this sense had come to resemble Adolph Lewy, the aging resident of Danzigerstrasse 26. Lewy tended to his two grown sons and to his butcher business and cattle trade. He passed the twilight hours at Falkenberg's pub watching his friends play skat.

This is where he was on Sunday afternoon, March 11, the night of the murder. After closing a deal out on the Hennigsdorferstrasse, Adolph Lewy retired to Falkenberg's pub from four o'clock to seven o'clock. He then walked back across the marketplace and went home for his evening meal, returning to the pub an hour later and staying until ten.[83] His sons had likewise been occupied that afternoon. Moritz, his eldest, had been at the Dunkershagen farm buying a calf until seven in the evening, when he also returned home for supper. After dinner, Moritz visited Elise Freitag, with whom he had something of an amorous relationship, and did not come home until after ten, when he looked after the horses and went to bed. Hugo, the younger son, had been away since ten o'clock in the morning, tending to business in various villages outside of Konitz until seven-thirty that evening. After a long day, he ate supper with his family and retired to bed at nine-thirty.[84]

Despite Lewy's alibi, people started to suspect him, and by April his customers, save for some Jews, ceased to come by.[85] The threats terrified him, and we can imagine old man Lewy, a "timid and anxious shadow of a man looking on" through the slits in his wooden shutters, to the violent streets below.[86]

The anti-Semites had high hopes that the inspector would

swiftly solve the crime and arrest the Jewish butcher, who they were convinced had murdered Ernst Winter.[87] They had good cause for optimism, for Braun's reputation preceded him. Raised in the Russian Caucasus, Johann Braun was a different class of investigator from the hapless Settegast or the simpletons of the local police force. A member of the Berlin homicide division for more than thirty years, he had developed a keen sense for the modus operandi of cold-blooded killers. "Whoever Braun arrests is the one who committed the murder," the detective supposedly said of himself.[88] Braun would soon disappoint the anti-Semites, however. For the notion of Jewish ritual murder, he had nothing but scorn—a shameful dark-age shibboleth, he thought, a product of ignorance and fanaticism.[89]

On May 29, Braun instead summoned and interrogated Gustav Hoffmann, the Christian butcher. Along with Inspector Wehn, he also interrogated Hoffmann's fifteen-year-old daughter, Anna.[90] Braun suspected that Ernst Winter had tried to seduce young Anna Hoffmann and that the father had discovered Winter in the act. Enraged, Hoffmann murdered Winter, as Braun's theory went, and later carved up his corpse as only a trained butcher could, disposing of it piece by piece.

Local officials found this theory utterly improbable.[91] A devout member of the Old Lutheran church, Gustav Hoffmann had been a town councillor for eleven years and the president of the butchers' guild for fifteen. By all accounts, he enjoyed a good reputation in Konitz. The father of nine children, he was, according to police reports, "a man of means," "a strict man," in whose house one could find "warm patriotism and real piety," who "with his family led a solid, reserved life," and "who was seldom to be seen in the taverns, and then only in those taverns in which the better society meets."[92] He had a stately, comfortable carriage, ample cheeks, a carefully waxed, wide-winged mustache named for the previous emperor, and a countenance that revealed a self-satisfied ease. That he had killed Ernst Winter seemed, as one official later put it, "psychologically almost unthinkable."[93] Moreover, Hoffmann did not act as if he had killed someone, the daughter did not seem especially distraught, and the Christian butcher had a perfectly good alibi.[94]

More important, the alibi could be corroborated. In the early afternoon of March 11, Hoffmann had guests for Sunday dinner; at three, he accompanied his guests to church, where they participated in communion. From church, he joined a group going to his friend Wilhelm Ziebarth, another butcher, who lived close to Schlochau gate. Hoffmann stayed at Ziebarth's until after 6:00 P.M. and then left with the other guests to return home, sitting down to his evening meal at 7:30. Half an hour later, two of Hoffmann's apprentices arrived. "In accordance with his strict ways," Hoffmann chided them for their tardiness and sent them off to bed.[95] At the butcher's house, lights went out at 9:00 P.M., a bit earlier than usual. That he might have left his house later to carve up the body seemed inconceivable, since neither his apprentices nor his maid heard anything out of the ordinary.[96] Even Hoffmann's dog slept quietly that evening.[97]

The relationship of Anna Hoffmann with Ernst Winter also appeared less salacious than Inspector Braun suspected. According to witnesses, it was "hardly more than a harmless flirtation," which Anna's father did not even know about.[98] As one of the officials involved in the investigation later put it, "It is already difficult to imagine that a girl, hardly fifteen, who seems morally upstanding, would have sexual relations with an eighteen-year-old high school boy. But if one wanted to assume this, then it could have happened only in a moment of passion and at a special opportunity, never as a result of previous arrangement on a cold March evening in a wooden shed in the space of barely a quarter of an hour."[99]

Inspector Braun began to wonder: perhaps he had gotten it wrong.[100] Hoffmann comported himself like a reasonable man eager to cooperate with the investigation. When the interrogation was over, Hoffmann patted Braun on the shoulder. "Had you been here from the start," Hoffmann said, "the killer would have long since been discovered."[101] Later that evening, Hoffmann's demeanor would grow more defensive and more sinister.

First, however, news of the summons of Hoffmann and his daughter "spread throughout the town like wildfire," galvanizing the anti-Semites.[102] Some of them were locals, like the men from the citizens committee; others were journalists from Berlin who had taken up quarters in Konitz, partly to report on the affair and partly to drive events forward. Although outsiders, the journalists ingratiated themselves with local personalities, like Ernst Winter's mourning father, and Julius Lehmann, the new editor of the local newspaper, the *Konitzer Tageblatt*.

Throughout the upheavals, the *Konitzer Tageblatt* had been a neutral newspaper. But on May 13 its editor and publisher, Friedrich Roehl, died, and the newspaper fell into the hands of his assistant, Julius Lehmann. Roehl was an educated and refined gentleman of an older era. A conservative journalist, he was committed to the enlightenment of the people. Julius Lehmann embraced a different kind of journalism, one more attuned to the popular pulse and the prejudices of the age. But something else also separated the two generations. Roehl had married a woman named Martha, whose maiden name was Caspari, a prominent Jewish family in Konitz. In the summer of 1900, Lehmann also fell in love with a woman named Martha. Strong willed and actively anti-Semitic, she was nineteen years old, the eldest daughter of Gustav Hoffmann.[103] When the police summoned her father, her fiancé's newspaper waxed indignant.[104]

The anti-Semites did not stand idly by. The citizens committee summoned its own witness, Bernhard Masloff, whom Wilhelm Bruhn, the publisher of the anti-Semitic newspaper *Die Staatsbürgerzeitung*, had persuaded to testify. A crude, barely literate worker, Masloff told the citizens committee that on the night of the murder he had been lying in the alley behind Lewy's house waiting to steal a slab of meat. While there, he had observed Lewy and two other men walking (two in front, one in back) to the Mönchsee, carrying a heavy package, presumably containing Winter's upper torso.[105] Masloff thus offered a counterstory to inspector Braun's theory, and this counterstory, which centered not on the Christian but on the Jewish butcher, set the stage for violent conflict.

I V

Around half past ten at night, cartloads of peasants, artisans, and workers rode into town.[106] The journalist Bruhn had set up the "main camp" for the anti-Semites in Kühn's hotel, where he was staying, and there was a constant procession into and out of the rooms he had rented. According to one of Zedlitz's contacts, the anti-Semitic organizers had even passed out cigars and schnapps.[107] Outside the hotel, a rumor began to spread among the crowd that Hoffmann would be arrested at one o'clock in the morning. This inflamed the crowd, which now included more than a thousand people.[108] Some tried to storm Lewy's house; others tried to break into Jewish homes along the side streets. Most contented themselves with yelling anti-Semitic epithets and tossing stones, first at Jewish houses and shops, then at local officials. The mayor tried to calm the people; when he could not, the gendarmes—eight men on horses, two on foot—drew their swords and, around three o'clock in the morning, dispersed the crowd. Later on, Zedlitz learned that a group of anti-Semites had banded together and, armed with sticks and clubs, prepared to liberate Hoffmann in the event of an arrest. "No one doubts," the county official reported, that "lynch justice against the Lewy family would have followed."[109]

The riots on Tuesday evening unsettled the authorities, and when it appeared that they would begin again the next morning, a market day in Konitz, Zedlitz no longer felt secure relying solely on his gendarmes. He requested that the Thirty-fifth Division of the Prussian army, stationed in nearby Graudenz, send a company (roughly 150 men) to ensure order. The government complied, and at half past four, troops boarded a special train headed for Konitz, each soldier armed with thirty rounds of live ammunition and emergency medical supplies.[110] Meanwhile, the mayor and the city council issued a plea to the citizens of Konitz, urging them to stay at home after sunset.[111] The police issued a similar plea, adding that further violent actions would be met with the use of firearms.[112]

The plea failed to impress. Throughout the day, local police received warnings that the crowd would go after Mayor Deditius, who they thought was overly protective of the Jews. They would satisfy their lust for "lynch justice" by dragging Lewy from his house. Moreover, a newspaper report in the evening edition of the anti-Semitic *Staatsbürgerzeitung* further inflamed the public by stating that the police had ordered a medical inspection to ascertain whether Anna Hoffmann had been deflowered.[113] A fabrication, the report nevertheless sharpened the animosity of a crowd already angry at the submission of a solid Christian citizen to the indignity of an interrogation.

The demonstrators began to gather at eight-thirty that evening. To their surprise, they were soon confronted by the Eleventh Company of the Fourteenth Infantry Regiment. The crowd grew nevertheless. Increasingly nervous about the confrontation before him, the company commander, Captain Hesse, ordered his soldiers to present their rifles. Meanwhile, someone had set off fireworks, and some people mistook the sharp crackle for rifle fire. "The detonations," according to Zedlitz, "aroused terror and bitterness."[114] But within a short time, Captain Hesse and his soldiers cleared the streets, dispersed the crowd, and roped off the marketplace.[115]

A threshold had nearly been crossed, not only by the Prussian army but also by the citizens of Konitz. "The threats to beat the Jews to death and to set fire to all four corners of the town are to be taken very seriously," a local Jewish lawyer reported.[116] Increasingly anxious, Baron von Zedlitz provided the Prussian minister of the interior with a résumé of the situation in Konitz: "For three months the population has been roused against the Jews with all the weapons of fanaticism. Many really believe that they are doing a good deed and protecting their children from the fate of Winter if they beat a Jew to death."[117] The soldiers of the Eleventh Company stayed in Konitz for six days, until

Tuesday. When they withdrew, there was also a brief respite from further violence. But a few days later, rioting started anew.

The third wave of violence began in an atmosphere thick with anticipation. Zedlitz feared that any new and unsuspected turn in the murder investigation would incite local riots all over again.[118] Partly, that turn came when Inspector Braun arrested Bernhard Masloff and his mother-in-law and charged them with perjury. Both had been key witnesses in support of the accusations of the citizens committee against Adolph Lewy. Now the anti-Semites and their increasingly large following became ever more convinced that the Prussian police were in the pockets of the Jews. The matter did not rest there, however. As had already happened when rumors circulated of Hoffmann's rather unlikely arrest at one o'clock in the morning on May 30, the anti-Semites fabricated another pretext for violence. On Thursday, June 7, the *Konitzer Tageblatt* reported that the police intended to pursue the investigation into Hoffmann's actions with renewed vigor.[119]

By eight o'clock on Thursday evening, there was already talk in the pubs that later that night the synagogue would be burned.[120] Around nine o'clock, women "who knew that something was about to happen" gathered in the center of town.[121] Then, at half past ten, a group of anti-Semites began to set fires to the fence that sealed off the synagogue, as well as to a number of nearby sheds, one of which belonged to Gustav Hoffmann. Since the sheds were extremely dry, the fires spread quickly, and the fire department did all it could to control the flames and to dampen the synagogue, the main target of the arsonists.[122] Local people, moreover, were loath to help put out the flames. When the fire department asked them to lend their draft horses in order to pull wagons of water, the people refused; and as the firemen tried to extinguish the flames, anti-Semitic demonstrators hurled stones at them.[123]

The next day, on June 8, the *Staatsbürgerzeitung* reported that the Jews had started the fires in order to expunge evidence against them. The sheds that burned, the paper claimed, were the sheds in which the Jews dismembered the body and drew the blood of Ernst Winter.[124]

The newspapers also reported that two Christian boys, eight and thirteen years of age, had been missing for over a week; the following night, on June 9, the rioting started once again.[125]

The pattern was already familiar. After dusk on Saturday night, a crowd gathered on the Danzigerstrasse, where Lewy and Hoffmann lived. After shouting epithets and insisting that Masloff and his mother-in-law be released, the rioters hurled stones and bricks at the houses of the Jews. Wasting no time, the police and the gendarmes charged through the streets, six men abreast, and dispersed the crowds.

But the clashes had only just begun. The next morning, anti-Semites rode their bicycles and went by train to neighboring towns and villages to round up farmers and rural laborers and anyone else who wanted to join the protest. According to one report, people came not only from the area around Konitz but also from the surrounding counties of Tuchel, Schlochau, and Flatow. Mayor Deditius even claimed to have seen a group of men with axes arriving by train from the east.

The situation appeared ominous. Crowds of angry workers and peasants, men and women "with a prayer book in one hand, club in the other," gathered at the marketplace in front of the Protestant church.[126] When a Jewish man walked by the crowd, a Christian gestured by sliding his hand across his neck: today, he signaled, throats would be cut.[127] But the Jews had already been warned the night before. Two women had told a Jewish merchant, "Watch out on Sunday, all the Jews are going to be beaten to death."[128] By eleven on Sunday morning, thousands of people had assembled in the marketplace. In addition to the usual anti-Semitic tirades, the demonstrators demanded the release of Bernhard Masloff and his mother-in-law, Anna Ross. The police arrested one of the troublemakers among them, Theodor Knievel, but the rumor soon spread that Hoffmann had been arrested. Irate, the throng pressed on to the town hall and threatened Mayor Deditius, who barricaded himself inside the building. The police and the gendarmes drew their swords. It would not be enough. For a moment, Zedlitz considered giving the order to present firearms and shoot. But he was hesitant. Women and children were everywhere in the crowd, and the sight of them lying face down on the ground, their hands over their heads, was too much for him to countenance. He also worried that a resort to violence would unleash a "storm against Jewish houses, especially in the side streets," and that the authorities could not offer the Jews sufficient protection.[129]

In the hope of quelling the riot, the town sounded the fire alarm, but the crowd seemed unimpressed. Instead, demonstrators attacked police inspectors from Berlin, throwing one of them to the ground and wounding another.[130] The demonstrators then marched to Lewy's house and pummeled it with rocks. They also damaged the shop of a Jewish merchant who had not shut his storefront grate. At half past four, a group of young men, trailed by women and children, marched to the synagogue.[131] Breaking inside, they smashed the wooden pews, yanked down the lamps, ripped apart the drapes, and tore pages out of the holy books. Fortunately, the Torah rolls had already been moved to a safe place, a precaution taken after the initial attempt to burn down the synagogue on the preceding Thursday night. The temple, the *Danziger Zeitung* reported, now "resembled a ruin."

Konitz, a local Jewish man wrote, was "in a state of revolt."[132] County officials agreed. When the crowd could no longer be controlled, Baron von Zedlitz, "obviously shaken and as pale as a chalkboard," called the Prussian minister of the interior, who once again ordered that the garrison in Graudenz send the Eleventh Company of the Fourteenth Infantry Regiment. As the train carrying the troops passed through the neighboring town of Tuchel, another demonstration gathered at the railway station to shout the troops down and stone them.[133] When the soldiers finally arrived in Konitz, at nine-thirty in the evening, Zedlitz read the riot act, and the infantry marched into town, with rifles loaded and bayonets fixed. Although no shots were fired, there were injuries in the clash, resulting mainly from people being struck by butts of rifles and cut by bayonets.[134] As this violence erupted in Konitz, the situation became so serious that the Prussian minister of the interior, Baron von Rheinbaben, met personally with Kaiser Wilhelm II in Berlin to apprise him of the situation. Sensing a revolt against state authority, the kaiser immediately ordered that not just a company but a battalion be sent to Konitz. The battalion, roughly 650 men, arrived on Tuesday, June 12, stationing a soldier for every sixty paces, as well as a cordon of infantrymen around the synagogue and a special guard around Lewy's house.[135]

Military occupation of the town put an end to the major incidents of anti-Semitic violence in Konitz, though isolated instances of anti-Semitic rioting continued to occur on the periphery of the region throughout the month of June: in Berent, north of Konitz, where there had already been an alleged case of ritual murder in 1894; in Mrotschen, in the province of Posen; and in Schlawe, in Pomerania.[136] In addition, anti-Semitic gangs again demolished the Jewish cemetery in Hammerstein, while in Janowitz, in the district of Bromberg, two men broke into the synagogue through the side window and proceeded to vandalize the temple.[137] Moreover, isolated acts of violence against individual Jews continued. On a country road leading out of Kamin, a village south of Konitz, a worker named Josef Krajetski attacked a sixty-four-year-old Jewish trader with a pitchfork, beating him senseless. As Krajetski dealt his blows, his wife encouraged him, shouting "hep-hep." Had the lord of the local manor not come to the trader's aid, Krajetski would presumably have left the Jewish trader for dead.[138] Similarly, in Prechlau, Ernst Winter's village, young thugs attacked a Jewish cantor and his seventy-year-old father, who had come to the town to perform a circumcision. The father had to be admitted to a hospital with serious head wounds.[139] And in Konitz anti-Semitic sentiments continued to smolder. "Despite the surface calm," Baron von Zedlitz reported two days after the occupation, "I judge the situation as more serious than ever before."[140]

Postcard depicting the ritual murder of Ernst Winter
by the Lewy family and other Jews in Konitz. "Remember
the 11th of March 1900. On this day the Gymnasium
student Winter was sacrificed in Konitz to the knife of a
kosher butcher." The publisher was sentenced to six
months in prison for making this card.

CHAPTER TWO

The Butcher's Tale and Other Stories

Where no wood is, there the fire goeth out:
so where there is no talebearer, the strife ceaseth.

—PROVERBS 26:20

The real author of the narrative is not only he who tells it,
but also, and at times even more, he who hears it.

—GÉRARD GENETTE

The advent of the twentieth century was remarkable enough, but the spring season that emerged in the year 1900 was particularly noteworthy. For the first time ever, a brilliant sheen of electric light illuminated the Eiffel Tower, completed eleven years earlier, as if to augur the technological advances of the coming years. Enthusiasts of speed would soon crank their engines and drive their Daimler-powered cars through dust-filled streets in the Paris–Lyon road race; Graf Zeppelin would launch the first of his famous cigar-shaped airships, which hovered far above Lake Constance; and by the end of the year, Max Planck would discover quanta as a measure of energy emitted by radiating atomic particles, thus opening the way for other physicists, Albert Einstein most prominent among them, to unlock further secrets of the physical universe.

It was a time of optimism, if not uncritical satisfaction, and contemporaries had a general sense that through reason they could overcome obstacles, conquer prejudice, and slay superstition. The events in Konitz, located on the eastern fringes of the German Empire, and on the western edge of a Slavic pogrom landscape, could hardly diminish the sense that, setbacks notwithstanding, mankind was moving forward. The superstitions that gave rise to anti-Semitism could still "turn the heart of a nation into stone," Thomas Masaryk wrote in the wake of the Polna ritual-murder accusations of 1899. Nonetheless, like most of the best and brightest of his contemporaries, Masaryk believed that these superstitions belonged to a "dying century."[1]

It thus seemed easy to dismiss the violence in Konitz as, at best, a Dreyfus affair à demi, a backwoods witch trial, an inquisition altogether out of step with the times. The anti-Semitic journalists, however, did not make this mistake, sensing in the murder story the possibilities of a public sensation—not just a story to be told but a spectacle, like a Wagnerian opera, to be created.[2] From late May onward, they traveled to Konitz and stayed there for weeks on end, the most dedicated among them taking up local quarters and throwing themselves fully into the cause. One of these journalists was Wilhelm Bruhn, whom we've already met, the thirty-one-year-old editor of the Staatsbürgerzeitung, an anti-Semitic newspaper that mixed news and prejudice so thoroughly as to render them indistinguishable.

Born in rural Pomerania, Bruhn had arrived in Berlin in 1894, after serving, like many other professional anti-Semites, as a schoolteacher, a lowly position that in Wilhelmine Germany paid all too modestly. He first purchased a printing press and published a local newspaper in Berlin-Weissensee; four years later, he joined the editorial board of the Staatsbürgerzeitung. Whether he joined this anti-Semitic newspaper for the money or out of conviction is difficult to say. Like many journalists barely scraping by, he no doubt needed a steady income and had already been arrested for gambling.[3] Now writing for the Staatsbürgerzeitung, he set out to create the anti-Semitic spectacles from which he and his newspaper lived.[4] He had already once before canvassed the Pomeranian and West Prussian countryside, spreading anti-Semitic invective.[5] On May 26, he headed east again, this time to take part in Ernst Winter's "solemn funeral."[6]

Bruhn undoubtedly boarded a train bound for Konitz at the austere, if spacious, Silesian Station in Berlin. The train crossed the Oder River, which after World War II became the dividing line between Germany and Poland, before heading deeper into the eastern territories, through flat empty spaces and row on row of rye fields.

As the landscape passed by, Bruhn may have focused his attention on the lead articles of the day's newspaper. The Boer War in South Africa continued, portrayed in the German press as a struggle of desperate, but valiant, settlers fighting for the soil—not to mention the gold and diamonds—of their homeland against the *Uitlanders,* rapacious foreigners supported by the brutal British armies of Lord Roberts and Lord Kitchener. More prominent still was the Boxer Rebellion, which, according to the German press, pitted bloodthirsty Chinese rebels against civilized nations in a conflict that would soon involve the murder of Christians and foreigners, including Germans, who had significant investments in China. Closer to home, there was the naval race, stirred with new vigor by the imperial government's plan to build ships at a pace so dizzying that it would force Great Britain to concede to Germany what the soon-to-be chancellor, Bernhard von Bülow, called its rightful place in the sun. These were important developments of the time: in provoking the aggressiveness of modern nations, each event foreshadowed the coming war whose horrors people would honor by calling it the Great War.

That conflict, of course, was still over a decade away, and more immediate issues concerned the journalist. After some five hours of travel, Bruhn's train approached Konitz through Pomerellen, a landscape known for its gentle fields and old-growth forests, for its small lakes and still smaller villages.[7] But the beauty of the Pomerellen deceived. This land was, as Max Weber once called it, "among the parts of the monarchy least blessed by nature."[8] The soil was sandy and stubborn, and the farmland dominated by the Junkers, reactionary Prussian lords who served as employer, magistrate, police, and judge. The common people led their lives in the shadow of these men, and most of them never had the chance to till their own soil. Instead, they worked as farmhands with yearly contracts or as day laborers, maids, or servants. There were some independent farmers, but as a result of agricultural depression, those who owned small plots increasingly fell into the ranks of the landless poor. And poor they were. The countryside around Konitz belonged to one of the most destitute regions in all of Germany. In Konitz County a day laborer earned about two marks per day in the summer, and slightly more than a mark per day in the winter. Women workers earned less still, just over half of a man's wage.[9] And children, when they worked scratching potatoes from the earth, earned twenty pennies per day, barely enough to pay for a loaf of bread.

The conditions in this rural region remained harsh and difficult, and the 1880s saw a powerful exodus from the area, part of the largest exodus ever from the German countryside. Young men and women, many of whom had never experienced so much as a whiff of economic independence, boarded ships destined for the United States, dreaming of five-acre homesteads on the great plains of Kansas. Although the wave of emigration to the New World had already subsided by 1900, migrations continued to western Germany's steel mills and smelting factories, and to the dark shafts of the coal mines of the Ruhr. As in many impoverished places throughout the earth, migration remained the bitter tribute the poor paid to their poverty, their requiem for the land they left behind.

More than just poverty marked the Pomerellen, however. If Bruhn left the compartment of his train to walk down the aisle, he perhaps looked north to an area populated mostly by Kashubians and Poles, who together made up the majority of the population in Konitz County. Warmly evoked in the novels of Günter Grass, the Kashubians spoke a Slavic language separate from the Polish and settled south and west of Danzig. In the countryside north of the broad Berlin-Königsberg highway, which cut a northwesterly diagonal through Konitz County, they were the oldest inhabitants, if also the poorest and least educated.[10] In 1886, a survey of Konitz County listed its inhabitants as 45 percent Kashubian and 15 percent Polish, but in 1900, more and more Kashubians claimed Polish as their primary language and identification.[11]

If Bruhn instead looked out of his compartment window, he would have seen the southern part of the county, populated by German Catholics whose forefathers had settled there in the sixteenth century in a belt of villages collectively known as the *Kochschneiderei*. He would also have seen villages of German Protestants and villages that were mixed: Protestant, Catholic, German, Polish. For although West Prussia was a hinterland, it was also an area of religious and ethnic diversity, and within this diversity, occupying a special position, though closely linked to the Germans, were the Jews. In the Pomerellen, many of the villages to the south of Konitz—like Krojanke, Cammin, Jastrow, and Zempelburg—once boasted significant Jewish populations. As late as the early nineteenth century, the majority of Prussia's Jews lived in the eastern provinces, most in small villages and towns and some in towns whose Jewish populations rivaled Berlin's.[12] But those days had passed. There were fewer Jews in the countryside now, though they could still be seen walking on the dirt road with their bundles, sitting atop their wood wagons, or leading their cattle to market.

Bruhn's train finally arrived at Konitz station, where he stepped out and was taken to Kühn's hotel by carriage along the Bahnhofstrasse, still full of ruts and holes from the April thaw and the recent rains. He had been here a number of days earlier, and the owner of the hotel, Paul Kühn, sympathized with the anti-Semitic cause. Here Bruhn could also join the *Stammtisch*, the common table, where he could converse and drink beer with men who thought and felt as he did. There he is likely to have met Franz Schleiminger, a bookseller, and Max Heyn, a photographer, along with the master mason Rudolf Hermann and the dentist Max Meibauer (a founder of the anti-Semitic citizens committee), Dr. Arthur Müller (son of the county medical examiner who performed the autopsy), and a number of prominent merchants, postal workers, a baker and a butcher, and the proprieter, Paul Kühn himself, who may have joined his anti-Semitic guests, "real German men," for a drink.[13] That Bruhn might have met any or all of these men over a glass of beer at Kühn's hotel was not a coincidence. In 1888, in fact, an officer of the church complained of the "veritable cancer" that Konitz counted "not fewer than fifty places to drink beer."[14] More than just the quality of beer separated the taverns of Konitz. One could discern differences by looking at the newspapers they displayed. Since February, Kühn would have undoubtably hung the *Staatsbürgerzeitung*, clamped into a wooden spine, on the wall for guests to read, pass along, and discuss.[15] One could also tell taverns apart by their clientele. Kühn's counted as a good middle-class tavern, the kind of place frequented by men like Gustav Hoffmann ("who went only to those taverns in which the better society meets").[16]

We don't know whether Gustav Hoffmann, the Christian butcher, met Wilhelm Bruhn, the editor of the *Staatsbürgerzeitung*, at Kühn's hotel, or at his home no more than a hundred yards across the marketplace and down the Danzigerstrasse. But that they met, on the evening of May 29, is certain. And their meeting proved to be a turning point of the events in Konitz.

I

On June 13, 1900, the day after the Prussian army marched into town, Wilhelm Bruhn's *Staatsbürgerzeitung* published a remarkable and lengthy document, carrying the date of June 5, 1900, called the "Petition of the Konitz Butcher Gustav Hoffmann Pertaining to the Matter of Winter's Murder," which set in print the butcher's tale.[17]

In this petition, Hoffmann began by describing his interrogation of May 29 and the substance of the inspector's accusation against him. Around seven o'clock in the evening of March 11, the police suggested, Hoffmann left his house to look for his daughter Anna and found her together with Ernst Winter, her body entwined with his. Enraged, Hoffmann first strangled and then stabbed the boy. The accusation,

Hoffmann told Inspector Braun, was baseless and the interrogation insulting. Here are Hoffmann's words:

> My daughter is the child of an upstanding middle-class family, and he [Inspector Braun] should know that daughters of this class are sexually unapproachable. My innocent child, who on that afternoon received, along with myself and the whole community, Holy Communion, this child should then have in this way committed a sexual transgression? Only a lowly Jewish fantasy could imagine such a thing. Not even the most depraved hussy would, on the day that she went to church and received Holy Communion, commit such a sin. But nothing is sacrosanct to the Jews, especially when the aim is to falsely accuse a Christian of murder in order to deflect the justifiable suspicions against them.

Hoffmann then recounted the events of the evening following the arrest. Until around ten o'clock, there had been isolated cases of boys shouting "hep-hep" and "here and there a window pane secretly smashed." But then, according to the butcher, "the Jews and their collaborators spread the rumor that I would be arrested in the night." This changed everything. "Upon hearing the news of my arrest, a few thousand grown-ups, mostly married men, gathered in a completely voluntary way in order to prevent the arrest of my person, a slap against all Christians." He then rehearsed his own credentials—a citizen of Konitz since 1876, homeowner for seventeen years, nine children, city council member since 1888, *Obermeister* of the general artisan guild from 1885 until its dissolution in 1899, currently *Obermeister* of the butchers' guild, and member of the adult-education board. He enjoyed the trust of all classes of people, he wrote.

The Jews need a Christian butcher on whom to pin their own guilt, Hoffmann averred, adding that he was disappointed in the Berlin inspectors for their inability to see through this Jewish machination. The inspectors did not even come up with the accusations by themselves; rather, they merely parroted what the Jews had already said.

Gustav Hoffmann also proposed reasons why he could not have been the murderer: his house—which was on the ground floor and consisted of the butcher shop, a living room, a kitchen, and four bedrooms—was full of people: his wife, his grandmother, eight of his nine children (ages three to seventeen), a servant girl, a journeyman, and two apprentices. The servant girl slept in the kitchen, which remained the only exit when the door to the Danzigerstrasse was closed. In this crowded abode, furtive movements were impossible. Hoffmann also had a solid alibi. He had spent the afternoon in company down the street at the home of Ziebarth, a fellow butcher, until six, when he returned to his own house, along with Reymann, the pastor, and Fengler, a city official, who soon left to catch the 6:53 P.M. train. Hoffmann's daughter, Anna, arrived shortly thereafter along with Fengler's daughter, who around six-thirty also caught the carriage to the train station. Anna then went for a walk but returned home by seven to help prepare the evening meal, which was served a bit earlier that night because the journeyman Welke wanted to go to the theater. The family sat down to eat at around seven-thirty. The two apprentices, Clemens Misiekowski and Albert Longear, did not arrive until around eight and were scolded for their tardiness. Thereafter, all the family members remained at home; because of the tight quarters, they could not have left unnoticed.

Other evidence against Hoffmann was mostly circumstantial. In the past winter, he had apparently seen his daughter talking to two young boys in front of the butcher shop when he called out, "Anna, come in! And if you louts don't get out of here, watch out!" The two boys ran off as quickly as possible, so Hoffmann did not even see who they were. Supposedly, one of them was Ernst Winter. The Jews, the butcher wrote, also invented the story of the intestines in the manure pile. When the Jewish merchant Isidor Fleischer emptied Hoffmann's manure onto his field (Fleischer gave straw for Hoffmann's horse in exchange for dung for Fleischer's field), he found human intestines.

Thus far the butcher's tale was about the "Jews"—conspirators who planted evidence to ensnare the innocent Christian butcher and his family. Hoffmann did not mention specific names; he did not accuse. But like a knife the butcher's tale turned. In Hoffmann's words:

> Now that this has been told to me from an official standpoint, I am forced for my further defense to officially request that the real murderer be arrested. I maintain that the butcher Adolph Lewy and his son Moritz Lewy were present and active at Winter's murder.

Hoffmann then put forward twelve arguments demonstrating the guilt of the Jewish butcher and his son. They were as follows.

First, on the day that the torso was found, Hoffmann went to the lake, where he could observe "the naked torso very precisely." He concurred that the torso was bloodless and that the sack containing it showed "no traces of blood whatsoever." Close examination of the body parts also showed that "they were completely bloodless." On these matters, the Christian butcher considered himself an expert. He also knew about cuts. "The cut, through which the head was separated from the torso, was a real kosher cut, as the Jewish slaughterer [Schächter] does it."

Hoffmann proceeded to describe the method.

> As a butcher, I have repeatedly had the opportunity to watch the slaughter of animals. In previous times, the slaughterer used to butcher calves in such a way that they hung the live animal from its hind hooves so that the head hung toward the ground and was held steady. The slaughterer then cut through the throat of the animal with a sharp knife below the larynx. To judge from the characteristics of the torso, this is how I think Winter was murdered. The cut on the throat below the larynx and the complete bloodlessness of the body leave no room for doubt. Winter must have been suddenly attacked by a number of people, prevented from screaming by being choked, hung up by his feet with his head pointing downward, undressed, and finally killed by a practiced kosher butcher who cut his throat as he would an animal's. The blood was carefully collected, and then the dismemberment of the body began.

This was an operation, Hoffmann further reasoned, that could not have been performed by an ordinary butcher. It must have been someone who knew how to slaughter humans. "I mean," Hoffmann clarified, "that the man who dismembered the body must have already killed and dismembered a number of Christian boys, so skillfully were the parts that I saw worked on." It must have been done in a lighted room, and the whole operation must have taken hours, since the torso was also packed in a sack. Finally, from information concerning the autopsy that he had read in the newspaper, the Christian butcher deduced evidence that pointed to a Jewish butcher. In kosher slaughtering, Hoffmann opined, the butcher, after he has partly opened the stomach, cuts the diaphragm and reaches in with his hand to examine the lung. If the lung is healthy, it does not stick to the ribs; if it is stuck to the ribs, the animal is unclean and may not be eaten. This is how it was done with Winter. "If the autopsy really is accurate," Hoffmann concluded, "then it is certain that Winter was slaughtered like a piece of cattle according to full Jewish ritual."

Second, the murderers or their abettors must have carried the wrapped torso to the Mönchsee; and because the torso was heavy, a number of people must have been involved. This could have happened only at a place hidden from the eyes of the night watchman or the glances of passersby. "When one walks past the row of houses in the Maurergasse, the Lewy house alone seems suitable for carrying out such a murder without being seen." In fact, Hoffmann continued, it was the only place "in the whole area in which the above-described hour-long work of killing and dismembering could have been done by light."

Third, the sack that contained the torso came from Plath, a tailor; every three weeks, Adolph Lewy's sister bought rags from the tailor, or rather from his helper, a Polish woman named Frankowski. In this way—from Plath via Frankowski to Lewy's sister—the sack made its way to the Jewish butcher. "It can be assumed with certainty," Hoffmann maintained, "that the butcher Adolph Lewy received this sack from his sister and used it to pack the body."

Fourth, Hoffmann also accused the Jewish butcher's first son, Moritz Lewy, then twenty-eight years old. Here are Hoffmann's words:

> The son Moritz Lewy was friends with the deceased; they were the same age and were often together. In all probability, Winter's penchant for the female sex was used as a lure by which Moritz enticed Winter into the back shed, where the murder victim was met not by womanly arms but by the fists of the murderers lying in wait.

Fifth, a day laborer who brought Lewy a cow was in Lewy's house on the Sunday afternoon of the murder, and the Jewish butcher allegedly touched and poked him and said to his wife, "He is pale, he has too little blood."

Sixth, the lady who cleaned for Adolph Lewy, Mrs. Ross, came by on Sunday evening between seven and eight and heard strange noises from the cellar. A few days later, she found a watch chain in the living room. When Mrs. Ross took the chain in her hand, Mrs. Lewy supposedly ripped it away from her and screamed, "The chain belongs to my son Moritz." The chain, Hoffmann reported, is now missing.

Seventh, the son-in-law of Mrs. Ross, Bernhard Masloff, walked by Lewy's at about eleven Sunday night and heard murmuring in the cellar; he went around to the back and saw Lewy come out with a light; later, three more men came out, one of them Moritz Lewy, carrying a heavy package to the Mönchsee.

Eighth, Wolf Israelski, the Jewish skinner, buried the head just beyond the shooting club, showing therefore that Lewy had help and "that the murderer is really only to be found among the Jews."

Ninth, a number of people must have participated in the murder, as the transportation of the arm and the head shows. Also, according to Hoffmann, the fact that a 20,000-mark reward did not bring forth a traitor pointed to a Jewish cabal.

Tenth, Jews from the outside had come to Konitz in the week of March 4 to March 11. They left thereafter because the "slaughter of Winter was a success."

Eleventh, in the shop of the Jewish merchant Meyer, a conversation was overheard by Mrs. Wiwjorra, the wife of a cabinet maker. She heard the name Winter, whereupon Meyer's daughter said to her parents, "No, let that go, that's pure murder."

Twelfth, a relative of Lewy's from the village of Bad Polzin allegedly visited him on March 11. A servant girl listening in the next room reported that when the man returned home his wife asked him, "How was it? Was he very strong, very powerful? Did he defend himself? Was it worth it? Did you bring me something?" "He was very strong," the husband replied; "six men had to hold him; but with time he became weak; it was worth it, and I brought you this." He then presented his wife with a bottle of blood.

Hoffmann concluded his tale with general complaints: that the Berlin police neither trusted nor listened to the Christian witnesses; that right after the murder the Jews had formed a committee that influenced the testimony of witnesses, sometimes through bribery; and that if the government would only send different investigators, the crime could be solved. But for now, Hoffmann, an innocent man, had to defend himself and the honor of his innocent daughter.

The butcher's tale, officially the "Petition of the Konitz Butcher Gustav Hoffmann Pertaining to the Matter of Winter's Murder," was published both in the newspapers and as a pamphlet with a print run of 50,000 copies, making it perhaps the most widely read piece of writing in all of West Prussia that summer.[18] Almost certainly, however, Hoffmann, a modestly educated butcher, did not write the tale alone, if, in fact, he wrote it at all. Its tone, style, and diction, and the felicity with which it mimicked the expressions on the streets and the printed word of the press, all point to the possibility that it was composed by one of the anti-Semitic journalists, probably Wilhelm Bruhn. The collusion began with Hoffmann's summons. "That's what we've been waiting for," Bruhn may have said.[19] When, in the morning hours, the police came to Hoffmann's door, Bruhn leapt into action, bringing Bernhard Masloff, the counterwitness, to his room in Kühn's hotel, where Bruhn pressured him to "tell the whole truth" so that he could "save the Hoffmann family from misfortune."[20] This was a day of great excitement and activity, with Kühn's hotel as the "flashpoint of social life for many Konitz residents and citizens."[21] That evening, Bruhn met Hoffmann for the first time. Hoffmann's lawyer, Carl Gebauer, who would emerge as the "center of the anti-Semitic movement in Konitz," set up the meeting.[22] Gebauer asked Bruhn to "represent the interests of Mr. Hoffmann, who has been unjustly attacked from all sides, in the *Staatsbürgerzeitung.*"[23] The substance of the conversations between Bruhn and the butcher cannot be reconstructed, but Bruhn eagerly complied with the lawyer's request. "That's what we did," Bruhn later said, "and in this sense the petition has to be understood."[24]

Upon Gebauer's request, Bruhn probably wrote the petition, or at the very least dictated it, and Gustav Hoffmann signed it.[25] The Christian butcher claimed authority, and the people perceived it as his statement. "Many now say that Hoffmann brought forward proof for a ritual murder in Lewy's house," the county official Zedlitz recorded on June 17.[26]

At first glance, the butcher's tale suggests the power of Berlin-based print over local, oral communication in the generation and dissemination of anti-Semitic ideas. Yet this conclusion alone remains too facile, failing to account for the stories within the butcher's tale—points five to twelve of the petition—which, based on fantastically dubious hearsay, widened the accusation against Lewy and the Jews.[27] More important, this one-dimensional interpretation rests on a false dichotomy between oral and print culture that ignores the mutual influence of these forms of communication at the turn of the century. Anti-Semitic journalists like Bruhn who penned these stories for the papers also spent their evenings in the pubs and on the streets drinking beer and wine with the townspeople; they listened to and coached them in their storytelling; they lived on rumors and propogated them. To understand this process, it makes more sense, as Robert Darnton has written, to discern how "two forms of communication worked together, defining, transmitting, and amplifying messages."[28]

More than mere messages—simple vehicles for transmitting

information—stories took hold of and transfixed the population of Konitz. Stories are fundamental to the way we understand ourselves and our world. When they are imaginary, they ask us, as Coleridge pointed out, to engage in a "willing suspension of disbelief"; when they are "real," we think of them as true. In either case, stories invite people to see from a certain perspective: through the eyes of the narrator, or from the point of view of a character, sometimes both. Readers and listeners come to understand, even share in, the way the events of a narrative are framed. In this sense, the narrative act is necessarily social, particularly when many people actively participate in the production and dissemination of the narrative—when they become, to use Barbara Meyerhoff's felicitous phrase, "authors of themselves."[29] In Konitz, the anti-Semitic journalists drew from a cauldron full of stories the people in the town had already told each other. In this sense, and especially with respect to the latter parts of the butcher's tale, it was the townspeople who provided the primary ingredients. They thickened its plot, deepened its cast of characters, and stirred in more and more damning detail.

I I

The accusation that the Jews murdered Ernst Winter surfaced soon after the boy's torso was pulled from the lake. Already the next day, the market hummed with gossip and speculation, traders and store owners, passersby and cleaning ladies exchanging news more feverishly than their wares. Well before Wilhelm Bruhn arrived in Konitz, many people had come forward to tell disparaging stories about Adolph Lewy and other Jews. Of these stories, the most influential was the intricate yarn spun by Bernhard Masloff and his mother-in-law, Anna Ross.

Masloff, a twenty-four-year-old bricklayer, came to the police on March 20, nine days after the boy's murder. Supposedly, he had seen a flickering light and heard strange noises emanating from the house of Adolph Lewy on the night of the murder. But because a 2,000-mark reward had been posted, the police were wary. "The manner in which he gave the whole testimony," one inspector said, meant that "from the beginning I gave it little weight."[30] But the bricklayer proved tenacious. A month later, on April 25, when the size of the reward had increased tenfold, Masloff returned to offer the following story.[31]

He claimed that on the night of the murder he had drunk four glasses of beer at Sänger's pub and three glasses of schnapps at his in-laws'. As he ambled home, he passed Lewy's house on the Danzigerstrasse and accidentally dropped the cork to his snuffbox. When he bent down to pick it up, he suddenly saw a light in Lewy's cellar and overheard people in the basement uttering sounds—"ho, ho, hoho!"[32] Curious, Masloff crouched on one knee and put his ear to the window. After about fifteen minutes of straining to hear, he went around to the back, took off his boots so that he could make a quiet escape, and, for two hours, listened. Eventually, he heard voices "murmuring" and saw a small man "in the shape of the elder Lewy" come out and warily look about. "Nothing shall be known," Masloff heard Lewy say.[33]

Masloff told this story in late April—in an atmosphere of deepening enmity after the first wave of violence. Perhaps he thought its reception would now be more favorable. Among the police, it was not. But six weeks later Masloff's day finally came. When the police summoned Gustav Hoffmann on May 29, the anti-Semitic journalist Bruhn persuaded Masloff to try again. Masloff now amended his story a third time.

To start, he had far less to drink: two glasses of beer, one shot of schnapps. He also had a new reason for kneeling down at the door of Lewy's back court for such a long time. Having eyed a slab of meat in the cellar eight days before, he now resolved to steal it. Masloff pulled the slab of meat down from the rack and, his boots in one hand, the five-pound piece of meat in the other, made his way home. More important, Masloff now claimed that not one but three men exited the cellar, among them Moritz Lewy: two men were carrying a heavy package, the third lighting the way to the Mönchsee with a kerosene lamp.[34]

Masloff brought forward a remarkable testimony, a detailed eye-witness account unequivocally incriminating the Lewys. But if his rough-hewn story of kneeling in his socks behind Lewy's house seemed to stretch credulity, it was more than matched by the complicated tale spun by his mother-in-law.

A forty-three-year-old woman, Anna Ross ran a maid service in Konitz, sometimes cleaning houses herself, sometimes coordinating the services of others. She had cleaned and washed for the Lewys for eight years.[35] She had also hired out her two daughters—the elder, Auguste Berg, and the younger, Martha, Bernhard Masloff's wife.[36] Both had cleaned for the Lewys as well.

At seven o'clock on Sunday night, March 11, Anna Ross went to the Lewys in order to set up maid service. While talking with the lady of the house in the living room, Ross heard "muttering whispers" from the cellar. Frightened, she was about to leave when Helene Lewy (Adolph's niece) supposedly came up the stairs with a kitchen lamp, which she blew out the second she noticed Ross. Three days later, and the day after the torso had been fished from the Mönchsee, Ross went to the weekly market to look for domestic help for the Lewys, but she could find no one, since the women of the town were so convinced of the culpability of the Jews. Ross told this to Pauline Lewy, Adolph's wife, and said that it would be easier to find help when the police discovered the killer. "The [killer] will never be discovered," Pauline Lewy supposedly replied. "The Jewish community is very rich," and "that Winter is not worth all the commotion."[37]

Over the next three weeks, Anna Ross rarely visited the Lewys. Then, on Palm Sunday, April 8, she picked up laundry from Pauline Lewy, took the wash back to her apartment, separated the clothes the next morning, and noticed a handkerchief "much cleaner" and finer than the others and with embroidered initials. Ross, who could not read, showed the handkerchief to her daughter Auguste, who identified the initials as "E.W."[38] Neither made a connection. Later in the week, Ross returned the wash to Pauline Lewy in a basket that belonged to Bernhard Masloff. She also sent her daughter Martha, Masloff's wife, to the Lewys to work as domestic help. While cleaning, Martha happened upon a white watch chain, like the one Ernst Winter possessed, which Lewy's wife, Pauline, grabbed from her, saying it belonged to her son Moritz. Martha also claimed that she found a cigar case with a picture of Ernst Winter inside.

The following Sunday was Easter Sunday. That afternoon, Anna Ross allegedly met a stranger, a farmhand from a village west of Schlochau, who told her that he had been in Konitz on the evening of March 11 and had observed near the synagogue three men carrying a heavy package who then disappeared in the narrow alley between the houses of Gustav Hoffmann and Adolph Lewy. On Wednesday, April 25, more than a week after Easter Sunday, and immediately following the first large wave of riots in Konitz and the surrounding area, it suddenly occurred to Anna Ross that E.W. might stand for Ernst Winter. The next day, she told Auguste, and on the day after that she went to the police station. Officer Block, who was temporarily stationed in Konitz, immediately charged over to the Lewys before they could get wind of what was happening. When he entered the house, he demanded to search Pauline Lewy's wash, sifted through it, and found nothing.[39]

The stories of Masloff and Ross quickly wended their way through the taverns, but even in the anti-Semitic camp, their family hardly inspired confidence. According to one account, the Masloff home was a mess, the parents fought, the mother refused to cook and clean, and the father drank himself senseless and told notoriously tall tales.[40] Bernhard Masloff, who had moved to Konitz in 1897, had a record for petty theft and, like his father, coveted his drink. Anna Ross herself was hardly an upstanding citizen. Although she had lived in Konitz longer, she had a reputation for mendacity and her two daughters had prior police records: Martha for stealing, Auguste for trespassing. Moreover, everyone knew that Bernhard Masloff and Anna Ross did not get along. In the past, Masloff had threatened his mother-in-law, even beat her, enough that she once called the police for protection and had her son-in-law charged with assault and battery. This incident occurred shortly after Masloff's wedding in May 1898, when, much to his mother-in-law's chagrin, he forced his new wife, Martha, to convert from Protestantism to Catholicism. Tolerance, apparently, was not something that ran in the family. Martha also took to beating her own father, once so badly with a broom that blood dribbled from his head.[41]

Still, the people of Konitz sided with Masloff and Ross, unlikely protagonists though they were. After all, the people of Konitz, with the help of Wilhelm Bruhn, were choosing to believe a story they themselves had helped create.

The town's collusion with these unreliable sources was most evident in the testimony Bernhard Masloff offered on May 29. On the day that Gustav Hoffmann was interrogated, three men—Wilhelm Bruhn, factory-owner Paul Aschke (Masloff's boss), and Karl Kuby, an engineer—invited Masloff for a drink of bouillon in the entertainment room of Kühn's hotel. The men spoke with Masloff for an hour, and Bruhn brought him to the police. That afternoon, the men went back to visit Masloff again, this time at his workplace, the gasworks.[42] We do not know what was said in that first encounter. In one version, it was this: "Look, Masloff, tell the truth. . . . People's lives depend on it." Another had it this way: "You can save an honorable man from prison; the butcher Gustav Hoffmann has been arrested. You can save him."[43] In either case, the pressures on Masloff were evident. On that morning, a crowd had gathered, with Masloff at the center; the crowd was already agitated, and the lines in the sand—here the forces for Hoffmann, there the protectors of Lewy—were already drawn. Moreover, the most immediate pressures came from wealthy, refined gentlemen in top hats, his employer among them.

Anna Ross was not alone, either, and the circumstances of her first testimony also reveal the highly charged atmosphere out of which these stories emerged.

She first made her accusations on the night of Wednesday, April 18, three days after Easter. Police Commissioner Block and his assistant were in pursuit of thugs they had seen disappear into the courtyard where Ross lived. It was late at night, and, according to Ross, Commissioner Block pried open her window with his sword and entered her bedroom, where she and her daughter lay in bed barely clothed. Upon seeing the policemen climbing through her window, Anna Ross jumped up and screamed and ran out into the courtyard.

"Why don't you go after the Jews and leave us alone," she yelled.[44]

"What do you know about the Jews?" Block replied.

"Yes, the Jews did it. . . . Search at the Lewys', in their house, there you'll find something."

"What do you know about the Lewys?" Block asked.

"I could tell you a lot but not like this," she said, after an initial silence.[45]

Commissioner Block pressed her, and she told the story about the farmhand from a village west of Schlochau, who had come by on Easter and pointed out to her where the two men carrying a heavy package had disappeared into the narrow alley between the houses of Hoffmann and Lewy, and how a third man had then followed.[46] But when she could not name the farmhand, the commissioner broke off the questioning. "You know," he said to her, "it would be best if you wait until the man comes back; then let me know, and I'll get him myself."[47]

But if Block did not pursue the lead, other people happily stepped in. Later that week, two schoolteachers, Thiel and Hofrichter, and a dentist, Meibauer, interrogated Anna Ross in her apartment. The date of the meeting is unclear: either Saturday, April 21, or Sunday, April 22.[48] Hofrichter had heard from a servant girl that Anna Ross knew something; the three men went to her apartment, a number of times, it turned out, and she recounted the story of the stranger. On another occasion, a journalist and "private detective" named Georg Zimmer, who had been writing that summer for the *Konitzer Tageblatt* (now edited by Martha Hoffmann's fiancé), also visited Ross in her apartment, and she recounted the story to him as well.[49]

At important points in the unfolding of Anna Ross's story, prominent townspeople, whether local notables or sensation-hungry, anti-Semitic journalists, lent credence to her story and framed it within the context of the town's struggle. Masloff's testimony became part of the larger divide between the faction of Hoffmann and that of Adolph Lewy, and Ross's testimony bolstered the conspiracy theory that the Berlin police, who treated the local Christians disparagingly, had dismissed clues that led to the doorsteps of local Jews. Ross's and Masloff's stories also gained significance when journalists elevated their status, and that of the people who told them, by publishing them in the columns of their national newspapers. On May 1, the *Staatsbürgerzeitung* ran a long article detailing the evidence that had surfaced in Konitz up until this point. Entitled "On the Konitz Blood Murder," the article emphasized those pieces of the puzzle that pointed to the culpability of the Jews and concluded with the dubious evidence offered by Masloff and Ross. The article implied that their stories were the culmination of sightings already made by "the people of Konitz." In the printed version, the stories of Masloff and Ross were not told from the standpoint of their problematic, often inebriated tellers. Instead, the focalization, as Gérard Genette calls it, was elsewhere: "the people of Konitz."[50] Rendered as a collective singular, the people of Konitz emerged as the real detectives, the ones who collected the evidence, who knew where it pointed, and who understood what the Berlin police did not: that the Lewys killed Ernst Winter.

The stories of Masloff, Ross, and family were recounted again, but between May 1, when the *Staatsbürgerzeitung* first printed them, and May 29, when Hoffmann was indicted, the *Staatsbürgerzeitung* mentioned the tales only once, on May 19, and then only as an aside, taking up the story of the white watch chain, which Martha Masloff supposedly saw while cleaning Lewy's house.[51] This changed dramatically on the day of Hoffmann's interrogation. In the evening edition of the Tuesday newspaper, May 29, the *Staatsbürgerzeitung* printed the following telegraph:

> Konitz, May 29, 1:26 P.M. The Christian population is very agitated; the Christian butcher Hoffmann has been apprehended

and taken to the station for an interrogation. Meanwhile, his house is yet again being searched. His definitive arrest awaits. A worker Masloff has today made very incriminating statements against the butcher Lewy and his sons. He says he saw three men in the night carrying a package from Lewy's courtyard to the lake.[52]

Thereafter, Masloff's story assumed greater centrality in the minds of the people and became tied to Hoffmann's summons. Suddenly, what Masloff supposedly heard became a standard refrain: "Nothing shall be known" appeared again and again as bylines for newspaper articles and for anti-Semitic pamphlets.[53] The catchphrase had even begun to surface in the stories other people told, and the citizens of Konitz imagined Jews whispering to each other in the streets, "Nothing shall be known." Through constant retelling in the press and in the pubs, the stories started by Masloff and Ross coalesced in the minds of the townspeople. They became part of a common store of local knowledge: what the people knew, their own story of how the murder happened.

Unimpressed by their testimony, Inspector Braun arrested Masloff and his mother-in-law and charged them both with perjury. For good measure, he also charged Ross's two daughters, Auguste and Martha. Still, the subsequent trial, which took place in November in the Konitz county courthouse, hardly untangled what Inspector Braun called a "powerful tissue of lies."[54] Rather, the trial became a spectacle of the first order, a farce in which witness after witness recounted stories incriminating the Lewys and other Jews in the ritual murder of Ernst Winter.

Spearheaded by Dr. Max Vogel, a prominent Konitz lawyer, the defense sought to prove the innocence of Masloff and Ross by demonstrating the credibility of their tales. To this end, and over a period of two and a half weeks, the defense called a series of witnesses testifying to suspicious circumstances in the house of Adolph Lewy. Beyond this, further witnesses testified against other Jews in the area. There was a Jewish conspiracy, the defense claimed, in which Adolph Lewy played the central role. And if the Lewys were guilty, the defense further argued, the innocence of Masloff and Ross followed.

Certain peculiarities of the justice system in imperial Germany favored the anti-Semitic strategy. The trial was held in Konitz, it was public, and it was to be adjudicated by a jury. Unlike the United States, imperial Germany possessed no legal provision for moving trials to neutral ground in cases where the local population proved especially partial. And in Konitz, the population was nothing if not partial. According to a report of the Anti-Defamation League, 90 percent of the people of Konitz assumed that the family would be found innocent of perjury.[55] Since the trial was public, the court attempted to appease the anti-Semites in the streets and among the spectators. "In order to calm public opinion," a ministerial memorandum reported, "every clue pointing to the Jews was carefully pursued . . . even far beyond what was necessary and appropriate."[56]

The jury, too, was not entirely unbiased. In imperial Germany, judges did not ordinarily screen jurors to ensure that they were impartial with respect to the case at hand. Instead, judges simply selected men whom they considered upstanding local citizens. As a consequence, the jury often reflected a conservative, even authoritarian, frame of mind, and its members often knew about the case before entering the courtroom. In the perjury trial against Masloff and Ross, there were twelve jury members and four substitutes: of the sixteen men chosen, nine were manorial landowners, and three owned and farmed smaller plots of land; in addition, there were two merchants, a town council member, and a teacher.[57] The teacher, Maximillian Meyer, served as the foreman of the jury. Like many of his colleagues in the Konitz Gymnasium, he also waxed anti-Semitic.[58] As if this were not enough, the wives of the jurors sat close by and often "let their sympathies and antipathies be known."[59] Finally, in the foyer of the courtroom, members of the unofficial citizens committee—especially Hofrichter and Meibauer—busied themselves by conducting their own investigation, interrogating witnesses before and after they took the stand, and influencing their testimony.[60]

The courtroom thus constituted a stage on which to rehearse the butcher's tale and other stories all over again. It was, moreover, an elevated stage, because the juridical rendering of the stories lent them an air of legitimacy, raising their status from marginal gossip to public evidence. As more and more townspeople became involved with the event, the courtroom drama pit the partisans of the butcher's tale against the defenders of local Jews in an epic confrontation, the "Konitz civil war," as one commentator called it.[61]

The war ended in a pyrrhic victory for the prosecution. The jury found the principal defendants, Bernhard Masloff and Anna Ross, guilty of perjury, and the judge sentenced Masloff to a one-year prison term and Anna Ross to a two-and-a-half-year term. But with respect to Masloff, the perjury charge only pertained to his deposition under oath of May 2 (following his testimony of late April), when he withheld "the fact" that he had stolen meat from Adolph Lewy on the night of March 11. On the second charge of perjury, pertaining to the sworn deposition of June 8 (following his statements at Kühn's hotel on May 29), the jury found him not guilty. "The untruth of the statement, which the defendant Masloff swore under oath on June 8, has not been proven," the jury proclaimed.[62] The jurors thus confirmed the credibility of Masloff's account of three men leaving Lewy's cellar carrying a sack to the Mönchsee. How exactly they reached this conclusion is more difficult to discern. The defense conceded that Lewy had a solid alibi, but argued that Lewy may have leased his cellar to the killers, and that the ritual murder could nevertheless have taken place as Masloff testified.[63] Moreover, the jury found Martha Masloff, Bernhard's wife, and Auguste Berg, the other daughter of Anna Ross, innocent, even though they actively colluded in the stories that Ross had told. These stories the jury found less credible, and concluded that Ross was guilty as charged.

I I I

The impact of the outside journalists and the elevation of Masloff's and Ross's sightings and suspicions to a courtroom drama of "us" versus "them" was considerable. Yet all of these efforts to blame the Jews would have been in vain had it not been for the people—for the treacherous acts they imagined and for the secret conversations they thought they heard. Fortified by their fears and anxieties, a disturbingly large number of people in Konitz and the surrounding area publicly proclaimed their suspicions of their Jewish neighbors.

The faltering investigation provided an opportunity—as long as the police had few leads, they were forced to pursue every shred of evidence, no matter how tenuous. They searched people's private homes on at least eighty separate occasions and took every story, every accusation, seriously.[64] And in Konitz, as we know, there was no shortage of accusations, especially since the advent of the 20,000-mark reward.[65] By July, there had already been four hundred separate incriminations by people coming to the police and to the newspapers with stories of what they saw, heard, smelled, even dreamed.[66]

These stories take us into the heart of the anti-Semitic imagination. Some stories were born of half-baked theories of how the murder must have happened, others came from conversations people imagined themselves as having overheard, and still others involved further evidence about Jews already suspected of being implicated in the killing. But few people came forward to tell the complete tale of ritual murder. More often, people imagined small parts of the whole story. But when soldered together, the bits and pieces formed an imposing edifice of tangled and twisted fictions.

The murder, many people assumed, was planned in advance. In Konitz, this belief structured a series of accusations against the Jewish merchant Matthäus Meyer, who owned a hardware store on the Danzigerstrasse, across from Adolph Lewy's house. Witnesses claimed to have seen a Jewish-looking man walk with a list under his arm into Meyer's hardware store. A discussion supposedly ensued, with Meyer's youngest daughter, Rosa, insisting that her father not sign the petition to slaughter Ernst Winter. "That is murder!" Rosa allegedly said, vexing her father greatly.[67] The mother, in one version of the story, also contributed to the conversation, saying, "We don't need the blood for Matzo but only for good luck," and later, "Drag him to the

Mönchsee."[68] But in another telling, the mother supposedly said, "The poor young man, he is really to be pitied." In this version, the father, upon hearing the resistance of his wife and daughter, returned the list, saying, "No, I will not sign, I am not going to do something like this, and I am not going to stay in Konitz."[69]

The Meyers had in fact moved to Berlin in early March, a week before the murder. But the accusations had a disturbing sequel. When Meyer's eldest daughter, Jenny, died, people accused the Meyers of having poisoned her in order to stop her from warning Ernst Winter of what awaited him.[70] The rumor gained currency, and officials in Konitz even discussed the possibility of exhuming the corpse. Fortunately, this was avoided. The daughter, it turned out, had fallen into a cataleptic trance.[71]

A second set of stories more specifically addressed the question of who killed Ernst Winter, where, and how. Here too, rumors echoed throughout the region.

Paul Orda, a wayfarer passing through Konitz after his release from prison, claimed to have been walking down a country road on his way to seek employment on a farm when two men—one older, one younger—approached a nearby fence. A wagon full of Jews pulled up, and one of their number lassoed the younger man, jerking him to the ground. "What do you want?" the younger man cried out. "I am Winter." Yet no fence existed where Orda claimed it had, and Orda was not in Konitz when he said he was. Furthermore, he had been arrested for false accusations before. Now he would be arrested again, find his way back to prison, and languish there for another five years.[72]

In the case of Paul Orda, money may have been the primary motive. In other cases, simple superstition may have fueled the imagination. There were, for example, a number of stories involving the synagogue as the murder site. In Konitz, a fifty-seven-year-old bricklayer, Christian Lübke, insisted that there were underground vaults and tunnels beneath the synagogue, and that the murder occurred within these vaults and tunnels—so he allegedly overheard some Jews as saying.[73] Partly through the agitation of the local press, this theory even began to assume a certain popularity, forcing Mayor Deditius to inspect the temple and to question the masons who had worked on the foundations a few years earlier.[74] Similarly, a washerwoman in Konitz reported that "many years ago" she had looked into the mikveh, the ritual bath, and had seen that there were stairs leading underground to a place with "many different alcoves." The sight made an "eerie impression on her," and she thought of it again after the murder of Ernst Winter.[75]

People not only claimed to have seen something suspicious, they also reported having overheard incriminating conversations—all of which pointed to a vast Jewish cabal. Thus, Johann Winkelmann the night watchman, who lived in a village to the east of Konitz, claimed that he had overheard a conversation between two beardless Jews, "one stout, the other lean," who had been contracted to slaughter Ernst Winter. According to the night watchman's testimony, the conversation, which took place in front of Meyer's hardware store, went as follows:

STOUT JEW: "What did you want with the Rabbi?"
LEAN JEW: "He had me come from Czersk; I'm supposed to come to Konitz to kill someone, to slaughter him."
STOUT JEW: "Man, don't do that. You've already done enough. Let someone else do it."
LEAN JEW: "I have to do it. No one else wants to do it, and we don't have any blood."
STOUT JEW: "Well, what sort do you have?"
LEAN JEW: "He is supposed to be a big guy, eighteen years old, from the Gymnasium." . . .
LEAN JEW: "He should be easy to get. He was supposed to have had a long conversation with our girls." . . .
STOUT JEW: "How will you kill him?"
LEAN JEW: "He will be stripped naked, and then he will be chopped under the knee."
STOUT JEW: "He will probably be drained of his strength?"
LEAN JEW: "No, the blood has to come out, his head will be cut off."
STOUT JEW: "While he is still alive?"

LEAN JEW: "Although he will be drunk, he will still know what we're doing with him."
STOUT JEW: "No, I wouldn't do this for 100,000 marks. What kind of a torture is this?"
LEAN JEW: "If only I could for my part get the half of that. But I'm getting a few hundred thaler."[76]

The police easily cast doubt on the veracity of the story. The Jews in question could not be found, and Winkelmann, who was Polish, barely understood German, making it difficult to imagine how he could comprehend what the Jews had said. Moreover, people in his village, such as Choinackinz, a teacher, assured the police inspector who followed up the lead that Winkelmann was "a man endowed with a prodigious imagination," while the county official Neumann described him as the village "mutton head."[77]

Whatever people may have thought of his intellectual qualities, Winkelmann appropriated themes that had circulated in and around Konitz, including the involvement of religious authorities in the murder, Winter's alleged transgression with Jewish girls, and the necessity of Christian blood for the Jewish community. The latter theme captured the imagination and resurfaced in conversations other people allegedly overheard. For example, August Steinke, a raftsman in Prechlau, said that just before the murder in Konitz, he had carried on the following conversation with Josef Eisenstädt, a Jewish cattle trader from Schlochau:

STEINKE: "The Winter family is a respectable family with a nice son."
EISENSTÄDT: "The son is fit for slaughter."
STEINKE: "He is too thin."
EISENSTÄDT: "He has a lot of blood."[78]

In a similar vein, Anton Hellwig, "Stutter Anton," a Catholic farmer from the village of Görsdorf, claimed that a Jewish grain dealer, Alexander Camminer, had told him, "This year blood is so expensive, it costs half a million marks."[79]

For the rumor mill in and around Konitz, nothing seemed too far-fetched, not even the alleged statements of Alex Prinz. A twenty-three-year-old Jewish man who had never made it past the fourth grade, he was known to everyone in Konitz as "Dumb Alex." A trader in rags, bones, and iron nails, Alex allegedly said to Auguste Schiller, the seventy-three-year-old wife of an innkeeper and a fortune-teller, that the Jewish cantor in Schlochau killed Ernst Winter with a slit to the neck. On the morning of March 13, before the torso was found in the Mönchsee, Alex came into her cottage, and according to Auguste Schiller the following conversation ensued:

> DUMB ALEX: "Yes, I will fetch water, but the Jewish cantor in Schlochau murdered Winter. Cut his throat."
> AUGUSTE SCHILLER: "A [kosher] cut? Oh my God!"
> DUMB ALEX: "Yes, a [kosher] cut!"
> AUGUSTE SCHILLER: "Alone?"
> DUMB ALEX: "No, three Jewish cantors. Haller from Tuchel, Hamburger from Schlochau, and the one from Elbing."
> AUGUSTE SCHILLER: "Where did it happen? It had to happen somewhere?"
> DUMB ALEX: "Yes, at Lewy's, in the cellar."
> AUGUSTE SCHILLER: "So! Who did it?"
> DUMB ALEX: "Lewy! Lewy!"
> AUGUSTE SCHILLER: "So! Well."
> DUMB ALEX: "He didn't have any money."
> AUGUSTE SCHILLER: "Alex, for God's sake."
> DUMB ALEX: "Yes, blood fetches a dear price."
> AUGUSTE SCHILLER: "Where did they put the blood?"
> DUMB ALEX: "It was sent away, and they got 100,000 thaler for the blood!"
> AUGUSTE SCHILLER: "So! But, Alex, the blood stains?"
> DUMB ALEX: "That will all be cleaned up. All cleaned up immediately."[80]

Despite its inconsistencies, the conversation took up standard motifs, concerning blood, money, ritual slaughter, conspiracy, and the use of Lewy's cellar. How did Dumb Alex come to say such things? Alex claimed that "the youngsters at Jeleniewskis got [him] drunk," and told him what to say, but according to his mother, Rosalie Prinz, Auguste Schiller served Alex the lines he was to repeat and, reading it in her cards, promised him a lot of money.[81] In court, a grinning Dumb Alex confirmed this and said, "Go to America!" Instead, his mother gave him a beating. Finally, Auguste Schiller did not go to the police with the news, but rather went to the butcher Gustav Hoffmann, and she did not go there until June 15, by which time she claimed that Dumb Alex had visited her twice again, each time with more news. At Hoffmann's there was also a "certain Mr. Bruhn," who took notes on the story.[82] This is how it landed in the *Staatsbürgerzeitung* and circulated throughout the town.

In the main, such stories came from marginal sources: from the drunken Dumb Alex; from the night watchman Winkelmann, the "mutton head"; and from the likes of "Stutter Anton," whose superstitions his fellow pupils in Görsdorf had earlier ridiculed.[83] Nevertheless, when dignified in print, the stories of Dumb Alex and "Stutter Anton" became part of the narrative of ritual murder. Like other pieces of evidence, their stories were discussed in the pubs and on the streets, adding, with every retelling, to the store of local knowledge.

What exactly did this "local knowledge" signify to the people who told the stories, and to the many more people who repeated them? In spite of the vast historical record of the events in Konitz, one cannot be certain about the inner thoughts of the townspeople. Separated by history and perspective, we remain beholden to the indeterminacy of interpretation; but I would like to suggest that when pieced together, the various stories imply an allegory about community, about the lines people draw between themselves and their neighbors.

Each tale—from that of Masloff and Ross to that of Dumb Alex—spoke about transgression, and transgression presupposes that boundaries separate communities, dictating limits and defining the company one may keep. Certainly, the repeated reference to Ernst Winter and the "Jewish girls" suggests as much. This reference surfaced in Winkelmann's story but had been circulating in the newspapers and in the banter of the pubs for many months. It was also the point of a song commonly sung in the taverns, one refrain of which went as follows:

> Ernst Winter, he was young and handsome,
> With a Jewess he wanted to take a stroll.
> And as he to the Temple came
> There the Jews him stole.[84]

On both sides of the religious divide, there were strong social sanctions against Christians' marrying Jews. Yet, as the story goes, it was the Jews who took revenge for the alleged sexual transgression. One version of the story even referred to a Jewish "blood court," which meted out a sentence to the Christian boy for seducing Jewish girls.[85]

The cautionary tale addressed this sexual transgression—at one level. At another level, it spoke, if obliquely, about social pollution through either religious or racial defilement. Blood is both material and metaphor, referring beyond itself. At the turn of the century, the blood of a dead Christian boy symbolized both the blood of Jesus Christ, signifying the Christian community, and the blood that defined race. What unites both meanings is the focus on a specified community, in the one case of believers, in the other of a people defined by unalterable genetic factors outside the reach of history and culture. What differentiates these meanings is that the former was an old idea; the latter, in its social Darwinist guise, a new one. Christianity has a long history of exclusionary practices, but race, to cite Henry Louis Gates, "is the ultimate trope of difference."[86]

It is impossible to discern the degree to which religion, or race, constituted the principal interpretive parameters people used to understand the stories they told. Still, in either instance, defilement remains central to the story: the Jews not only took the blood of a German Christian but also cannibalistically consumed it, mixing the fluid of the two bodies, the one German and Christian, the other Jewish. Finally, one may understand this mixture as the crime itself, against which the tale is told. In this way, too, the tale admonishes: to police the boundaries of community, to keep separate what belongs separate, and to recognize a well-defined "we" opposed to, and distinct from, an increasingly alien "they." An allegory of community, these tales were implicitly hostile to the century of Jewish emancipation and assimilation.

The social origins of the stories—born of hearsay and furtive observations possible only in an integrated community—also points to their function as allegories of that community, warning itself against the dangers of social pollution. Many stories came from people who seemed to know intimate facts about the Jews in question. This was especially true of the tales told by female servants. In addition to the involved narratives of Anna Ross and her daughters, two other stories proved particularly spectacular.

The first came from Mathilde Rutz, who claimed that Adolph Lewy had tried to rape her as she was carrying winter potatoes into his cellar. When she dumped out the potatoes, the lantern went dark. "I can't find my way out," she screamed. Lewy then relit the lantern, and as she was running out they came face to face and Lewy began to press against her. "Don't say anything," he said. "I'd like to cut you off a piece of meat." She then tried to get out, but Lewy grabbed her breasts and pulled her into the straw. "I just want to have fun with you," he supposedly said. Struggling, she brushed him aside with a sweep of her arm, and then her son, who was there the whole time, took her by the hand, and together they ran out of the cellar.[87]

Good evidence speaks against such accusations: Lewy was, by all accounts, a shy and reticent, if sometimes cantankerous, man; Mathilde Rutz was a woman who liked to tell tall tales.[88] Like her husband, who was registered on the police list of town drunks, she drank excessively, though she claimed that during work hours she had only a shot of schnapps a day, and was never so drunk that someone had to carry her home.[89] There was also a great deal of yelling and screaming in her house, and she often beat her husband.[90]

The second story involved seventeen-year-old Rosine Simanowski, who developed such persecution anxiety that she left Konitz and moved to Berlin, saying that the Jews were "following" her and trying to stab her with knives.[91] She had a gift for inventing conversations in her mind, which, via the courts and the press, reached the wider public. She reported, for example, the following conversation with Heinrich Friedländer, a Jewish merchant, in his store in Konitz:

FRIEDLÄNDER: "The Jews need blood."
SIMANOWSKI: "Why?"
FRIEDLÄNDER: "They just need it."
SIMANOWSKI: "That's why you slaughtered Ernst Winter."
FRIEDLÄNDER: "I don't know about that."

She was just about to leave, when Friedländer allegedly said, "You don't have to go talking about this," and then repeated, "Don't say anything, I'll buy you a nice present."[92] Simanowski had more stories, so many that they ceased to be credible, even to the people of Konitz. But the stories and denunciations, especially from servant girls, kept coming. In Kamin, a village due south of Konitz, Josef Rosenthal's servant claimed that she overheard him saying to his wife that "he could not live on after his deed." Soon after saying this, Rosenthal allegedly tried to hang himself on a nail, but was pulled down by his brother.[93] In Bütow, a town to the north, young Marie Schmidt allegedly saw her Jewish master, Max Grossmann, return home from Konitz on March 11 with blood stains on his clothes and a bottle of blood in his hand. Grossmann, it turned out, had been in Berlin.[94] The original story, moreover, may have been twisted by the newspapers, as Schmidt later claimed that she saw blood stains only in the sink, and a dry patch of blood on Grossmann's pants, which she herself rubbed out with a dry brush.[95]

I V

Why did so many people side with the butcher's tale and the fantastic stories that, like baroque columns, both supported and adorned it?

The answer lies, in part, in the way the people of Konitz constructed a collective narrative, a script they wrote and read and, in violence, acted upon. The butcher's tale was the centerpiece of their
narrative. It gathered together narrative strands from the various stories
on the streets, some of which had already made it into print, and it
wove them together into a stronger, more intricate pattern. But the
butcher's tale was more than a series of interlacing accusations—it was
also a story with a plot.

In *Reading for the Plot*, the literary critic Peter Brooks has pointed
out that the "original sense" of the idea of plot "is the idea of boundedness, demarcation, the drawing of lines to mark off and order."[96]
Plots include and exclude, defining who belongs and who does not. In
the butcher's tale, the plot limns the lines of community. It opposes a
protagonist, Hoffmann, to the villain, Lewy. Although both men are
butchers and neighbors, Hoffmann belongs to the respectable middle
class, whose daughters are innocent; Lewy, by contrast, to a "lowly
community" for whom "nothing is sacrosanct." Behind each is a chorus. For Hoffmann, the chorus consists of the demonstrators on the
streets: respectable, upstanding, honest citizens from Konitz, "mostly
married men" who have come out into the streets to defend the honor
of a man and a girl and the faith of Christ. Women do not appear,
except to be protected by men. On the other side, the Jews who help
Lewy are the ragged, skulking characters of a provincial underworld.
There is poor and pitiful Wolf Israelski, the lean "beardless" Jew who
will kill for a hundred thaler, and the unnamed cantors from nearby
towns. They are mostly men, but women support them in ancillary
roles, like Lewy's elder sister, as bearers of implements or carriers of
body parts, or as Lewy's wife, Pauline, quick to cover up evidence, or
as the characteristically unnamed Jewish girl who lures Ernst Winter to
his death trap. Because Jewish women also bear the mark of Cain and
wander the earth, they are as deceitful as their men.

Neighbors thus do not share the same world, an impression
sharpened by the story's use of visual description. Whereas Hoffmann
is described in great detail, and photographs of him as a model citizen

abound, Adolph Lewy remains a shadowy historical figure. We do not know what he looks like or how long he has lived in Konitz. The butcher's tale also uses the predictable clichés of light and shadow to express its point. Hoffmann's property is open to plain view, while Lewy's back shed remains hidden in a dark alley (in reality they abut in the same back street). The murder takes place in a still-darker cellar, lit only by the light held by Lewy's niece. The cliché is further extended from sight to sound. The Jews, generally, do not speak in sentences; preferring to "murmur" or repeat curt phrases—"nothing shall be known," "tie him up," "Mönchsee." Between Christians and Jews, there is barely a common language. Like the "niggers" of Joseph Conrad's "dark continent," they are a civilization apart, and, as if peering into the "Heart of Darkness," one questions their humanity.[97] They are also portrayed in the story as particularly cruel, not simply in killing a young man, but in the more precise and graphically detailed sense of kosher slaughter, which in the 1880s had been the subject of parliamentary debates, often misinformed, about cruelty to animals, but which by 1900 had become an issue mainly of the anti-Semites. This imagined cruelty, in which Jews are bereft of feelings, reinforces their estrangement. By casting shadows and muting voices, the tale further highlights difference by portraying Lewy as dark, secretive, inaudible, and cruel, while implicitly rendering Hoffmann as white, truthful, audible, and innocent. The tale thus encourages the binary strategies of identification, but it also cries for popular justice—to punish the crime of a singular act (ritual murder) carried out in the name of the collective, against an individual (Ernst Winter) but aimed, symbolically, at the entire Christian community. The crime, finally, occurred because of a transgression—sexual, spatial—and because Jews, whose crimes are timeless and outside the civilizing effects of history and culture, have done this many times before.

The butcher's tale, after all, was not a wholly new creation. Cobbled together "in the age of the telephone and x-ray" in a West Prussian town, it harked back, in its figurative language as well as in its detail, to an old trope of the Western literary imagination handed down through Chaucer. In the *Canterbury Tales*, in "The Prioress's Tale," we read,

> Fro thennes forth the Jues han conspired
> This innocent out of this world to chace.
> An homycide thereto han they hyred,
> That in an aleye hadde a privee place;
> And as the child gan forby for to pace,
> This cursed Jew hym hente, and heeld hym faste,
> And kitte his throte, and in a pit hym caste.[98]

The butcher's tale bore lamentable testimony to the enduring force of fiction, and in particular to those places, to quote Toni Morrison, "where imagination sabotages itself, locks its own gates, pollutes its vision."[99]

North Sea

Baltic Sea

Konitz •
1900

BERLIN •

G E R M A N Y

Posen •
1736

Xanten
• 1891

POLAND

Neuenhoven
• 1834

Weissensee
1303
•

Dormagen
1819

Fulda
•1235

Oberwesel
1287 •

Prague
•1305

•Mainz
1283

CZECH REPUBLIC

Weissenburg
1270 •

Polna
•1899

•Pforzheim
1267

Regensburg
1476 •

Endingen
1470 •

Überlingen
1331

Munich
• 1285

Passau
1476

Krems
1293 • VIENNA
•

Pösing
1529

• Ravensburg
1429

A U S T R I A

Bern
• 1294

•Judenstein
Chapel
1670

SWITZERLAND

•Lienz
1442

Trent
• 1475

0   200 km

Chazaud

I T A L Y

*Detail of map of central Europe showing the major cases of
ritual-murder accusations throughout history.*

‎࿊‎

CHAPTER THREE

History

Ez bringent noch alliu jar
die juden Kristes marter dar
ein kristen sie mordent

In every year it happens still
the Jews Christ's passion offer
when a Christian boy they kill

—SEIFRIED HELBLING,
thirteenth-century knight and poet

The butcher's tale was based on a story even older than the poetry of Chaucer. "In every year it happens still . . . ," Seifried Helbling wrote at the end of the thirteenth century, his words suggesting that the ritual-murder tale had already firmly lodged itself in the dark recesses of the Christian imagination.[1] Yet the tale, like hatred of Jews generally, had not always been there, and while one can only speculate about the long half millennium between Augustine and Abelard, filled as it may have been with more sympathy than antagonism, more tolerance than tension, it does seem that the Christian world that created tales of Jewish ritual murder belonged squarely in the millennium we just recently left behind.[2]

The first officially documented accusation of ritual murder occurred in 1150 when, in the first volume of his *The Life and Passion of Saint William the Martyr of Norwich*, Thomas of Monmouth described the murder of a young boy that took place in Norwich,

England, in 1144 as a symbolic crucifixion.[3] The tale of murder, with Thomas's embellishments, then found its way into the *Anglo-Saxon Chronicle* penned by the monks of Peterborough Abbey, a scribe having brought it up to date in 1154.

> Now we wish to tell some part of what happened in King Stephen's time. In his time the Jews of Norwich bought a Christian child before Easter, and tortured him with all the same tortures with which our Lord was tortured, and on Good Friday hanged him on a cross for love of our Lord, and afterwards buried him—imagined that it would be concealed, but our Lord showed that he was a holy martyr, and the monks took him and buried him reverently in the minster, and through our Lord he performs wonderful and manifold miracles; and he is called St. William.[4]

In this brief passage we can already see in bold outline the major motifs that would inform the tenacious tale for centuries: that Jews killed Christian boys before Easter; that because they hate Christians, the Jews tortured the boys; that the killing was in imitation of the killing of Christ; that Jews were not only a timeless menace but also a present threat; and that the murdered boy, as a martyr for the Christian community, performed miracles.[5]

The tale started as a learned tale, for Thomas of Monmouth was an educated monk from Wales whose *Life* made him a notable hagiographer.[6] But because few copies of the *Life* were made, subsequent dissemination of the story depended on the monks of Peterborough, who incorporated it into the *Anglo-Saxon Chronicle*. Probably, some people of Norwich believed that Jews had killed the boy when the murder occurred in 1144; but the idea that it was a ritual killing in all probability stems, as the historian Gavin Langmuir has argued, from the all-too-creative fiction of Thomas. In the canticles that sounded throughout the abbeys of Christendom, this was a new and terrible note.[7]

It resonated in the twelfth-century northern European world of Bernard of Clairvaux and Thomas à Becket, a world that brought forth the love affair of Abelard and Heloïse, the troubadours of Languedoc, and the heart-wrenching, illicit, pining of Sir Lancelot for Arthur's Guinevere. In the shadows of the great Cathedrals—Durham and Canterbury, St. Denis and Chartres—new learning flourished, as men like Peter Lombard and John of Salisbury labored to understand the astronomy of Ptolemy, the geometry of Euclid, the mathematics of the Islamic world, the verse of Ovid and the orations of Cicero, and, just beyond the turn of the century, carefully guarded in select scriptoria across the Alps and on the other side of the Pyrenees, the ethical and metaphysical works of Aristotle. This was a world marked by a great renaissance.[8] At the same time, however, it was marred by a deteriorating image of Jews, a distended sense that Jews were the implacable enemies of Christendom, not just blind to the truth but deceitful, threatening, and dangerous.[9]

The idea that Jews murdered Christians soon found its way into the Christian faith. The early tales of ritual murder were not isolated alcoves beneath an otherwise glorious cathedral. Rather, these tales, and tales like them about other groups, provided a firm foundation for a newly constructed "persecuting society," begun in 1096 with the First Crusade, which unleashed a destructive fury against the Jewish communities along the Rhine. In the course of the twelfth century, this emerging "persecuting society" also erected walls of intolerance against heretics, lepers, and homosexuals. Buttressed by the stiff legalism of the Fourth Lateran Council in 1215, the new persecutions culminated in the Inquisition, entrusted in 1232 to the Dominican friars.[10]

By the mid-thirteenth century, a shift in the motifs inscribed in the tale of murder had occurred. The initial tales involved murders, sacrifices, and crucifixions; they did not, however, involve the ritual use of blood. That was a German invention, mentioned for the first time in 1236 in the *Annals of Marbach*. The reference is to the Fulda case of 1235. While a miller and his wife attended mass on Christmas Day, their mill, which was outside the city walls, burned down and their five sons perished. Local Christians, though perhaps sojourning crusaders, accused the Jews of killing the boys, drawing their blood, carrying it away in wax bags, and using it for curative or religious purposes.[11] Three days after Christmas, on December 28, citizens (or crusaders) "put to the sword" thirty-four local Jews after two Jews, in order to escape torture, confessed to the crime. The citizens (or the crusaders) later brought the exhumed corpses of the children to Emperor Frederick II in the Alsatian city of Hagenau. Although Frederick did not find the accusation made in Fulda credible, he nevertheless summoned spiritual and secular authorities and solicited their opinions. But their opinions conflicted, and Frederick brought together a commission of converted Jews from all over Europe, who in the spring of 1236 denied that Jews used Christian blood. Indeed, they argued, the opposite was true: blood, of any kind, polluted, and the Torah and Talmud strictly forbade its consumption. On the strength of this recommendation, Frederick, in an imperial bull of July 1236, "fully acquitted the Jews of Fulda of the crime attributed them, and the rest of the Jews of Germany of such a serious charge."[12]

The populace, however, was not so easily convinced. The blood libel spread, and violence against Jews ensued. In the following spring, another major case occurred, this time in Valréas, a village in the Vaucluse, in southern France, after two Franciscan monks accused the Jews of crucifying and exsanguinating Meilla, a two-year-old Christian girl. Some Jews were tortured in order to draw their confession; others were simply murdered. Desperate, the Jews of Valréas appealed to the Holy See for protection, and in two papal bulls, both issued on May 28, 1247, Pope Innocent IV condemned the persecution of the Jews in Valréas.[13] Just over a month later, in a third papal bull, on July 5, 1247, he declared as erroneous the charges that Jews slaughtered Christians in order to use their blood.[14] The response of Innocent IV, motivated as much by fear of uncontrolled violence as by a genuine conviction of the untruth of the blood libel, inaugurated a long tradition of Vatican condemnation of the ritual-murder charge.

Although disclaimed by the high church, the ritual-murder charge at Fulda occurred in a climate of concern about heresy. The more immediate pressure, however, came from a more general persecutorial brooding, particularly evident in southern Germany, the domain of Conrad of Marburg, the severe confessor of Elizabeth of Thüringen. In 1231, the archbishop of Mainz, the most powerful prelate of the Holy Roman Empire of the German Nation, made Conrad an inquisitor. Formidable and fanatical, Conrad rode from town to town (on a donkey, we are told, in imitation of Christ), thundering against the heretical demons of his phantasmic imagination. The heretics he accused were put to the sword or tossed into a lake or consumed by flames. Against apostates, especially the Rhineland Cathars, he preached vigilance. A storm of denunciations and counterdenunciations now descended on southern Germany; one of the charges was that the heretics profaned the wafer—degrading, befouling, even stabbing it.

This was the specter of host desecration. It stuck at a sensitive question concerning the Eucharist: whether the wafer and the wine was the real body and blood of Christ, a mystical corpus and fluid, or, as some heretics had it, merely bread and wine, a symbol.

Starting in the late twelfth century, theologians increasingly argued that the Eucharist constituted a sacrament involving the real presence of Christ.[15] This reorientation was then sanctioned by the Fourth Lateran Council in 1215, which asserted that "the body and blood" of Jesus Christ "are truly contained in the sacrament of the altar under the forms of bread and wine, the bread and wine having been changed by God's substance, by God's power, into his body and blood."[16]

A remarkable claim, no less wondrous for its ritual recurrence, the doctrine of transubstantiation came to rest not on the wisps of mystical insight but firmly on the logical and categorical constructions of Aristotle, the man whom the medievals called "the philosopher," "the master of those who know." In the early discussions concerning the true nature of transubstantiation, the influence of

Aristotle, mediated by Boethius, was mixed with Augustine's sym-
bolism and Plato's forms. In the eleventh and twelfth centuries, the
question of the real presence of Christ in the host thus remained
open. But in the course of the thirteenth century, as Aristotle's texts
were newly translated, his influence, not only in logic but also in sci-
ence, became more palpable.[17]

The resulting epistemic shift turned on the nature of substances,
which for Aristotle were not the magical numbers of Pythagoras or the
unchanging essences of Plato but perceptible things, the ordinary
matter of the world. Substances consist of both matter and form,
which in Aristotelian logic are separable, just as Eve was made from
the rib of Adam. A substance that exists in matter may thus appear in
a form external to it. Analogously, the body of Christ may take on the
appearance of bread. "All the substance of the bread is transmuted
into the body of Christ," Aquinas writes, and this transmutation "is
not a formal conversion but a substantial one."[18] Aquinas's caveat is
crucial and thinkable only within Aristotelian logic, for it means that
the wafer does not *become* Christ but rather the *substance* of Christ,
and substance is separable into matter and form. When a Christian
devours the wafer, it is the accidental form that he eats. "Whatever is
eaten as under its natural form, is broken and chewed as under its natural form," Saint Thomas tells us, "but the body of Christ is not eaten
as under its natural form, but under the sacramental species."[19]
Christians, thanks to this Aristotelian nuance, do not practice what the
anthropologist Beth Conklin has in another context called "compassionate cannibalism."[20]

To our symbolically impoverished sensibilities, this line of reasoning may stretch credulity, but it is nevertheless important to recall
that in the thirteenth century Aristotelian categories possessed all the
force that the Hegelian dialectic did in the two centuries before our
own. Like the followers of Hegel, those who argued on the wings of
Aristotle were not stuck in a mire of obscurantism but rather soared
among the most widely acclaimed thinkers of the day.[21] And just as in
later centuries when men like Lenin committed unspeakable crimes,

and poets like Mayakovski justified them, because they thought themselves instruments of larger historical forces, so in the thirteenth century the wonder of the Eucharist brought forth new patterns of power and persecution. It inaugurated, *inter alia*, centuries of host-desecration charges: that Jews tortured the wafers until they bled and that it was Christ the savior who was bleeding. The new emphasis on the corporeality of the host, on Christ's real presence in the sacrament, also secured the emotional context for the ritual-murder charge, of which host desecration was merely a symbolic variation.

The key, in one way of thinking about it, is the psychological process of "projection," which simply states that one person imputes to another what he himself really thinks or does. This particular psychological defense mechanism is especially powerful when a person thinks or acts in a way that is shameful to himself or his community. According to this line of reasoning, there was something disturbing about a ritual in which the body and blood of Christ was consumed as food and sacrificed to God. That disturbing element was imputed to the Jews. To put it in terms of the relational structure of the two rituals, one imagined, the other real: ritual-murder accusations represented a projection onto Jews of the ineffable—that in the celebration of the Eucharist, Christians, not Jews, practiced ritual cannibalism.[22]

The charges of ritual murder and host desecration rested on a projected fantasy of the medieval imagination. No one ever saw a Jew commit ritual murder or desecrate a host, and in the scores of cases that would follow those in Fulda and Valréas, no Jew, except those who suffered the pain of torture, ever admitted to participating in such acts. Yet the cases, first of ritual murder, later of host desecration, continued unabated—in Pforzheim (Baden) in 1267, in Weissenburg (Alsace) in 1270, in Mainz in 1283, in Munich in 1285, in Oberwesel (the Rhineland) in 1287, in Krems (Lower Austria) in 1293, in Bern in 1294, in Weissensee (Thuringia) in 1303, and in Prague in 1305. The accusations were not all cut from the same cloth, however. In some cases, townspeople saw miracles. In Oberwesel, the corpse of the tortured fourteen-year-old "good Werner" supposedly swam up the Rhine

River and healed the sick. In Pforzheim, the murdered girl allegedly bled anew when the populace inspected her; her face also seemed to blush and her hands to levitate. In other cases, the drawing of the blood defined the legend, as happened in Weissensee, where the Jews were said to have opened all the veins of Konrad, a schoolboy. And in still other cases (in Prague, for example), the story centered on a cruci-fixion. In terms of motif, most instances of alleged ritual murder involved the killing of boys, though not all, for the cases in Valréas and Pforzheim began when townspeople discovered the lacerated corpses of young girls. The murders sometimes happened in the spring, around the time of Passover, but this was by no means always true, for in Weissenburg the events took place in June or July, in Pforzheim in July, in Munich in October, and in Fulda in December. Still, in almost all cases, the accusations focused on blood.

In the medieval period, folktales about the magical powers of blood abounded. Variations on these tales recounted how Jews used Christian blood to prepare sauces for Passover, and how they baked matzo in it; they told of Jews who ate the hearts of Christian children, and of Jews who purged themselves of sin by washing in Christian blood. Some of the folktales referred to the role of Christian blood in specific religious rituals: that the Jews used it for communion on the Sabbath, for example. A different genre of tales described Jewish use of Christian blood as a talisman against the tribulations of everyday life. According to these legends, Christian blood cured illnesses, espe-cially leprosy; it eased childbirth and coagulated the wound made by circumcision; it rejuvenated; it diluted the Jew's own stench; it even served as an aphrodisiac.[23]

By the end of the thirteenth century, as eucharistic devotion intensified, host-desecration charges against Jews also broke out. The first major case was in Paris in 1290; it then spread, at first tentatively and then with ferocity, striking in 1298 a spate of Franconian towns: Röttingen (near Rothenburg ob der Tauber), Iphofen, Lauda, Weikersheim, Möckmühl, and Würzburg.[24] From Franconia it traveled down the Danube, bringing the scourge to two communities near

Vienna, Korneuburg in 1305 and St. Pölten in 1306. Thereafter, out-breaks were intermittent, until they erupted in full force in 1338, wreak-ing severe havoc in Pulkau, a town northwest of Vienna, and in the Bavarian town of Deggendorf, where, at the signal of the church bell on Sunday, September 30, the locals attacked their Jewish neighbors, plundered their wares, and burned their houses to the ground, killing, in the course of the day, every last Jewish man, woman, and child.[25]

The destruction sometimes followed its own pathways, and at other times it seemed that there was a grim stalker, bringing worse calamities still, on its heels. This was true of the cases in Franconia, a dangerous landscape where power devolved into the hands of many. In 1298, a leader named Rintfleisch, perhaps a knight, more likely a butcher, arrayed a private army of men to massacre Jews, citing charges of host desecration sufficiently odious that "God permitted such per-secution."[26] It is impossible to ascertain the total number of Jews killed by Rintfleisch, his peasant followers, and the city magistrates who col-luded with them. In a Hebrew elegy, part question, part plea, we hear that "once Abraham brought his only son to sacrifice," but "how many thousands have been brought to you as sacrifice now."[27] More pro-saically, the Christian chronicler Gottfried of Ensmingen estimated the death toll at ten thousand souls.[28] The blossoming Jewish communities of Franconia, like Nuremberg, Bamberg, Würzburg, and Rothenburg ob der Tauber, were trampled underfoot, and many smaller communi-ties, like Forchheim and Hollfeld, would never recover.[29] "May my viol become a mourning song and my flute the voice of tears," intones another Hebrew lamentation of the time.[30]

The first fifty years of the next dark century proved like our own "ravaged century," particularly destructive.[31] Within a generation of the Rintfleisch massacres of 1298, and in many of the same towns, another army of men, first following a self-anointed king named Armleder, then following his successors, roamed from town to town, ax, pick, and cudgel in hand, and murdered Jews. Although the marauders started in Franconia, they spilled blood far beyond its boundaries, in Hessen, in the Rhineland, along the Mosel, and in Swabia; then in

Alsace and in the lands of Austria, Bohemia, and Moravia.[32] "Jew bashers" they called themselves, as they clubbed the Jews of more than a hundred communities with their primitive and blunt tools of death. The motives of these people are unclear. They were peasants and townsmen. This one wanted plunder, another revenge, a third deliverance from his tedious days. Some evidence points to the nobility's indebtedness to Jewish creditors. There had also been rumors of host desecration, and forgeries charging the same.[33] And the night had only begun. "For there followed the absolute saddest days for the Jewish communities in almost all of Europe, as far as the cross is prayed to," the great Jewish historian Heinrich Graetz wrote in the middle of the nineteenth century.[34]

The massacres followed on the accusation that the Jews had poisoned the wells, first articulated in Spain, then in France, then in the great cities of the Holy Roman Empire, where Jews were now killed at a dizzying pace. In February 1349, they were murdered in Strasbourg, where two thousand Jews were driven to a cemetery, pressed into a hastily constructed barn, and in the course of six days burned. In March, they were attacked in Worms, where to avoid the hatchets of the butchers the Jews set their own homes on fire, they and their families inside. And they were besieged in the large and venerable Jewish community of Mainz, where in August of that same year, six thousand Jews fought the ravaging army and killed many of its members before they, too, torched their own dwellings, thus reducing the Jewish quarter to a soft blanket of ash.[35] The killings, which began in November 1348, almost always occurred on the weekends and on holy days, as confused and credulous peasants, landless laborers, wandering journeymen, and angry artisans vented their wrath, typically on the signal given by complicitous town magistrates and lords locked in a struggle for power and jealous of Jewish assets.[36] The result, more planned than spontaneous, was unabated killing in the many Jewish communities in southern Germany, such as Memmingen and Reutlingen, Haigerloch and Horb, Ravensburg and Meßkirch, Speyer and Konstanz, and in the north as well, in cities like Dresden, Braunschweig, Halle, and

Dortmund.[37] In all, misery rained on more than three hundred communities, almost the only towns spared being in areas where the bubonic plague raged less savagely. For many Jewish families, this was simply the end, and those who survived must have thought of Job. "As water wears away stones / and torrents wash away the soil / so you destroy man's hopes."[38]

By the mid-fourteenth century, a great divide, visible on the streets of German cities, had been cut into the history of Germany's Jewish communities. In Nuremberg, for example, the authorities razed a number of Jewish houses, tore down the synagogue and built the Liebfrauenkirche in its stead, and created an open marketplace (the Hauptmarkt, where the famous Christmas toys are sold). Townsmen also plundered the cemetery, using the cut stones to build a spiral staircase for the Laurentiniuskirche.[39] Although Jews would live in places like Nuremberg again, few returned to the same ashened streets and blood-stained hometowns of their fathers. We know this because we can compare the lists of martyrs with the family names of those who gave offerings for the dead a generation later, and the names are not the same.[40] Rather than return, Jews who survived the ordeal, especially the poorer among them, wandered, eventually settling elsewhere in a German empire sufficiently fractured that they could find a place to reside in it.

Their wanderings shifted the center of gravity of German Jewry away from the old Rhenish cities in the west to the center, to Hessen and Franconia, and to the southwest, to the patchwork of territories that later made up Alsace, Baden, and the northern parts of Württemberg.[41] In the course of the next century, many Jews, especially the wealthier among them, also migrated south to northern Italy and east to the more hospitable lands of Poland and Lithuania.[42] The greater part, however, found refuge in the countryside, families here and there settling in small villages, typically without a synagogue or a *shul* of their own.

But wherever they went, the tale of ritual murder followed them. In the fifteenth century, it resurfaced at the time of the early witch trials and concurrently with the smoldering pyres of the Spanish Inquisition.[43] That ritual-murder charges should again come to the fore reminds us of the degree to which such charges served as a sensitive barometric needle for a wider history of tolerance and persecution. Like the guidelines for the persecution of witches, which were codified and set to print in the famous *Malleus Maleficarum* of 1486, ritual-murder charges were also standardized. By the late fifteenth century, the many strands of mystical belief that had informed these charges began to converge, creating, according to the historian R. Po-Chia Hsia, "a single tradition of discourse."[44] This tradition became manifest at the ritual-murder trial of Trent in 1475, where, in the course of a savage torture, the Jews accused of murdering a two-year-old child (who would later be martyred as Simon of Trent) confessed to the crime in terms of an increasingly standardized story of how and why, when and to whom, ritual murder occurred. The central elements of this story consisted of Jews who, during Passover, murdered and drew the blood of prepubescent Christian boys in order to reenact the killing of Christ.

The trial at Trent represented a turning point in the history of ritual-murder accusations. It was, for one, paradigmatic for the increasing involvement of the offices of the court in these cases generally. As a result of the court's involvement, the language of accusation became ever more standardized, at the same time that the uncontrolled effects of ritual-murder charges, the massacres that accompanied them, declined in importance.[45] Trent proved to be a turning point in another way. Aided by the powerful, newly invented printing press, the "facts" of the case were more easily disseminated (in chronicles, pamphlets, and broadsheets) than ever before. No longer primarily the stuff of rumors and hearsay, ritual-murder accusations now became part of the more solid material of printed history.[46] The encyclopedic *Nuremberg Chronicle*, for example, included a story of how nine Jews held a young Christian boy named Simon, drained blood from his penis, and collected it in a vessel. A woodcut, one of nearly two thousand in the *Nuremberg Chronicle*, identified each Jew who allegedly participated in the murder by name, though the overall composition of the picture rendered it abundantly clear that the Jews acted in concert, with each Jew assigned a precise role in the event. Copied from the chronicle and pirated in cheap editions, this particular woodcut, as well as many others, made its way across the Holy Roman Empire and, in penny pamphlets and broadsheets, reached a wide audience.

The ground was thus prepared for the expulsion of the Jews who, in the aftermath of great trauma, had reestablished communities in the years after the plague. Cologne banished its Jews in 1424, Speyer in 1435, Konstanz and Augsburg in 1440, the bishopric of Würzburg in 1453, the archbishopric of Mainz in 1470, Passau in 1478, Nuremberg in 1499, Brandenburg in 1510, and Regensburg in 1519. Perhaps more than any other Christian fantasy about the Jews, the charge of ritual murder, along with host desecration, served to justify the expulsions.[47]

I

Soon thereafter a shift occurred. If ritual-murder accusations had been centered in the German-speaking lands of central Europe, they began to drift eastward, and to some extent southward. Partly, this was the result of the Jewish migrations of the fourteenth century and the expulsions of the fifteenth. It was also a direct consequence of the Reformation. Martin Luther, hardly a philosemite, vigorously attacked the realms of superstition, to which ritual murder belonged. He also severed the theological buttresses, most significantly the Catholic doctrine of transubstantiation, that lent credence to ritual-murder charges. If, as Luther now taught, wine merely symbolized the blood of Christ, the host his body, then the logical construction on which ritual murder was founded—involving the sacrifice of real bodies and real blood— came crashing down. Luther was not the first to question the validity of transubstantiation. In his critique of eucharistic devotion, John Wycliffe in Oxford had preceded him by more than a century. But Luther's critique cut deeper.

The reformers also subverted the authority of the Catholic clergy, who, so they believed, fabricated lies and superstitions in order to hide their own malice and incompetence. In 1540, the first sustained Christian defense of Jews in a ritual-murder case stemmed from a theologian, Andreas Osiander, who became famous as the man who published writings by Galileo. He excoriated the medieval clergy for whipping up the charge of ritual murder in order to fool and deceive Christians and persuasively argued that in the Old Testament the drawing of blood is strictly forbidden: "Whoever sheds the blood of man, by man shall his blood be shed" (Genesis 9:6). Dietary laws forbade it as well: "But you must not eat meat that has its lifeblood still in it" (Genesis 9:4).[48] There were other reasons to doubt the occurrence of ritual murder, some practical (if Jews needed blood, they did not have to kill for it), some related to the flawed nature of past trials (previous confessions had been extracted by torture). In all, Osiander offered twenty reasons why Jews could not commit ritual murder. He then suggested twelve reasons why in the case at hand (the supposed ritual murder in the Hungarian town of Pösing in 1529) Jews could not have committed the crime. He also gave seven hints as to how the real killer might be found.[49]

Osiander's treatise figures prominently in the story of how the Reformation helped reverse the tide of ritual-murder accusations. Yet the treatise also stood for another development that would have a profound effect on Christian-Jewish relations: it signaled the emergence of Christian scholars, mostly Protestant, who could read the Hebrew texts. These scholars dramatically altered the possibilities of biblical exegesis and managed to liberate Jewish texts from the shroud of superstition that enveloped them. In the process, certain beliefs about Jews, the ritual-murder charge foremost among them, proved increasingly difficult to maintain.[50]

In the wake of the Reformation, accusations of ritual murder in the German-speaking lands waned, especially in Protestant parts of the Holy Roman Empire. Moreover, magistrates discontinued torture as a means for extracting confessions, at least in German-speaking lands.

As a result, Jews were no longer put to death for allegedly committing the crime of ritual murder. There were, however, isolated Protestant intellectuals who propagated the legend. In the year 1700, for example, Johann Andreas Eisenmenger, a professor of oriental languages at the University of Heidelberg, penned an ill-spirited work alleging the veracity of ritual-murder charges.

Eisenmenger's two-volume work is useful—both for gauging the state of ritual-murder beliefs in Protestant Germany and for understanding the subsequent fate of these beliefs throughout Europe. For more than twelve hundred pages of these weighty tomes, Eisenmenger denigrated the Jews and their faith. Yet for all its subsequent notoriety, the section on ritual murder seemed anemic by comparison, receiving only six pages, which begin with the concession that "in present-day Germany one no longer hears about such gruesome deeds." Although Eisenmenger attributed the demise of ritual murder to effective punishment against it, his tone struck unwanted notes of ambivalence. From printed sources, he had unearthed two cases from the ancient period, eight from the medieval era (Aragon, 1250; London, 1257; Munich 1282; Weissensee, 1303; Prague, 1305; Munich, 1345; Trent, 1475; and Regensburg, 1486), three from the sixteenth century, and two from the seventeenth. Of the fifteen cases, he communicated detailed information about only one: Trent. For the rest, he drew most of his evidence from second- and third-hand accounts. Finally, and quite uncharacteristically, he concluded the section on ritual murder with a question.

> Since many diligent authors have written that the Jews need Christian blood, and have documented this with examples that the murdered children are usually killed at Easter, one can assume that not all of it is necessarily untrue. But I leave it open whether the case goes this way or that.[51]

Eisenmenger's skepticism was in step with his time. In Protestant Germany, chimeras of Jewish magic slowly ceased to capture the learned imagination.[52]

Did such illusions nevertheless retain a hold on the popular imagination? Eisenmenger assumed that they did. So too did Johann Jacob Schudt, whose four-volume work *Jewish Curiosities* constitutes a rich source of early eighteenth-century folklore by and about Jews, especially in Frankfurt am Main.[53] In this work, Schudt wrote of a woman who brought a saucer of blood to the cattle market, hoping to sell it to the Jews as human blood; and of people who, when they lost track of their children, immediately went to the Jewish quarter to look for them.[54] Unlike Eisenmenger, however, Schudt attempted to dispel such fantasies—products, he thought, of a superstitious mind. "As certainly and as truthfully as I am sure of my town," he wrote, "the Jews do not eat or drink Christian blood, nor do they bake it in their easter cakes, nor do they drive away their stench with it, nor ease the process of birth with it, nor stroke the dying with it."[55] Yet, while arguing against particular charges, especially as they pertained to the Jews he knew, Schudt nevertheless left open the possibility that ritual murders might have occurred, especially because "in the past 1,300 years so many writers have provided credible news of it."[56] Indeed, in Frankfurt there was a daily reminder of ritual murder. As one walked underneath the bridge tower, one could observe a depiction of Simon of Trent, the martyred child, his body punctured by awls and covered in blood. In 1609, the Jews of Frankfurt petitioned to have the painting removed, but the Frankfurt city council rejected the plea. In 1678, the painting was even renovated, and it would remain on the bridge tower for nearly another century, long enough for the young Goethe to have seen "the infamous and derisive painting."[57] There is no doubt that the painting, though perhaps also the copy of Eisenmenger's work in his father's library, encouraged Goethe's initial aversion to the Jewish quarters. "It took a long while before I dared go there," he wrote in his autobiographical *Dichtung und Wahrheit* (*Poetry and Truth*). "I had in my mind the old legend of the cruelty of the Jews toward Christian children. . . ."[58] Though no longer as widely prevalent as it once had been, the ritual-murder charge did not simply die out in Protestant Germany, but rested in repose.

In predominantly Catholic Germany, the idea of ritual murder retained more of a hold on the learned as well as on the popular imagination, though here, too, it slowly loosened its grip. In the seventeenth century, the case with the greatest public resonance was, significantly, a historical one: the alleged murder of young Andreas Oxner of Rinn. The murder supposedly occurred in 1462 after the boy's father sold his son to traveling merchants, who then killed the boy in a forest. At first, suspicion did not fall on the Jews, but after the events in Trent, which occurred thirteen years later, in 1475, the story of Andreas Oxner of Rinn took on the semblance of superstition; the populace became convinced that the Jews had tortured the boy on the "Jew stone," and a cult was created around Oxner's remains. Yet even this critical version of the events, which derives from late nineteenth-century scholarship, can no longer be verified. Recent research suggests that a child named Andreas Oxner perhaps never existed, the date 1462 in all likelihood a product of a seventeenth-century invention, the work of a doctor named Hippolytus Guarinoni from Hall, in the Tirol, who had heard of the story and collected evidence, however dubious, to support it.[59] Once in print, the legend assumed new legitimacy. By 1670, the people of Rinn had built a parish church on top of the "Jew stone" and named the village around it Judenstein. They also collected and published documents detailing the boy's torment, and appealed to the Holy See for approbation. The church granted their plea, as it had the one for the martyred Simon of Trent. In 1753, Pope Benedict XIV sanctioned religious ceremonies paying homage to Andreas Oxner of Rinn as a victim of Jewish ritual murder.[60]

The legend of Judenstein, and its subsequent consecration in the church, was not a unique moment of darkness in the light of the Christian world. Instead, it served as an important part of a Catholic religious revival centered on fascination with the martyrdom of saints and the innocence of children, visible in the changing iconographic representation of Simon of Trent. In the fifteenth century, artists rendered the two-year-old boy as a small man, emphasizing the drawing of blood from his penis; later, in the Baroque era, they portrayed him as a cherubian baby-child, his sexual organs hidden, the cuts placed elsewhere.[61] The renewed interest in ritual-murder and host-desecration charges also manifested itself in local acts of preservation. In Endingen, near the southwest German city of Freiburg, a fading panel showing how the Jews murdered a Christian family of beggars in 1470 was renovated in 1614.[62] In 1619 and again in 1722, the people of Lienz, in the Tirol, renewed the stone documenting the martyrdom of four-year-old Ursula, who "in Anno Domini 1452 . . . was tormented and killed by the Jews on Good Friday, and since then rests here."[63] In Pulkau, near Vienna, a chapel had been erected on the site of the alleged host desecration of 1338, and now, in the seventeenth century, painters refurbished the fresco that portrayed the scene.[64] In Korneuburg, new depictions of the alleged host desecration of 1298 were painted in 1660, and in Deggendorf, likewise the scene of a 1338 massacre supposedly following a host-desecration charge, local Catholics carried, as the centerpiece of their procession, a host, a shoe-maker's awl, and the prick the Jews supposedly used to torture the host.[65] In 1732, a fresco describing the "discovery of the host" was painted in the Grabkirche, the text to one of the pilgrimage scenes reading, "The Jews were killed by the Christians out of a zeal for jus-tice pleasing to God. God grant us that our fatherland is at all times free of this hellish scum [*Höllengeschmeiß*]."[66] There was also a popular song, "The Deggendorfer Song," that described the event, and, until the turn into the nineteenth century, the citizens of Deggendorf per-formed a play commemorating it.[67]

The revival of interest in the ritual-murder charge, itself part of a larger religious renewal, also found its way into printed texts. Many of the ritual-murder cases of the medieval period—Munich, 1285; Weissensee, 1303; Ueberlingen, 1331; Lienz, 1442—had long since languished in obscure Latin chronicles and learned treatises. As Catholics in the seventeenth century became fascinated with local tra-ditions of piety, they produced regional martyrologies, such as

Matthew Rader's *Bavaria Sancta*, which, replete with detailed engravings, reinforced anew the image of martyred children suffering just as Christ had suffered on the cross. Such themes were also taken up in popular plays at the time, an important part of the culture of the Catholic Reformation. In southwest Germany, *The Endinger Judenspiel*, whose first documented staging occurred in 1610, dramatized the "ritual murder" of 1470. In the play, Jews freely confess to the crime of ritually killing a beggar family; miracles then occur, and the Jews are burned at the stake.[68] From the surrounding area, pious Catholics streamed into Endingen to watch the play, and the relics of the slain family became a popular site for pilgrimages.[69] In the Tirol, a similar spectacle commemorated the trial and tribulations of Andreas Oxner ("Anderl") of Rinn. Written by a Jesuit in 1621, the play enjoyed considerable popularity and was staged many times.[70]

In these myriad ways, then, Catholic culture (in pictures, plays, print, and the stones of commemorative chapels) shaped the superstitions of common Catholic folk. It is possible that many of these superstitions survived on their own as part of a rich oral culture, passed down from parent to child, but they also received fresh sustenance from a Catholic religious revival that attempted to render the suffering of Christ and the community of saints as something of great immediacy. Even as the universal church marked its official distance from the ritual-murder charge, local Catholics, clergy and laity alike, continued to reinvent it.

In the course of the seventeenth century, however, the main stage for new ritual-murder accusations dramatically shifted eastward, mainly to the Catholic territories of Poland, where, as a result of successive expulsions from the west, more than one-third of the world's Jews lived. In a recent study of ritual-murder accusations between 1547 and 1787, one team of scholars counted eighty-two public accusations in Poland alone, though not all of these charges ended up in court.[71] The cases tended to be concentrated in flash points, most spectacularly in Sandomierz province, in Galicia, but they also flared up more modestly in places that would soon be part of Prussia:

Bromberg (Bydgoszcz) in 1713 and Posen (Poznan) in 1736.[72] Although there were chronological concentrations as well, what impresses is the even stretch of cases from the end of the fifteenth century to the eighteenth —a time when, in other parts of Europe, the rays of Enlightenment seemed to render ritual-murder charges an atavism of a darker past.

Unlike large-scale witchcraft accusations, however, these charges survived into the modern era, fostering divisiveness, enmity, and violence wherever they were made. And as they were increasingly invoked in eastern Europe, they again took on different hues. In 1475, the events in Trent had established an archetypal narrative, centered on Jews drawing the blood of prepubescent Christian boys at Passover. Its passage to eastern Europe, however, caused the tale to unravel all over again. The single story was then told in variations in which girls counted as victims again—at Czechry (Poland) in 1600, for example, and at Orcuta (Hungary) in 1764, though the majority of accusations still involved the ritual killing of Christian boys. In its various manifestations, the miraculous and multifarious powers of blood also reappeared as a central motif in the accusations. In Szydlow in 1597, Jews allegedly blessed their synagogue by sprinkling it with Christian blood. In Sandomierz in 1698, and in Michnow in 1747, blood supposedly squirted from the body of the slain when the killer stood in its presence. Most, but not all, ritual-murder accusations continued to surface at Passover. The girl "slaughtered" in Czechry in 1600 was killed in May; another case in Sandomierz in 1710 involved the death of a child in August; and the case in Orcuta began when a child was found "dead in a brushwood on June 25."[73]

In Poland, as in Catholic Germany, the printed word of the educated elite rendered the accusation of ritual murder sharper still and emphasized its broad appeal. Of the pamphlets and broadsides written against the Jews, the most famous, *A Criminal Case about an Innocent Child*, stemmed from the spiteful pen of Abbé Stephan Zuchowski. Published in 1713, the pamphlet recounted the charges leveled at the Jews of Sandomierz, who, after their torture, met death by execution.[74] In well-worn arguments, Zuchowski also pointed out that there were ten reasons why Jews needed Christian blood, primarily because they hated Christians, especially Catholics. Like other authors before him, Zuchowski buttressed his argument by appealing to an authority, in particular to Eisenmenger, but also to Polish and Lithuanian authors. He also used history to great effect, listing, as the genre now demanded, eighty instance of Jewish ritual murder that had allegedly occurred in Poland over the preceding three hundred years.[75]

During the eighteenth century, the situation in Poland deteriorated. Around midcentury, the Jews of Poland issued a desperate plea, entreating Pope Benedict XIV to intercede on their behalf against the ritual-murder charge. "Over the past ten years," it was claimed in 1758, "whenever anyone coincidentally found a Christian corpse, a murder was assumed to be certain and, without further reflection, it was assumed that the Jews of the area committed it for reasons of the aforesaid superstition."[76] The Vatican passed the issue on to Cardinal Ganganelli, who studied the recent spate of ritual-murder cases in Poland and found all of the accusations groundless. On the basis of Ganganelli's researches, Pope Clement XIII instructed the Polish nuncio, who in turn informed the prime minister of Poland, that the Vatican considered the charges of ritual murder leveled against the Jews of Poland to be without foundation in fact.[77]

Ritual-murder accusations had declined in Poland by the end of the eighteenth century, as a result partly of papal admonitions against them and partly of the Polish parliament's (the Sejm) abolition, in 1776, of the use of torture to extract confessions. The Jews of Poland no longer had to corroborate fantastic stories in order to save themselves and their loved ones from a horrible fate that, not so long ago, included the amputation of hands and feet, tearing off skin in strips, and burning at the stake.[78] "Who can count the dust and ashes," the rabbi of Posen asked on his way to the gallows, "of those who were burned and quartered for the faith of Israel?"[79]

III

For nearly two centuries, German Jews, most of whom now lived quiet impoverished lives in the countryside, had been spared major outbreaks of violence directed specifically at them. Having survived the Thirty Years' War more safely than the Christians around them, Jews had also been less affected by the subsequent calamities of the crisis-ridden seventeenth century. Moreover, the one major anti-Jewish upheaval, the Fettmilch uprising of 1614 in Frankfurt am Main, ended with the triumphant return of the Jews to their homes in Frankfurt's Judengasse and the execution of the pastry baker who incited the riot. The riot also failed to spread, and many Jews found refuge in Christian homes. For Jews, the seventeenth and eighteenth centuries were not the best of times; but they were far from the worst.

After a nearly two-hundred-year hiatus in accusations, ritual murder resurfaced. In 1819, in Dormagen, a village on the left bank of the Rhine between Düsseldorf and Cologne, a missing girl caused the local Catholic population to accuse the Jews of murder, even though the police had yet to find the girl's body. On October 14, 1819, the local chronicler of Dormagen wrote,

> There are thousands of opinions. The prevaling one is that the Jews captured the child because at times, according to an old legend, they must have Christian blood. And since the disappearance of the child coincides with the end of the Feast of the Tabernacles, there are all kinds of witnesses who claim to have seen either the Jew Sekel with a sack or the Jew Schimmel lurking around houses at midnight.[80]

The accusations drew sustenance from the popular cult of "the good Werner," the fourteen-year-old boy allegedly murdered by the Jews in the village of Oberwesel in 1286. The cult enjoyed great renown in the late Middle Ages, but with the advent of the Reformation its popularity began to wane. Still, it did not disappear—in part because of the influence of an entrenched oral culture as well as the newer power of the printed word. In a Westphalian almanac of 1745, for example, the calendrical entry for Easter Monday, April 19, was simply "Werner." Ordinary people, the writer must have assumed, understood that on this day, many years ago, "good Werner" had fallen into the hands of bloodthirsty Jews.[81] Eagerly exploiting the legend, the bishopric of Trier consecrated him as a "diocese saint" in its own calendar of holy days. Around this time, the Oberwesel parish also renovated a relief depicting the boy's brutal slaughter. And every year until the French Revolution, the locals participated in a procession to his supposed birthplace, the village of Womrath.[82] Accusations of murder thus resonated in the collective memory, and their immediacy was now reinvigorated as the town of Dormagen became, for a time, a place of pilgrimage for the pious.[83]

The murder accusation also occurred in an atmosphere of fervent hatred. Only two months before the murder, in August 1819, violent anti-Jewish riots, the so-called Hep-Hep riots, flashed from Würzburg through the Franconian hinterland to Frankfurt am Main, the towns of northern Baden, and then all the way to Hamburg, Danzig, and even Copenhagen.[84] Staged against the background of an economic downturn and the resultant pauperization of the artisan class, these riots— the first supraregional outbreak of anti-Semitic violence in Germany since the Middle Ages—laid bare the widespread disapproval of an incipient Jewish emancipation and revealed people's chagrin at the return of Jews to cities from which they had been expelled.[85] If the murder accusation in Dormagen occurred in this tumultuous context, it also inspired violence of its own. On October 30 in the nearby village of Hülchrath, rioters stoned the Jewish schoolhouse, demolished gravestones in the Jewish cemetery, and bloodily assaulted local Jews.[86] All of this—the return of ritual-murder belief and the violence that accompanied it—constituted a dismaying vestige of an era insufficiently past.

A second accusation came fifteen years later, this time in the Rhenish hamlet of Neuenhoven, not far from the town of Neuss. Although the substance of the charges recounted a familiar story (Jews

had murdered a six-year-old boy and drawn off his blood), the resulting violence wracked the local Jewish communities with considerably
more force than had been felt at Dormagen. According to a local newspaper, the *Elberfelder Zeitung*, "a numerous crowd" attacked "the
dwellings of two Jews living in Neuenhoven, and they were almost
entirely laid to waste together with the furniture and goods in them,
while at the same time the Synagogue at Bedburdyk was stormed and
completely destroyed."[87] For months on end, scenes of anti-Semitic
violence erupted in town and country, marring the idyllic landscape of
the left bank of the Lower Rhine. In some towns, only the presence
of the Prussian military saved the Jews from additional attacks.
Moreover, the Neuenhoven case encouraged further denunciations: in
Willich, in the county of Krefeld, in 1835, Jews were again accused of
committing ritual murder, as they would be in Düsseldorf in 1836 and
again in 1840.[88]

What is most striking about these cases is the clash between the
world of popular religiosity, steeped in the lore of medieval accusation,
and the rational reaction of public officials. In a decree dated July 26,
1834, two weeks after the murder in Neuenhoven, the president of the
district of Düsseldorf denounced the ritual-murder accusation as "a
superstition sprung from the barbarism of centuries long past" and
pointed out that the facts of the case should have "completely banished any thought of the reality of the silly tale."[89]

This statement marks an important moment in the history of the
ritual-murder accusation. Infused with optimism, enlightened officials
supposed that by decree they could mold a less superstitious, more
informed public sphere. This was a time when officials began to believe
in the emerging power of public education and the printed word to
eradicate baseless fantasies, such as those about ritual murder, that
bedeviled the popular imagination. And there were indeed grounds for
hope. In Germany, literacy had become the common property of an
increasing number of men and women. In 1840, according to one rough
estimate, 40 percent of Germans could read; in 1870, 75 percent; in
1900, 90 percent—a "revolution in reading," as one historian called it.[90]

To be sure, not all Germans steeped themselves in the works of Goethe, Schiller, and Lessing, but a great number of people read newspapers, almanacs, and penny pamphlets. As newly created knowledge was more easily disseminated, and as a public sphere based on the free exchange of ideas began to form—so early nineteenth-century reformers thought—the belief in magic and miracles, monsters and demons, would slowly but surely disappear. "The disenchantment of the world," to use Max Weber's phrase, would bring forth a more rational man.

Yet the ritual-murder accusation persisted. In Germany, accusations surfaced in Bavarian Swabia in 1845, in Cologne in 1861, in the Westphalian village of Enniger in 1873, in Xanten in 1891—in Catholic, not Protestant, regions. To enlightened German liberals, there was no riddle here. Since the 1830s, religious revival had swept the Catholic countryside. Reinforced by social tensions between town and country and by a political conflict over mixed marriages, the revival spoke in an increasingly secular age to deep desires to reenchant the world. But to German liberals, self-appointed eradicators of superstition, the revival raised the specter of mass mystification. They saw before them a long, drawn-out struggle for civilization against barbarism, for the forward claims of the modern against the backward pull of the medieval.[91]

The printed word, they thought, would be a weapon in their arsenal. But with respect to ritual murder, as had already been true in Trent in 1475 and in Sandomierz in 1710, it turned out to be a double-edged sword. Print could be wielded by the purveyors of prejudice as well as by the combatants for civilization. Book production constituted a case in point. In nineteenth-century Germany, a dramatic increase in titles addressing aspects of the blood libel occurred, with the bulk of books following major cases that elicited wide discussion—first in Damascus in 1840 and then again in Tisza-Eszlar (Hungary) in 1882. By the end of the century, there existed a sizable literature on the problem of ritual murder, with authors ranging from Grub Street pamphleteers to well-meaning Protestant pastors and theologians on both sides of the question. The discussion was also international. Books on ritual murder, pro and contra, appeared not only in German but also in Russian, Hebrew, French, Yiddish, Polish, Italian, English, Hungarian, Czech, Dutch, and Greek. Moreover, major works were often translated. Penned by Isaac Baer Levinsohn, the most important work defending the Jews of Russia against ritual-murder accusations, *Efes Damim* (*No Blood*), was originally published in Wilna in 1837 and included text in Hebrew, Latin, Russian, and Polish. The book was subsequently translated into German, French, and English. But on the other side of the debate, the scribblings of August Rohling, a fraudulent professor of Catholic theology who had taught in Milwaukee, Münster, and Prague, were also translated. Originally published in German by established Catholic publishing houses, Rohling's work was translated into Polish, Czech, Hungarian, Dutch, French, and English.

Nineteenth-century works on ritual murder differed radically in sophistication, style, and scholarly rigor. It should not be surprising that works defending Jews against the ritual-murder charge were typically composed in a high academic style and adhered to the strictest canons of evidence. Hermann Strack, Regius Professor of Theology at the University of Berlin, whose work *The Jew and Human Sacrifice* remains the best general book on the subject, devoted much of his career to showing—by close and critical readings of sources—that the ritual-murder charge had been a hoax from the start, and its modern purveyors nothing but frauds in pseudo-scholarly dress. Yet his style was forbidding, and his prose often choked on the garlands of endless textual citations. Equally forbidding for all but the most learned was Moritz Stern's *Source Contributions to the Position of the Popes on the Jews*, which gathered together the medieval papacy's impressive record denouncing the ritual-murder accusation. Yet Stern refused to translate some of his sources, letting the Latin- and Italian-language documents speak for themselves. Some authors, however, attempted to appeal to a wider audience. In 1901, Friedrich Frank, a Bavarian priest, wrote a popular refutation of the ritual-murder accusations. Relying heavily on the work of Strack, while forgoing Strack's elaborate scholarly apparatus, Frank showed that the accusations had almost always been fabricated and that in almost all cases the church, as well as many learned men, had opposed them.

On the other side, authors of Rohling's ilk had far fewer inhibitions when it came to popularizing the ritual-murder charge. Not only did anti-Semitic authors forgo serious source criticism; some could hardly read Hebrew. This was true of Ippolit Liutostanskii, a Polish-born, defrocked Catholic priest, who, after being tried for rape, turned to anti-Semitic polemics in order to earn money. He succeeded for a time in the 1870s and 1880s, aided, no doubt, by a depiction he had made of himself studying the Talmud wearing a tallith and tefillin. But when he was brought to court by the editor of a Hebrew newspaper, it became clear that Liutostanskii could not read Hebrew; indeed, he could not even decipher the alphabet.[92] Other authors were not quite as crass, but August Rohling, easily the most widely read and cited anti-Semitic "authority" on ritual murder, desisted from a similar public challenge issued by a young rabbi from Galicia, Joseph Bloch. If Rohling could translate a randomly selected page of the Torah in a public forum, Bloch would hand him the handsome sum of three thousand Austrian gulden. Rohling, however, refused to countenance such a public embarrassment.[93] In the course of the dispute, it also emerged that Rohling had simply plagiarized most of the translations in his *The Talmudic Jew* from Eisenmenger's *Judaism Discovered*.[94]

Anti-Semitic authors also unscrupulously appealed to recorded history as proof of the veracity of the ritual-murder charge. Typically, they published long lists of historic cases complete with the text of Jewish confessions. In 1700, Eisenmenger had already composed such a list, reporting but fifteen cases while assuring his readers that there were many more. By the mid-nineteenth century, the list had greatly expanded. In 1866, Constantin Ritter Cholewa von Pawlikowski, an Austrian anti-Semite, cobbled together in his *Talmud in Theory and Practice* a list of seventy-three "human sacrifices" between 169 B.C.E. and 1860.[95] After Pawlikowski's work appeared, plagiarisms of the expanded list abounded. Rohling reproduced much of Pawlikowski's material in 1870. So too did Henri Desportes, a French priest whose *Mystery of Blood among the Jews of All Times* appeared in 1889 and devoted nearly two hundred pages to the enumeration and description of at least one hundred ritual murders that had allegedly been committed since the twelfth century.[96] For readers with anti-Semitic proclivities, these lists no doubt hardened the belief in ritual murder. For even if one claimed that some cases seemed dubious, it proved harder to demonstrate that all of them were fabrications of anti-Semitic fantasy.

It is exceedingly difficult to gauge the popularity of these specific works. Some, like Rohling's, went into many editions in many languages and, as even Rohling's detractors admitted, reached a wide audience. Joseph Bloch, for example, conceded that Rohling's work had made the Talmud "a universal topic: in coffee houses, ale and public houses, in club meetings and in popular assemblies," and that pamphlets for and against "were carried even to the miserable huts of laborers."[97] What was retained in these "miserable huts" one may only surmise: perhaps Rohling's claim that in the Talmud Christians are called dogs and asses; or perhaps his equally notorious contention that the cabala demands the slaughter of Christian virgins.

I V

Violence had come in great waves, the unsteady climate of the Crusades and the rise of eucharistic piety creating the first massive swells that overwhelmed western Europe's oldest Jewish communities. That this violence was something new we can deduce from the lamentations of the Nuremberg poet Mose b. Eleasar Hakohen, who around 1300 hoped that the Rintfleisch massacres of 1298 would be "the final scene of a fifth millennium overly rich with persecution."[98] The Christian year 1240 was the Jewish year 5000, and, as we know, Hakohen's hopes were not fulfilled. Already the fourteenth century of the Christian calendar had brought still greater calamities as well as a permanent break in the civilization of German Jewry. In the three centuries that followed, violence erupted less dramatically but still repeatedly, especially in Poland, where most Jews now lived. A period of relative calm ensued, marked by the hope of enlightenment and the promise of emancipation. But there were serious forebodings: the Hep-Hep riots of 1819, the spillover violence of the revolutions of 1830 and 1848, and smaller tremors in between.[99] The seas began to stir.

In 1881, the storm broke; on this, modern historians agree. "The year 1881 marks a turning point in the history of the Jews as decisive as that of 70 A.D., when Titus's legions burned the Temple at Jerusalem, or 1492, when Ferdinand and Isabella decreed the expulsion from Spain," writes Irving Howe.[100] "If 1933 and the years immediately subsequent to it mark European Jewry's culminating agony," the historian David Vital has recently argued, "1881 marks the first great milestone on the road to it."[101]

That year witnessed the worst outbreak of anti-Jewish violence in modern history prior to the twentieth century. Starting in the district capital of Elisavetgrad, in Ukraine, during Easter week, the riots swiftly spread as the government reacted with insufficient resolve and as angry workers and peasants traveled by rail, river, and road from the cities to the towns and villages throughout the countryside. It was a modern massacre: urban in origin, driven by ideology, fueled by the press, and abetted by politicians from afar. Incoherent and unorganized, the actual violence remained more imitative than planned.

The pogroms were framed by political events that provoked people to act. All across central and eastern Europe, the onset of a severe economic depression in 1879, combined with a series of political realignments, brought about the collapse of liberal influence in the halls of government. In the Russian Empire, the collapse was especially abrupt. On March 13, 1881, the liberal Czar Alexander II, whom Disraeli called "the kindliest prince who has ever ruled Russia," was assassinated.[102] His heir, Alexander III, tightened the grip of autocratic rule and, following the counsel of a mystical prelate, Konstantin Pobedonostsev, pursued a policy of "orthodoxy, autocracy, and nationality." Clearly, this signaled a turn for the worse. Still, the government, contrary to what many historians used to believe, did not incite violence. It merely reacted so slowly that those who attacked Jews with sabers and clubs could think the czar looked approvingly upon their savage work. By the end of 1881, there had been an estimated 259 separate pogroms; they left tens of thousands of Jews homeless, caused millions of rubles worth of damage, and involved unsettling physical attacks as Jews were killed, beaten, and maimed and Jewish women raped.[103] Like the medieval massacres of Rintfleisch and Armleder, the pogroms effected a trauma and left a vast Jewish community wondering what place on this earth they might still call home.

Other pogroms, some involving ritual-murder charges, followed—in 1903, 1905, 1906, and 1911. These pogroms, and the deteriorating situation of Russian Jews generally, also inaugurated a stream of emigration that, when the dam broke in 1881, turned from a modest trickle into a raging torrent: from roughly 40,000 in the 1870s, to 135,000 in the decade following the riots in Elisavetgrad, to nearly a million Jews in the twenty years thereafter. It was the largest movement of people in Jewish history, as more than a third of eastern Europe's Jews left "the land that held the dust of their ancestors" behind for the New World.[104]

The violence spread far to the west, to Hungary, Galicia, and West Prussia and Pomerania, where in 1881 in Neustettin a synagogue fire, blamed on the Jews, led to the only other late-nineteenth-century outbreak of anti-Semitic rioting in Germany commensurate with that in Konitz in 1900. It happened roughly in the same area and included many of the same towns, not least, Konitz itself.[105] Throughout Europe, the number of ritual-murder cases also increased. One erupted in the spring of 1882 in the town of Tisza-Eszlar, in the northeastern part of Hungary. Like the Russian and German empires, the Austro-Hungarian empire had also undergone an abrupt political transition brought about by deepening economic depression and inflamed national passions, and this perhaps explains the atmosphere of uncertainty that enveloped the case of a servant girl, Esther Solymosi, who had disappeared. Pulled by popular sentiment, the Hungarian police arrested a number of Jewish citizens, though they had little evidence against them, until a fourteen-year-old boy implicated his father by claiming that he had seen him taking part in the ritual killing inside the synagogue. The trial, which took place in the summer of 1882, culminated in a confrontation between the boy and his father. "I don't want to be a Jew anymore!" the son said. "Won't you be sorry if they hang me?" the father replied. The excited gallery cheered at the son's every word, but the police later determined that the son could not have seen what he had claimed to see, and the Jews of Tisza-Eszlar were acquitted.

For the Jews of Hungary, the acquittal seemed like "the victory of truth" over the "phantoms of dark centuries."[106] Still, these phantoms proved tenacious, not least, in Germany. On January 22, 1884, in the small town of Skurz, about fifty miles east of Konitz, a fourteen-year-old boy had been found brutally murdered, his throat slit, his face slashed seven times, his limbs severed from his body, his legs expertly separated in two at the knees, his intestines ripped out, and his white body parts naked and drained of blood.[107]

"The Jews committed the murder in order to have Christian blood for the Easter holidays," the good people of Skurz, a town of about two thousand, concluded, most of them German and Polish Catholics.[108] Mankowski, a worker, came forward to claim that he had seen a poor Jewish butcher and rag seller named Hermann Josefsohn walking away from the scene of the crime on the morning of January 22. As if to foreshadow the events in Konitz, the police arrested Josefsohn after Mankowski claimed to have seen him "carrying a heavy sack on his back" with "a round object that looked like a human head sticking out of the lower corner."[109]

The police also arrested two other Jews, the sixty-five-year-old, "well-to-do" merchant Bloos and his son.[110] One witness noticed a commotion in the merchant's house, where many Jews had supposedly assembled. The witness heard someone with "a Jewish accent" call the boy in, and two other witnesses corroborated the story, adding details. Mrs. Reimann, a widow, who lived in the same house as Bloos, said that she had heard a loud noise and then the sound of something falling coming from the goat pen. The story received further embellishment from the servant girl Katharina Kowalewska. She had come home around four o'clock in the morning and gone to visit Mrs. Reimann, when she heard the sound of broken glass coming from her master's apartment. The next day, a Catholic butcher named Josef Behrend identified a vessel of blood in the possession of Bloos as the blood of the slain boy.[111]

The blood turned out to be oxen blood. Bloos and his son were released, and so was Hermann Josefsohn. Yet Josefsohn, who had spent several months in prison awaiting trial, could not easily return to his home town without "placing himself in danger of being beaten to death."[112] In May 1884, the mood in Skurz was indeed portentous and the local police, anxious about impending riots, called for reinforcements. Meanwhile, the Berlin police inspector who had come to solve the crime charged the two men who had supposedly seen Josefsohn carrying a sack with perjury and another with the murder of the fourteen-year-old boy. The man charged with murder was Josef Behrend, the Catholic butcher.

The case went to trial in late April 1885 in Danzig, then a predominantly German city, where it was judged by a jury of twelve men, six Catholics and six Protestants. The Berlin police thought they had their man. Mankowski, the worker who had testified that he had seen the Jewish butcher Hermann Josefsohn carrying a sack near the scene of the crime, admitted that he had lied. In fact, he had seen Josef Behrend. The case against Behrend appeared damaging. But on the witness stand, Mankowski retracted his statement, saying he could no longer be sure whether he had seen the Jewish or the Catholic butcher skulking around the scene of the crime with a sack on his back. Faced with conflicting evidence, the jury deliberated. In a split decision, it found Behrend "not guilty," the verdict falling, according to one source, along religious lines: Protestants found him guilty, Catholics moved to acquit.[113] As was the practice with split decisions, the court was required to let Behrend go. After the trial, Behrend fell into penury and resorted to begging on the streets. The Berlin-based German Anti-Semitic League even took up a collection for him.[114] Evidently, the effort was not a success, for soon thereafter Behrend emigrated to Minnesota, where it was rumored that on his death bed he confessed to the crime.[115]

These ritual-murder cases in the 1880s demonstrated the continuing emotional resonance of the blood libel. They also revealed that the anti-Semitic ritual—starting with general suspicion, moving to specific accusation, and culminating in waves of violence—needed little rehearsal. The "ruts in the pathways of the mind," to use Karl Mannheim's phrase, had been furrowed many times before.[116]

Far from abating, the accusations multiplied. In its bimonthly newsletter, the Berlin-based Association against Anti-Semitism counted seventy-nine bona fide ritual-murder charges made in Europe between 1891 and 1900. It actually counted more, but some cases were so self-evidently planted by anti-Semitic politicians that they never took hold. It may, however, have missed other cases, since some went unreported and others got lost in small-town newspapers. Yet the association's list constitutes the most comprehensive survey we have for a ten-year period. Moreover, the pattern that results when we consider these accusations as a whole proves revealing.

The accusations occurred throughout all of Europe, the vast majority east of the Rhine. The seventy-nine incidents break down as follows: thirty-six in Austria-Hungary (with thirteen in Hungary, eight in Bohemia, six in Moravia, six in German Austria, and three in Galicia); fifteen in Germany; eleven in Bulgaria; five in Russia; two in Romania; and one each in Serbia and in France. Of the seventy-nine accusations, fourteen escalated into some level of violence against Jews. In more than half the cases, specific charges were made against individual Jews, as opposed to the more general claim that "the Jews did it." When not listed as a crowd, the accusers typically came from humble backgrounds, though rarely from the peasantry. Of those named, eight were servants, seven were mothers of the victims, and one was the grandmother. There were also two apprentices, two peasants, two beggars, a worker, a nun, a soldier, a father of a missing child, and three young girls and two young boys. Not one member of the upper classes filed an initial accusation (except in one case where a lawyer did so on behalf of a mother). In six cases, the accusation came directly from the pages of an anti-Semitic newspaper. Conversely, the Jews who were incriminated typically belonged to the middle and upper classes. They were usually merchants (unless butchers) and, in a disproportionate number of incidents, were masters who employed Christian girls as maids.

The relationship between a Christian maid and her Jewish master constitutes an important motif in turn-of-the-century ritual-murder accusations, as many of the stories came from the maids themselves. For example, at Easter in 1894 in the Bohemian town of Lobositz, on the Elbe, a maid named Maria Lincha from the village of Wottitz supposedly overheard her master and his brother conspiring to ritually slaughter her. She had even seen the vessel they were to use to collect her blood. Further investigation showed that other women had told her stories about a similar case that had occurred the preceding Easter in the nearby town of Kolin, where the dead body of a servant girl was found in the Elbe. The girl, Marie Havlin, had committed suicide, but a Czech anti-Semitic newspaper claimed that she displayed stab wounds on her body; in bold headlines, the paper accused the girl's master of killing her for her blood.[117] Similarly, in 1896 in the town of Mährisch-Trübau, two servant girls spread the rumor, soon dignified in print, that the Jewish merchant Moritz Moller had drawn the blood of his former maid, Philomena Waclawek, by pricking her arm and leg joints with a needle. Medical examiners, however, found no such pricks, and Waclawek spent three months in prison for the fantastic stories she told to her credulous friends.[118] Stories of this sort spilled over into Germany as well. In Schoppinitz, Upper Silesia, in 1898, a servant girl accused her Jewish master of slicing her breasts while she slept. The officials charged with the investigation declared the story an invention and dismissed the case.[119]

Historians, however, must take such imagined tales seriously, for they open windows onto the mentality of people who otherwise leave few documentary traces. Servants were ordinarily of lower-class background, born in a village or the countryside, and usually undereducated. As Christian maids, they lived and worked in near-intimacy with Jews, who tended to be from the middle or upper class, generally from the town or city, and who were typically more educated than they. It may have been the maids' first time away from home and their first close encounter with members of another religious group. Moreover, as the accusations make clear, the fear of men and perhaps of rape (not unknown in master-maid relations) imparted emotional force to at least some of the charges involving mutilation.

But the maids were not alone. Their fears were often corroborated by rumors among friends and by the propaganda of anti-Semitic newspapers. Thus, in the Hungarian village of Szenicz in June 1894, a washerwoman never returned after having delivered clothes to the Jewish family Keszler. Immediately, local people thought it a case of ritual murder. Another maid claimed to have seen a number of rabbis and a kosher butcher gathered in the Keszler house. The missing girl, it turned out, had fallen into an overflowing stream during a flash flood.[120] Rumors of this type were also spread in print. In Vienna, during Passover in 1897, the anti-Semitic *Deutsche Volksblatt* listed the names of four maids who had served in Jewish households and were now supposedly missing. In all four cases, it was easy to document their whereabouts.[121] Nonetheless, the paper never printed a retraction, and the rumors, once let loose in the public realm, were not easily dismissed.

A second genre of murder accusations involved missing children. Mothers brought their children to market, sometimes to Jewish stores, and when the children wandered off, the mothers quickly concluded that the Jews had taken the children away. A case in Bucharest, in the kingdom of Romania, whose status as an independent country was not yet two decades old, proved typical. One day in August 1893, two Christian women entered Pascal's porcelain shop and somehow lost track of the child. The younger woman, the mother, immediately yelled at Mrs. Pascal, the Jewish proprietor, "Give me back my Jonica," and "You have hidden him to kill him." Meanwhile, according to one report, the older woman wrung her hands in anger. Then a crowd began to gather, and the mother again cried out for her boy: "My Jonica, my Jonica, now they are going to cut your throat." Within minutes of the commotion, a peasant woman brought the child back to the mother.[122]

Such incidents, many of which were never reported, were not confined to the far eastern corners of Europe. Seventy kilometers north of Konitz, in the town of Berent, a very similar event occurred. In April 1894, Mrs. Hermann, a Catholic widow, sent her son to sell a goat to a Jewish butcher named Werner. But when the son did not return, Mrs. Hermann marched over to the butcher shop, grabbed Mrs. Werner by the collar, and demanded that she return her child. Unfortunately, no child was forthcoming. Incensed, Mrs. Hermann ran down the street shouting, "The Jew slaughtered my child." An angry crowd gathered and marched to the town hall and demanded that the mayor liberate the boy. The boy, it turns out, had taken a side street and sold the goat to someone else. When questioned by the police about her anti-Semitic outcries, Mrs. Hermann replied she had "often read such things in the newspaper."[123]

Ritual-murder charges also served to obscure the mistreatment of children and infanticide. This happened in Labischin, in the German province of Posen. In June 1894, the Kuniszewskis seemed to have lost their five-year-old boy, and he was found hastily buried in a nearby wood. The mother, it turned out, had badly maltreated her son and, as the autopsy later revealed, had buried him alive. The Jews, she had told both her husband and the authorities, had taken the boy away to be slaughtered.[124]

Finally, ritual-murder accusations often deflected attention from an act that at once fascinated and disgusted turn-of-the-century European society: sexual murder. That Jews signified sexual danger was an old trope of anti-Semitic imaginings. In 1888, it had resurfaced anew in connection with the notorious case of Jack the Ripper. According to one theory, encouraged by Viennese newspapers, Jack the Ripper may have been an east European Jew who, in accordance with the injunctions of the Talmud, murdered Christian girls with whom he had sexual relations.[125] If the specific charge did not convince London society at the time, the general idea nevertheless achieved considerable currency in the cultural milieu of central Europe.

V

Of the seventy-nine cases documented in Europe, one merits attention because it shows that not only the motifs but also the modus operandi of the ritual-murder charge followed a predetermined path. On the feast of Saints Peter and Paul, June 29, 1891, in the small Catholic town of Xanten, in the county of Mörs, a five-year-old boy was murdered, his throat slit from ear to ear, his body found in a barn. As if on cue, local Christians accused Adolph Buschhoff of the murder, a Jewish butcher who lived near the scene of the crime.

The first to incriminate him was Heinrich Junkermann, the Catholic butcher. On the night of June 29, Junkermann had seen the fresh corpse lying in the barn; the next morning, at six-thirty sharp, he went to the mayor and urged him to arrest Buschhoff. The Jews need Christian blood, Junkermann said; his son, a medical student, told him so. As a butcher, he could also attest that the cut resembled a kosher slaughter.[126] By noon, the people of Xanten had already begun to single out Buschhoff as the primary suspect. As people talked, the stories grew more elaborate.[127]

A stonecutter, Heinrich Wesendrupp, Junkermann's brother-in-law, contended that unless a narcotic was used, blood should have squirted out from the neck more vigorously than it did. Perhaps Buschhoff had collected the blood, Wesendrupp reasoned.[128] His friend Hermann Mölders supported this view. A sixty-eight-year-old gardener who could neither read nor write, Mölders was mentally slow, and he enjoyed a few glasses of schnapps at daybreak. On the morning of June 29, his consumption quota already reached, Mölders witnessed an unusual sight at Buschhoff's house. "An arm came out from a grown-up person" (*"et kam en Arm von einem erwachsenen Minsch"*), he said. "They dragged him in" (*"Sie trock ihn herein"*).[129] The sightings and overheard conversations accumulated. Countless people now came forward to report that Buschhoff had been acting suspiciously, that he seemed upset, that his "color had changed," that he often ignored people (he was nearly deaf), and that he reacted defensively to the accusations.[130] Mathilde Biesenkamp said that Buschhoff had told her to shut her mouth because she didn't know anything about it (*"Ji sallt man die Mul halde, ji weet von de ganze Sak nix von"*).[131] Others claimed to have overheard conversations: the servant girls Selma Roelen and Anna Moritz heard Buschhoff and his son saying, "If they can't prove it, they can't do anything to us," and "As long as it doesn't leak out."[132] According to other witnesses, local Jews were involved in the cover-up. "We have to keep it secret," one Xantener Jew allegedly said to another, "and take care that you don't babble."[133]

It is a pattern we have seen countless times before: starting with an initial denunciation, accusations amassed and became more and more concrete. As time went by, it also grew safer to go after one's Jewish neighbor. The pattern, moreover, was already evident to contemporaries. "The people make an image," the state judge Brixus complained, "a few pieces of which they themselves experienced, then they gradually work themselves into the image, and to this is added what other people say."[134] The people, the judge pointed out, became more, rather than less, precise in their descriptions as time went by and as they believed in the images of their own imagination.[135]

The initial accusers were local anti-Semites. Junkermann had spent the day of the murder at the beer festival on the Fürstenberg complaining about the Jews. "I can't stand them," he said; "the Jews are a bad people, the dregs, and a bunch of cheats." When news of the murder came, his first reaction was to say, "Surely a Jew did it."[136] The same may be said of his brother-in-law Wesendrupp, hardly an upstanding citizen himself. A violent man with a bad temper, he beat his wife for many years, allowed his business to fall into ruin, and, after his wife's death, placed his three children in an orphanage.[137] He too hated the Jews, in particular Buschhoff, who had fired him on the Friday before the murder when he (Wesendrupp) showed up to work

Konitz, circa 1900.

*The marketplace, with the Protestant church in the foreground, the
Catholic church in the background, and the house of
Mrs. Wiwjorra in the right-hand corner.*

Danzigerstrasse, circa 1890.

View of the Gymnasium (the high school) that Ernst Winter attended.

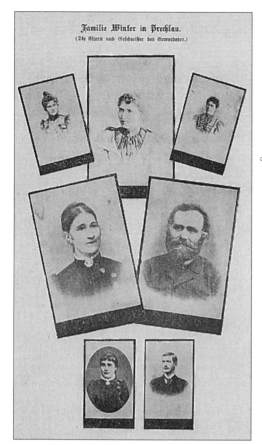

The family of Ernst Winter.

Townspeople gathered at the basin of
the Mönchsee after the discovery of
Ernst Winter's torso.

*The discovery of Winter's head in a ditch
at the Dunkershagen farm.*

*The discovery of Winter's vest in January 1901,
which led to a break in the investigation.*

Gustav Hoffmann and his daughter, Anna.

Funeral procession for Ernst Winter on May 27, 1900.

Moritz Lewy.

Anti-Semitic postcard depicting the Lewys as devouring, satiated lions.

*A postcard photograph featuring the synagogue,
taken after the attempt to burn it down, with Prussian soldiers standing guard.
The caption reads, "Greetings from Konitz in West Prussia."*

Jews burning in a pit—a woodcut from the Nuremberg Chronicle *of 1493.*

A popular depiction of the ritual murder of Simon of Trent, which allegedly took place in 1475.

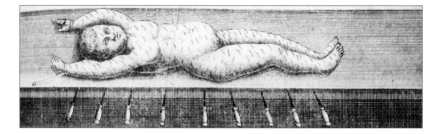

Depiction of the murdered child, Simon of Trent, on the Frankfurt Bridge Tower.

inebriated, as he often did. As he left Buschhoff's premises, Wesendrupp threatened that he would fix things so that his Jewish neighbor "wouldn't have another Sabbath."[138] The animosity Junkermann and Wesendrupp felt toward Buschhoff has even led one modern historian to speculate that they might have committed the murder themselves and subsequently directed attention toward Buschhoff.[139] For Wesendrupp, whose alibi was questionable and whom locals thought perfectly capable of committing such a heinous crime, there may even be something to that theory. Two years later in pubs in the nearby town of Kalkar, he allegedly confessed to the crime.[140] But if it is easy to understand why Wesendrupp attempted to frame Buschhoff, it is more difficult to discern a motive for the murder in the first place.[141]

From the start, the accusations were also supported by educated people, like Dr. Steinert, the medical examiner who first observed the corpse and against better evidence determined that blood was missing, or Junkermann's son Carl, the medical student who thought Jews need blood for baking matzo.[142] In Xanten, the local priest, Chaplain Bresser, also contributed to the baleful situation by gathering evidence against the Jews, especially among local children, and printing his findings in the Xantener newspaper, the *Bote für Stadt und Land*.[143] He also wrote an essay for Junkermann, as Bruhn would do for Hoffmann, attesting that the cut on the neck resembled a kosher cut. Bresser then dictated the essay to Junkermann, who wrote it down, word for word, signed it, and published it as his own.[144]

If initial accusations drew the support of the educated, they were also fostered by a dynamic of violence and community. In the weeks after the murder, there had been frequent demonstrations in the streets of Xanten. As these demonstrations gained momentum, and certainly by July 12, townspeople publicly engaged in rituals of "exclusionary violence"—taunting Jews on the streets, smashing windows, smearing Jewish houses with anti-Semitic graffiti.[145] Moreover, by July 12, an outside newspaper had intervened. The conservative anti-Semitic *Das Volk* reported that the boy's body had been found "completely bloodless."[146]

A few weeks later, an anti-Semitic newspaper published in Dortmund, the *Westfälische Reform*, wrote of an "authentic ritual murder."[147]

The Jews of Xanten now recognized the precariousness of their position. With the help of Rabbi Horowitz of Krefeld, they wrote a formal letter on September 14 to the Prussian minister of the interior. "The disturbances increase daily," they claimed; "only through the swift discovery of the evildoer can we be helped."[148] The government sent Inspector Wolff from Berlin. Like Braun in Konitz, Wolff quickly made an arrest, but he arrested the Jewish butcher, whose name, like Lewy's, was Adolph. Buschhoff struck the boy in a fit of anger, Wolff reasoned, because the boy had damaged gravestones. When the five-year-old fell unconscious, Buschhoff, realizing what he had done, was seized by panic and asked his daughter to carry the boy to the barn under her apron; the father then followed and slit the boy's throat.[149]

Wolff's theory rested on the veracity of Mölder's testimony ("an arm came out from a grown-up person"). It was also supported by numerous statements that Buschhoff seemed to be in an agitated state, and it was buttressed by a declaration Buschhoff's wife allegedly made to Wesendrupp: "She was happy and relieved that the child was not found at their house, because of their identity as Jews," she supposedly said.[150] For Inspector Wolff here was the motive that "must have moved them" to kill the boy in the barn.[151] On October 14, he arrested and incarcerated Adolph Buschhoff and his family. The case was then turned over to Judge Brixus, who, after a two-month investigation, sensibly concluded that Inspector Wolff's theory rested on unsupported suppositions and specious evidence. Mölders, for example, could not have seen what he claimed from where he was standing.[152] With insufficient evidence for a prosecution, Brixus recommended that Buschhoff's family be released. On December 23, they were free to go (though not home, since Xanten was no longer safe for them).

With renewed vigor, the public debate started all over again. Not only the anti-Semitic press but also the Catholic press and that of the Conservative Party portrayed Buschhoff's release as a travesty of justice.[153] Suddenly, the Xanten affair became a national issue. It was even the subject of a debate on the floor of the Prussian Landtag, where a Conservative delegate from rural Saxony, "Krautjunker" Baron von Wackerbarth-Linderode, got up and explained to the assembled deputies that Jews did, in fact, commit ritual murder and that they were getting off scot-free because the Prussian judiciary was in their pockets.[154] By early February, the time of the baron's harangue, the national political climate had already forced local authorities to reconsider the case. In the process, the county medical examiner, Dr. Ferdinand Bauer, discovered something new: a tear in the boy's shirt was caused by a notch on the blade of a knife found in Buschhoff's home—knife number 13.[155] State forensic experts dismissed the claim (many things could have caused the tear), but Bauer held fast to his evaluation. At this time, moreover, a series of new witnesses came forward and reported having seen Buschhoff in an agitated state. The police arrested Buschhoff and his family once again, and the case went to trial in Cleve District Court on July 4, 1892.[156] The trial lasted ten days, at the end of which the jury reached a verdict of not guilty. It could hardly have done otherwise. By then, even the district attorney, responsible for the prosecution, admitted that the evidence against Buschhoff seemed specious, and he urged the jury to decide accordingly.

For the anti-Semitic press, however, and the people in the area, no evidence could have exonerated Buschhoff. The decision sparked a hail of criticism and another round of violence.[157] Over the next two weeks, incidents occurred in Neuss and Grevenbroich, south of Xanten, as well as in their hinterlands. In Grevenbroich, anti-Semites desecrated a Jewish cemetery, "tearing the gravestones from the earth and breaking them to pieces."[158] In nearby towns and villages, they also desecrated cemeteries and in at least two communities, Hemmerden and Gierath, people threw rocks smeared with blood through the windows of Jewish houses. In Grevenbroich itself, anti-Semites taunted Jews on the streets, smashed shop windows, and shattered the windows of the Grevenbroich synagogue, which later, in August, someone even tried to blow up. In Neuss, the situation was hardly better. Jewish houses were plastered with hateful placards and, on the night of

Saturday, July 23, anti-Semites painted "large blood red crosses" on them.[159]

As it had in countless cases of alleged ritual murder and host desecration, the violence in the summer of 1892 told a symbolic story of exclusion and expulsion. Xanten was not a hometown—not for the Jews. The violence was of course real, but blood red crosses also evoked centuries of Christian animosity toward Jews, a history of barely concealed enmity and the thinnest veil of conditional tolerance. And still, the worst was yet to come.

By 1900, the vengeful anti-Semitic heart had behind it the full force of nearly a millennium of historical experience. Or to borrow from the historian Edward Muir: "Blood boiled not so much for natural as for learned reasons."[160] What was learned was not always already there, nor was it simply the flat screen of prejudice. Rather, the people had come to know a series of stories, a collection of murderous tales, which served as alibis for aggression.[161] The stories also came with a familiar script, powerful in its specificity. People got to know characters and understand their roles. There was the down-and-out Jew walking around with a head in a sack. In Konitz, this was Wolf Israelski. But such a figure also appeared in a dream to a woman in Skurz in 1884. In her dream, the dismembered fourteen-year-old Onofrius Czybulla came to her, dressed in white, complaining that a Jew "carried him in a sack."[162] The topos was also present in Dormagen in 1819 and in Ravensburg in 1429. In the latter case, the Jews allegedly stole a Christian boy from a wedding, ritually slaughtered him, and carried his corpse around in a sack.[163] The marginal Jew who reveals the secrets of the murder also constituted a recurring motif. Drunken Dumb Alex, in other words, was not alone. He had a counterpart at the trial in Trent in Giovanni da Feltre, a criminal, but also a convert, who claimed that his father had used Christian blood in Passover rituals.[164] Then there was Reichart of Mospach, a star witness at the Regensburg trials in 1475. A thief, three times baptized, now a Jew, now a Christian, married thrice, he gave insider testimony that the Jews of Regensburg tortured the host.[165]

On the Christian side, too, witnesses were not always cut of the finest cloth. "Liars, criminals, crazy people, or the feebleminded," the scholar Wolfgang Treue has argued, "easily assumed the role of star witnesses in the trials against the Jews."[166] Thus the likes of Stutter Anton and Rosine Simanowski, to say nothing of Bernhard Masloff and his mother-in-law, took their place in the ritual-murder drama, as such people had often done in the past. The same may be said of Christian maids whose bodies were allegedly violated by bloodthirsty Jewish masters. Here the instances of denunciation involving women and girls who served in Jewish houses are too numerous to recount. Suffice it to say that the alleged rape of Mathilde Rutz reflected a recurrent theme, especially at the end of the nineteenth century. The women were not completely alone, however. The imagined touch of the Jew also sent shivers down men's spines. In Konitz, the peasant Joseph Laskowski swore that Adolph Lewy had touched his arm muscles and hips in order to size him up for slaughter.[167] But this, too, was a topos people had learned. In Xanten, eight years earlier, the father of the murdered boy felt a bloody hand when Adolph Buschhoff, the Jewish butcher, touched him on the back.[168] Finally, there was the Christian butcher, perhaps the killer himself, who identified the incisions as the cut of his Jewish neighbor and fellow butcher. This is how it happened in Skurz. This is what occurred in Xanten. And this is the script that, at least in one sense, Gustav Hoffmann followed as well.

Adolph Lewy's house on the Danzigerstrasse.

◈

CHAPTER FOUR

Accusations

They do not speak peaceably,
but devise false accusations
against those who live quietly
in the land

—PSALMS 35:20

There is no doubt that witchcraft persecutions
were made between people who knew each
other intimately.

—ALAN MACFARLANE,
Witchcraft in Tudor and Stuart England

I

By August 1900, murder investigators had taken nearly eight hundred depositions from people who believed they had seen or heard something relevant to the murder of Ernst Winter.[1] Even if one considers that some people were deposed more than once, the sheer number of people who volunteered information overwhelmed the police and produced a mountain of paper, with incriminations, mostly of Jews, filling eighteen separate binders.[2] To make matters worse, most of the information was hardly credible, as witnesses came forward with all sorts of "stories, incorrectly overheard or misunderstood utterances, and dreams."[3] One person even claimed to have discerned the killer via spiritual communication with the dead.[4]

And then there were the sightings. How could so many people have seen the Jews of Konitz in incriminating circumstances?

In Konitz—overwhelmed in 1900 by fantastic claims about Jews who committed ritual murder—the actual sightings can often be traced to individual motives. Although some of the files of the murder investigation have been lost, we can query the more than forty extant cases and ask questions that bring us closer to these individual motives: Who were the accusers, and what was their relationship to the Jews they accused? Under what circumstances were the accusations made? And what did the accusers hope to gain? No general formula governs the responses to these questions. It was not always the poor who accused the rich, or the harmed who denounced a perceived oppressor. Anti-Semitic ideology sometimes played a role, but not always. Some of the accusations were outright lies, but others stemmed from the confusions of distorted memory. Still, taken together, the accusations yield a pattern: they were a way for individuals in the community to exercise power over the Jews, and more specifically over the Jews they knew. The dynamics of community also shaped these accusations, defining who belonged and who "sings not with us today"—as the Russian poet Mayakovski ominously wrote.

The immediate context, however, was a German town that, like any town, contained rich neighborhoods and poor sections, dust-filled back streets and pleasant promenades. With a population of ten thousand, Konitz was large enough that differences were palpable and that contrary to the popular saying, not everyone knew each other. By 1900, "the good old days" of extended families, of sons learning the trades of their fathers, and of families staying in one town, one generation after the next, had long since passed.[5] There were many newcomers to Konitz, though this fact did not make the town any more cosmopolitan. Since most of the new arrivals hailed from the surrounding area, they typically brought old ways, not new.[6] An aura of provincial backwardness thus pervaded the town—an aura reinforced by the many petty officials who resided here.

Despite the presence of these Prussian bureaucrats, Kafkaesque figures in a distant outpost, Konitz remained a relatively poor place. With 60 percent of the heads of households earning less than 900 marks per year, the minimum threshold below which one did not pay income tax, it lagged far behind the more prosperous communities of the western parts of the empire.[7] Anyone walking, riding on a wagon, or bicycling into Konitz would have noticed the indigence of its inhabitants right away. Crammed in dark houses—"each somehow livable space occupied by half a dozen children and a couple of grown-ups"— the workers lived on the fringes, in the makeshift quarters of the northern edge of town, near the Dunkershagen farm, where Winter's head was found, or in the working-class streets, Ziegelstrasse and Hohe Höfe, which led into town from the Jewish cemetery.[8] Workers also lived on the south side of Konitz, in the rows of humble houses on the Hennigsdorferstrasse, especially near the noisome banks of the Mönchsee, or on the Pulverstrasse, near the gasworks, or outside the old city walls along the Rähmestrasse, which was often used as a dumping ground (there was as yet no organized trash collection).[9]

The poorest workers dwelled among themselves or in dank apartments alongside widows and invalids hanging on to their meager pensions. In contrast to this group, better-paid workers typically lived in mixed neighborhoods, together with artisans, store clerks, and petty officials. When the soldiers occupied Konitz, most of them were billeted "among the small artisans and the many subalterns and lower civil servants," some of whom fell into debt as the result of costs associated with providing quarter for the troops.[10] In Konitz, these mixed neighborhoods were nestled just inside the old city walls and along back streets like the Postallstrasse. This is where Bernhard Masloff and Anna Ross cohabitated, their back window allowing them to peer into the house of Hermann Lange, the baker, and into the room rented by Ernst Winter. The more well-to-do addresses were located in the center of town, save for a few nice homes along the newer Bahnhofstrasse and Bismarckstrasse and around the Wilhelmsplatz and Denkmalplatz, where the fine houses of the anti-Semitic lawyers, Dr. Max Vogel and Carl Gebauer, stood.

Outbreaks of anti-Semitic violence
in Konitz and towns around it,
1900

■ Repeated incidents
● Single incident

Chazaud

It was, however, along the Danzigerstrasse, which led from the Wilhelmsplatz to the marketplace, that the actors most intimately involved in the Konitz drama resided. Starting from the corner of the Wilhelmsplatz, Danzigerstrasse 1, was the home of the cigar dealer Fischer, who would briefly become a suspect because of his affection for young boys. Matthäus Meyer, the hardware store owner accused of signing a death list that the Jews had sent around, dwelled two doors down. A few doors farther on resided Hermann Lewinski, whose cellar an anti-Semitic police inspector would later suspect as a more suitable place for a ritual murder than the cellar of Adolph Lewy. Across the street, at Danzigerstrasse 31, the house of Gustav Hoffmann cast a long, low shadow over the first bend in the Danzigerstrasse. And three doors down, their back gates abutting, was the house of Adolph Lewy.

I I

Within the cramped alleyways of Konitz and the towns around it, Christians denounced the Jews they knew. They either worked for the Jews they accused or had long been in close business relations with them, the only exception being the battery of students who came forward to claim that they had seen Moritz Lewy and Ernst Winter together. Consistent with the long history of ritual-murder accusations, the accusers generally came from the lower or lower middle classes: they included unskilled workers and day laborers, masons and a civil servant, a prison guard and a night watchman, a poor farmer and his family, a handful of apprentices, and a larger number of servant girls. Men and women came forth with accusations in roughly equal numbers (in the Third Reich, by contrast, it was primarily men who denounced their fellow citizens).[11] Not surprisingly, some of the accusers were poorly educated. Aside from Franz Hellwig, who was "mentally somewhat slow," Anna Ross could not read, nor could the night watchman Friedrich Russ, who claimed to have seen Ernst Winter and Moritz Lewy promenading up and down the Danzigerstrasse almost every night after ten.[12] Finally, a few accusers had criminal records, including the key witness Bernhard Masloff, arrested for assault, Russ, a habitual drunkard, and Margarete Radtke, who had been caught stealing.

One tradition of historical analysis would view the denunciations of middle-class Jews by poorer Christians as a rudimentary form of economic or class protest. Motivated by social and economic disadvantages, Christians falsely accused their Jewish neighbors and set off the storm of riots that beset Konitz in the summer of 1900. Yet the patterns are not so simple as this seamless theory of social protest might suggest: not all the Christians who denounced Jews were disadvantaged, and not all the Jews accused were middle class. More important, economic issues hardly figured in the actual dynamics of accusation, which were more significantly bound up in the tangled web of personal relations. The prominence of servant girls among those who came forward brings this complicated issue into focus. Of the forty-six accusers, eight were domestic servants, most of whom lived in the houses of their Jewish employers. If we count Anna Ross, Martha Masloff, and Anna Berg, who washed and cleaned but did not live with the Lewys, the number is higher still.

At first sight, it seems remarkable that girls who lived in such close proximity to Jewish families should be the ones who accused the Jews they knew of something as fantastic as ritual murder. Physical proximity, however, does not imply emotional intimacy or even trust; moreover, toward the end of the nineteenth century, domestic servants increasingly existed on the margins of the middle-class family: they no longer dined with the family and often lived in a tiny room of their own, usually set off from the kitchen. Within the household, the whole weight of manual labor fell on their shoulders, and the status of a middle-class woman rested on the fact that she did not perform housework. The relationship, then, between a female servant and her employer was marked not only by proximity but also by an extreme imbalance of power.[13] Denunciations reversed this imbalance, often with disastrous results for the Jewish middle-class family. This was obviously so for Adolph Lewy, who was denounced by women who performed domestic work in his own house. A similar fate befell Moritz Zander in Konitz and Max Grossmann in Bütow.

Virtually no Jew in the region was immune. This became evident through the case of Josef Rosenthal, a merchant and the wealthiest man in the village of Kamin, located about eight miles south of Konitz.[14] In the beginning of July, amid the storm of anti-Semitic violence following the summons of Gustav Hoffmann, Rosenthal's domestic servant, Margarete Radtke, claimed that her Jewish employer had participated in the killing of Ernst Winter and "was going to confess to everything."[15] Burdened by guilt, he even tried to hang himself from a hook, she said. The police pursued the lead and inspected Rosenthal's home, but could not find the telltale hook. The Jews had obviously hidden it, anti-Semitic critics countered. The police soon returned to Rosenthal's home, this time with an expert from Berlin who tore away part of a ceiling in order to expose the beam with the alleged hook from which Rosenthal had tried to hang himself. But when they, too, could find no hook, Rosenthal sued Margarete Radtke for defamation; she, in turn, accused him of pressuring her to commit perjury. Along with other family members, he had allegedly tried to persuade Radtke to retract her statements. For reasons the documents do not specify, the police arrested Rosenthal and his family, and not Radtke, and they spent several months in prison awaiting trial. While languishing in the hot and humid jail cells, two of the family members fell ill and had to be transported to a local hospital. One of them died soon afterward. The case, it turned out, never went to trial.[16]

What moved Margarete Radtke to envision her employer hanging himself from a hook? Rosenthal apparently believed that she was mentally unstable and no longer capable of accounting for her behavior. As the trial approached, he asked the presiding judge to have medical experts examine her psychological state, but the judge demurred, fearing that this would only encourage public wrath.[17] Moreover, certain pieces of evidence suggested a girl who well knew what she was doing. She had, on a previous occasion, accused a different master of rape after he had fired her for stealing. Certainly, sexual abuse of female servants was common enough to seem credible, but the authorities investigating the case concluded that not a word of her story was true. With this second denunciation, then, one could begin to detect a pattern: Radtke accused her employers in order to spite them.[18]

In addition to the employer-servant relationship, the entanglements of sexual intimacy, especially across forbidden boundaries of class and religion, provided another point at which the dynamics of personal and social power could be reversed. This was evidently the case with Rosine Simanowski, the seventeen-year-old girl who imagined that the Jews of Konitz were chasing her with knives. In her original story, she had allegedly overheard a conversation of Heinrich Friedländer, in which Friedländer said, "The Jews need blood," and supposedly offered to buy her a "nice present" if she did not remain silent. As it turned out, Friedländer, twenty-three years old, had been sleeping with Simanowski for nearly two years. According to Friedländer, he had known the girl since November 1898 and "had slept with her often, always in [his] apartment."[19] Friedländer denied having paid her, but he admitted to having bought her presents and given her money, once to buy new shoes and once to pay off her debts to a tailor. Since July 1899, Simanowski had been under the "moral supervision" of the police and had to report for medical examinations. She was, in other words, a prostitute. But Friedländer refused to admit that he "used her" as such, even if, for him, there was nothing more to their relationship than sex.[20] Essentially, Simanowski's story corroborated his own. In closed court ("to protect public morals"), Rosine Simanowski admitted that she "gave herself to him" shortly after her confirmation in the Catholic church, and on Christmas Day 1898 he seduced her.[21]

Whether she was a virgin at this point is unclear; Friedländer did not think so.[22] She also admitted to sleeping with him often, which begs the question of when did they stop, who stopped it, and why? On this matter, their testimonies proved enigmatic and contradictory. According to Simanowski, she had ceased to have sexual relations with

Friedländer after the death of Ernst Winter, in mid-March; according to him, he "used her for the last time" in early April.[23] They also gave contradictory accounts of their meetings in Friedländer's store on a weekday in summer 1900. She recounted having been there twice to purchase clothing; he said she had been there but once. More important, she claimed to have told him that she knew that Moritz Lewy and Ernst Winter had spent time together and that Friedländer had talked about the case, saying, "The Jews need blood."

One can only speculate about what motivated her accusations. Perhaps Friedländer was responsible for her troubles; perhaps she loved him, but he did not reciprocate. Clearly, she was the less powerful of the two: her class and social standing, not to mention her age, positioned her beneath him, and her dubious reputation made her even more vulnerable. One can therefore imagine how she might have bent his words. When he said, "I'll buy you a nice present," he may have been paying her for sex, a secret he would not have wanted publicly revealed. Though enamored of him, she probably resented being treated like a common prostitute; spurned, she struck back with a vengeance, accusing him of saying that Jews need blood.

Simanowski was not the only person to exact public revenge for a private slight. Joseph Laskowski, a rural laborer who recounted fantastic stories about Adolph Lewy's sizing him up for slaughter, also had reason to be bitter. Laskowski's story begins on the day of Winter's murder, March 11. Hugo Lewy, Adolph's youngest son, had arranged for Laskowski to drive a cow from the nearby village of Frankenhagen to Konitz, a distance of about four miles. For the work, Laskowski expected to be paid one and a half marks, but Lewy offered him only one and a quarter. Lewy also asked Laskowski to buy a new rope to lead the cow. Instead, Laskowski tied two used pieces of old rope together and pocketed the money himself. When Adolph Lewy heard about this, he confronted Laskowski, and when police sergeant Kühn happened to walk by, Lewy told the policeman what Laskowski had done.[24] What happened thereafter is unclear.

According to Laskowski, Adolph Lewy asked him to bring the cow around back and to come inside the house, where, "afraid in his heart," Laskowski trembled and allegedly heard Adolph Lewy say the following: "we need blood," "high school students walking," "the cantor has much to do," "the cantor will prepare a bath," and "ropes, chains, Mönchsee." Then Adolph's wife, Pauline, came into the room and inquired about Laskowski's age, whether he was married, and whether he had children. Sizing him up, Lewy demanded to see Laskowski's arm. "Too white, too white, pale, pale," Lewy allegedly muttered, and let Laskowski go.[25]

Naturally, the Lewys denied every last syllable of Laskowski's testimony, which Laskowski had in any case given in "a condition of severe inebriation."[26] For the anti-Semitic press, however, no state of intoxication disqualified evidence against the Jews. By dint of constant reprinting, Laskowski's story became an established part of the Konitz narrative, in which the Lewys sized up Christians—like pieces of meat—before preparing them for ritual slaughter.

I I I

Of all the denunciations in Konitz, perhaps the most tragic involved a series of sightings of Ernst Winter together with Moritz Lewy, Adolph's elder son. Moritz Lewy denied knowing Ernst Winter, though he conceded that he may well have been standing in his company at some point and that it was possible that he had in passing greeted the young man on the street. In all probability, Moritz Lewy was telling the truth. Willi Rahmel and Erich Boeckh, Ernst Winter's two best friends, saw Winter nearly every day and shared intimate details with him, but even they could not recall Winter's having ever mentioned Moritz Lewy's name.[27] Still, a series of witnesses claimed the contrary, and in October 1900 the police arrested Moritz Lewy for perjury. By the time of Lewy's trial, in February 1901, thirty witnesses had come forward to claim that they had seen the two together—a remarkable phenomenon that highlights the various ways in which

Christians, in an environment rife with accusations, marshaled dubious evidence against the Jews of Konitz.

The story of the sightings begins with the accusations of Richard Speisinger, a seventeen-year-old dropout, who claimed that Ernst Winter had carried on flirtations with two Jewish girls, Meta Caspari and Selma Tuchler, as well as with Anna Hoffmann, and that a jealous butcher's apprentice, whom Speisinger could not identify but who may have worked for Hoffmann, had allegedly said to Winter one evening in the fall of 1899, "Wait until the next time, when we're both alone, I'm going to make sure that your lights are knocked out for good."[28] The accusation, reported to the police in the town of Jastrow on March 27, did not implicate the Lewys, or even the Jews. If anything, it pointed the finger back at the house of Gustav Hoffmann.

The police did not take Speisinger's initial accusation seriously. It could not be corroborated, and Speisinger's former teachers thought him lazy, boastful, and mendacious. But when the investigation began to falter in the wake of the ill-fated Hoffmann interrogation, the police called Speisinger to Konitz to testify, and this is where the real trouble began.

When Speisinger left the Konitz county courthouse on the morning of June 23, he was immediately greeted by the anti-Semitic journalist Wilhelm Bruhn, who invited Speisinger out for a few drinks, and then lunch, and told him that he, Speisinger, was a star witness, terribly important to the case. In the afternoon, Bruhn took him out to meet still other anti-Semitic journalists. Together they had coffee and cake and later went to the shooting club. The next morning, Speisinger had a terrible headache, but he well remembered Bruhn's anti-Semitic tirades. His story suddenly began to take on a different hue.

In the Monday paper, Bruhn published an article detailing Speisinger's sensational story, excluding the parts that might have involved one of Hoffmann's apprentices and emphasizing that Winter's relationship with Tuchler and Caspari was more intimate than that with Anna Hoffmann.[29] Still, however, Speisinger had not mentioned Moritz Lewy.

Lewy had already come into the story on Sunday. As Speisinger strolled down the Danzigerstrasse, Martha Hoffmann called him into the house to discuss the accusations. She asked him about Winter's relationships and whether he knew that Moritz Lewy and Ernst Winter had spent time together. Speisinger replied that he knew this, but it was not confirmed. "We have to prove him [Moritz Lewy] guilty of perjury," Martha then said to Speisinger; "it lies in our interest."[30] Speisinger then left for twenty minutes, supposedly to consult a friend; on his return, he said, "Now I know it, now I can swear it under oath."[31]

For Martha Hoffmann, however, this was still not enough. She told Speisinger that he would commit perjury if he withheld details and that it would be wise to set his accusation down on paper. After consulting with a friend, he did just that. At his subsequent interrogation, on July 6, Speisinger stated, "Moritz Lewy knew Winter. In the fall of last year, I saw them together on the Danzigerstrasse. Another time, I saw them standing in front of Lewy's door."[32]

It is difficult to know what moved Martha Lehmann to pressure Speisinger into helping her "prove Lewy guilty of perjury." She herself could not have seen Winter and Lewy together, because she was in Warsaw at the time. She did, however, concede that she "hated" Lewy and that, like her father, she had no objective evidence for her claims.[33] The Hoffmanns, moreover, did not spin their tangled web of intrigue alone. When Speisinger returned to Hoffmann's house the second time, two other men were present, the journalist Max Wienecke and a mysterious man with a white beret and a mustache.[34]

By the beginning of the perjury trial of Moritz Lewy, in February 1901, nine additional witnesses had come forward to claim that they had seen Moritz Lewy and Ernst Winter together. Of these, two claimed only that Lewy had greeted Winter on the street, which Lewy did not necessarily deny. Of the seven others, the first person to come forward was Friedrich Russ, the night watchman responsible for overseeing the Danzigerstrasse and the area around it. After having seen the photograph of Ernst Winter in Heym's studio, Russ claimed to have seen Lewy and Winter together, at least three or four times a week, if not more, and always after 10:00 P.M., even though fellow schoolmates at Lange's boardinghouse insisted that Winter was usually home by then.[35] Russ was hardly a reliable witness, however. Illiterate and barely audible, he constantly quarreled, drank more than his share, and neglected his duties on the job. He also begged, and Moritz Lewy had even given him small change.[36] Why Russ accused Lewy is therefore unclear, but few people in Konitz took him seriously, except for the anti-Semitic journalists, who eagerly printed his story—albeit without attribution—on the front page of the evening edition of the Saturday newspaper, on June 23.[37]

A number of the sightings of Ernst Winter together with Moritz Lewy stemmed from the creative imaginations of people who had already provided spurious testimony. There was Rosine Simanowski, who had accused Heinrich Friedländer of saying, "The Jews need blood," and who now claimed to have seen Ernst Winter and Moritz Lewy talking together in Lewy's doorway on the Danzigerstrasse. Christian Lübke, the bricklayer who produced the strange story of Jews hiding Winter's body parts in the secret vaults underneath the syna-gogue, likewise deposed that he had seen Moritz Lewy and Ernst Winter together—on at least twenty separate occasions. He did not know Ernst Winter, however, and recognized him only retroactively, after he saw his picture in Heym's photography studio. Moreover, by late June, the anti-Semitic papers had begun to publish reports of these sightings, specifically those of Ernst Winter with Moritz Lewy. In early July, Lübke came forward with his own testimony, as did his daughter Anna.[38] But before she appeared in court, Anna Lübke spoke to a woman with whom we have already become familiar: Martha Hoffmann.[39]

At least two of the further sightings may be traced to special ani-mosities. The first involves Karl Nagorra, a former policeman and now an assistant prison guard, who despite his terrible eyesight claimed to have seen Moritz Lewy and Ernst Winter walking together three times. As it turns out, Nagorra had an ax to grind: Adolph Lewy had regis-tered the complaint about Nagorra that had led to his dismissal from the police force back in 1896.[40] The second witness to whom one can trace a personal vendetta was Gustav Schlichter, a seventeen-year-old journeyman plumber, who first testified that he had once seen Ernst Winter and Moritz Lewy on the Danzigerstrase, but later "came to the conviction that I saw them often" and sometimes felt "as if I could still see them there."[41] At a subsequent trial, however, another plumber's apprentice testified that "with his testimony Schlichter wanted to pull one over on Moritz Lewy."[42] Equally revealing, Schlichter later admitted to having helped set fire to the synagogue on the night of June 9.[43]

Schlichter's alleged sightings may have inspired Franz Hellwig, a printer's apprentice, to register that he, too, saw Ernst Winter and Moritz Lewy walking back and forth along the Danzigerstrasse and standing in Lewy's doorway. Given that Hellwig was "mentally somewhat slow," his sighting, reported a year and a half after the event, constituted a remarkable feat of memory.[44] He did not know Ernst Winter and later confused him with someone else. But as a friend of Schlichter, the gullible Hellwig may have simply wanted to go along with his friend's attempt to "pull one over on Moritz Lewy."

Of the original seven accusers, only Elisabeth Tuszik, a "pious, truth-loving" domestic servant, remained. She allegedly saw Lewy and Winter walking together, but exactly when she could not say, either in 1898 or 1899, in the summer or the winter. She claimed to have known all along that Moritz Lewy was involved in Winter's murder. Two or three days after the murder, Tuszik leaned out her window, and as Moritz Lewy walked by she supposedly called out, "Moritz, Moritz, what did you do with Winter?" "What are you talking about, Elisabeth?" Klara Niewolinski, the lady of the house, asked. Tuszik then allegedly said, "People are saying that the Jews did it. And if he [Moritz Lewy] didn't do it, then he probably lured him somewhere into a trap." "I can say this," she added, "I have seen him walking with Ernst Winter." "You would be a good witness," Mrs. Niewolinski then said. But Tuszik did not report her sighting until late September 1900. She was afraid, she said, "I could also be locked up."[45]

During Moritz Lewy's trial, many more people came forward. As more people testified, the risks associated with public denunciation decreased. Among those who testified against Lewy were Regina Schultz, the Polish-speaking domestic servant of Lewy's next-door neighbor, Hermann Aaronheim; Anna Schnick, a domestic servant who lived two doors down; a number of students and young apprentices; and Anna Hoffmann. Hoffmann's testimony is interesting in its display of caution. When asked whether Ernst Winter knew Moritz Lewy, she fell strangely silent; like the others, though, she also said that she had seen the two together in the street.[46]

Indeed, the sightings came to focus on two motifs, Lewy and Winter walking along the Danzigerstrasse, and Lewy and Winter standing in the doorway. These scenes, one may recall, had originally been reported by Richard Speisinger, whose visions postdated his conversation with Martha Hoffmann. The trail of denunciation circled around and, once again, led back to the Hoffmann house.

Lewy's trial had, like Masloff's, turned into a grand spectacle in which one witness after another claimed to have seen the two boys walking or standing together. To outsiders, it seemed like a clear case of "suggestion," but it was less than that. Among the witnesses against Moritz Lewy, there was an obvious hint of malice. Nevertheless, on February 16, 1901, the jury found Moritz Lewy guilty of three counts of perjury and sentenced him to four years of incarceration in the Graudenz prison and the loss of his citizenship for the duration. The Lewys also had to pay costs. Two days later, the family moved to Berlin, and soon thereafter Moritz Lewy began his prison term, his release date set for May 10, 1905. According to a police report, "the judgment against Lewy was received by . . . the great majority of the local people with satisfaction and has done much to calm their sentiments."[47]

I V

The rhetoric of modern anti-Semitism depicted Jews as all too powerful. They controlled the press, the justice system, and the financial world and used their power in conniving ways: charging peasants usurious prices, for example, and aiding each other. In Konitz, as in many small towns and big cities throughout Germany, this image of the powerful, conspirational Jew proved pervasive. It was propogated in the newspapers and in broadsides. It was disseminated from pulpits and in schoolrooms. And one encountered it on the streets.

Still, the reality of the allegations against Jews suggests a different relationship. Especially in the initial months of the investigation, most of the Jews denounced in Konitz were themselves outsiders, in some sense marginal within the community and certainly vulnerable. There are notable exceptions. Rosine Simanowski's denunciation of Heinrich Friedländer does not fit this pattern, for it served to reverse a relationship of power. The same may be said of many of the domestic servants who accused their employers. Yet, in other cases, the salient feature of the relationship of the accuser to the accused is the latter's vulnerability. When the Christians of Konitz denounced Jews, they did not, as a rule, point to the powerful; instead, they focused on the powerless.

Of the Jews in Konitz, Wolf Israelski—an inebriate skinner, a man who could not hold down a job and who, by his own admission, was "weak of thought"—proved an easy target.[48] That Israelski was once a skinner is also relevant because in the symbolic economy of the artisanal guilds, skinners, unlike butchers, had long ranked among the "dishonorable" and "defiled" trades. They handled "cold flesh," and it was their job to dispose of carcasses. In earlier eras, they sometimes did the work of hanging as well, leaving the privilege of beheading to the executioner, who was also "dishonorable" but of higher status than the lowly skinner. Like the executioner, and in some cultures the shepherd, the miller, and the latrine digger, the skinner was historically condemned by the laws governing social pollution to be a permanent outcast.[49]

The initial accusation against Israelski came from the subaltern Friedrich Fiedler, who claimed to have seen Israelski limping along with a gray sack over his back, carrying the head of Ernst Winter to a ditch on the outskirts of town. Other witnesses later followed Fiedler's lead: the railroad worker Julius Dühring; Klara Streubing, the wife of a harness maker; and August Steinke, a raftsman from Prechlau who had allegedly overheard Josef Eisenstädt saying that Winter was fit for slaughter. Steinke overheard another conversation as well. Near the train station, someone mentioned Israelski's name, and Steinke heard, "Hey, everything is paid for."[50] Meanwhile, the newspapers generated mendacities on their own accord. On May 1, the *Staatsbürgerzeitung* reported that Israelski had traveled to Xanten to receive directives, that he was related to Adolph Buschhoff (the Jewish butcher in Xanten), and that the *A* on the torn handkerchief stood for Alma, Israelski's sister.[51] Later on, the paper also reported that Alma had often gone to Berent (the site of an alleged ritual murder in 1894) and that when Israelski was in prison, he had received a note scribbled on a piece of paper. Stuffed into a potato, the note supposedly instructed Israelski on what he was to say during his interrogation.[52]

Obvious fabrications, such stories nevertheless hardened the conviction that Israelski could not have worked alone, and this in turn led to further denunciations, widening the circle of incrimination around him. In this context, Paul Brüggemann, a thirty-two-year-old carter, claimed that he had on the Wednesday before Easter seen Adolph's sister, Pauline Lewy, carrying underneath her arm a package roughly as large as a head. Known in Konitz as "Rag Lewy," Pauline (who had the same name as Adolph's wife) had drawn her shawl tightly around her so that no one could identify her. She was an old woman who could hardly hear, could neither read nor write, and barely eked out an existence by selling her wares, rags and string. Powerless, she perfectly conformed to the pattern of accusations against marginal Jews. Brüggemann claimed that Adolph Lewy was walking "ten to twenty paces" behind her. It was sometime after 10:00 P.M. on the Danzigerstrasse, and they were, so Brüggemann opined, carrying the head to the house of Wolf Israelski.[53]

Israelski stood trial on September 8, 1900. Despite extremely specious evidence, Chief Prosecutor Settegast pleaded, if halfheartedly, that the court find Israelski guilty as an accomplice to murder, and he requested a sentence of five years' imprisonment. To support his case, Settegast called a chain of witnesses, two of whom claimed to have seen "a suspicious-looking man" near the ditch, and one of whom saw a person who walked like, but did not look like, Wolf Israelski. Further witnesses included Dumb Alex and the barmaid Przeworski, who claimed that "twelve Jews must be the killers, since the Jews have twelve tribes."[54] Przeworski testified that on a day in March she had seen a man carrying something long, perhaps the arm. To round out her story, Stolpmann—another barmaid, whose husband had denounced Selig Zander—took the stand and maintained that, at the time of the murder, Israelski had been in a suspiciously bad mood; her eleven-year-old daughter, who was also called to testify, said so as well. This parade of less-than-stellar witnesses left Settegast with his initial witness, the subaltern Fiedler—who allegedly saw Israelski carrying a sack with something round in it—and the known indiscretions provided by Israelski's wife, who complained that her husband was a drunk.

Accordingly, the judge found Israelski innocent, much to the chagrin of the angry throng that packed the seats of the court as well as the anti-Semitic demonstrators on the street outside. The latter desisted from further rioting however, since it was September, and the Prussian army still controlled the center of town.[55] Though substantial violence was, at this point, narrowly avoided, one denunciation supported by a series of vague secondary sightings managed to ensure the temporary incarceration, and near-condemnation, of a man already in many ways on the margins of local society, both Christian and Jewish.

Denunciations of the vulnerable also fueled the central accusation of our story. Here one must, to be sure, measure words. People pointed to Lewy because he was a Jewish butcher and because he lived near the supposed scene of the crime. Yet his position in local society lent credence to the accusations. Adolph Lewy was a cantankerous recluse. In the past, he had been quick to report others to the police, and a few of his accusers, including Joseph Laskowski and Karl Nagorra, now incriminated him in turn. Even among his Jewish neighbors, he was an isolated figure. With the merchant Hermann Aaronheim, his next-door neighbor, he had for a time lived in "conflict," and the two men "almost never" spoke to each other. After the accusations, this changed slightly. "He came to me," Aaronheim said, "and I could not just show him the door."[56] Lewy did occasionally go to Falkenberg's pub and watch the other men play cards, but with the exception of Moritz Brünn, none of the pub regulars seem to have come to Lewy's house.[57] Lewy was rarely in the company of the notables among the Jewish community in Konitz, men such as Rabbi Kellermann and City Councillor Fabian, or even Gustav Caspari, the wealthy merchant who lived across from him. Whether Lewy maintained close ties to the synagogue is more difficult to say, though his son Moritz admitted, "I seldom go to synagogue."[58] By all accounts, Adolph Lewy kept to himself; few people, Christian or Jewish, knew very much about him.

But when the accusations began to fly, Adolph Lewy's private world quickly collapsed. Already in April, he had to close down his butcher shop, and his son Hugo had to travel to Berlin to look for work.[59] When Adolph Lewy tried to sell meat at the marketplace, crowds gathered around. "Christian meat," they screamed; Lewy "butchers Christians."[60] The assaults were not only verbal, however. In May, a worker threatened to stab him with a knife; in June, a number of men broke into his house with axes and demanded money.[61] Thereafter, Adolph Lewy could walk the streets only with armed guards. For his wife, too, the accusations made life intolerable: "I have suffered so much grief and unhappiness," Pauline Lewy said in October, when the trial of her son was still to come.

Gustav Hoffmann's public accusations of the Jewish butcher fell within the context of the humiliation and eventual destruction of Adolph Lewy and his family. Printed on June 13, the denunciation had been completed and presented to the investigating officials on June 5, having been composed sometime during the week before, in collusion with the reporter Wilhelm Bruhn. Although no doubt a distressing time for Gustav Hoffmann as well, it was a perilous period for Adolph Lewy and his family. During the demonstrations, Hoffmann could watch as thugs repeatedly hurled bricks and stones through his neighbor's windows. The people who darkened the streets clearly and unmistakably sided with Hoffmann against Lewy. More distressing is Hoffmann's appropriation of public outrage. "I only wrote down what the people already knew. Everybody thinks as I stated it there," he later said.[62] When asked under oath whether he had any objective evidence for what he had seen and heard, he replied, laconically, "no."[63]

A number of possibilities might explain why, lacking evidence, Hoffmann offered the butcher's tale. Perhaps, one might speculate, there was a feud between his family and Lewy's. But there is no evidence of open conflict, only icy separation. As far as one can tell, the two men hardly exchanged a word, though they lived next to each other and shared the same occupation. Lewy, a butcher, was a competitor, and perhaps this motivated Hoffmann, but the Christian butcher was already by far the more successful of the two. His business was flourishing, and he had a number of apprentices and domestic servants. Lewy, by contrast, had no apprentices, save for his two sons, and—in his most solvent days—he could not even afford a live-in servant.[64] By early June, when Hoffmann made his accusation public, Adolph Lewy and his family were on the edge of ruin. What could have driven Hoffmann to accuse his neighbor? Perhaps he was merely trying to deflect attention from an unpleasant investigation, which would include indiscreet questions about his daughter's virginity. Or perhaps he desired something more simple and base: the cover-up of a crime and the destruction of his Jewish neighbor's life.

V

Whatever his motive, Hoffmann's denunciation of Lewy was an act of power over someone increasingly powerless, and, as such, it conformed to a more general pattern. Unlike isolated acts of violence, personal denunciations depend on a communal context. To have force, they must be credible—in the eyes of the people and, eventually, the legal authorities. In the case of Adolph Lewy, it was enough that the people of Konitz found the denunciation credible; in the unfortunate case of his son, the courts concurred as well. In Konitz, denunciations accumulated as the communal conflict deepened, as the lines dividing Christians and Jews sharpened, and as the bonds between them loosened and broke.

Analyzing the quickening pace of the denunciations, we can perceive the communal influence on the actions of otherwise independent individuals. Although it is impossible to reconstruct the chronology of accusations exactly, it remains clear that the denunciations came in clusters and that the clusters centered on specific events that shook the community. The chronology also reveals that very few specific denunciations occurred immediately following the murder—except for Bernhard Masloff's initial deposition and Joseph Laskowski's drunken ravings against Adolph Lewy.[65] But if initial accusations were sparse, this all changed in April, after the first journalists arrived in town. Around April 10, the first accusations were leveled against the Meyer family (whose case we will address shortly) and were reported in the newspaper.[66] On April 15, Friedrich Fiedler saw Wolf Israelski carrying a sack, an accusation that led to the skinner's arrest. Building on these initial accusations, others came forward, with denunciations often focused on the same person. The first wave of violent demonstrations, on the weekend of April 20, added momentum to the accusations. By the end of April, a number of newspapers had unequivocally identified the Jews as the killers, and on April 28, the Prussian government upped the reward to 20,000 marks. In early May, people's willingness to denounce their Jewish neighbors palpably increased.

The lines separating Christians from Jews had grown clearer, and by the end of May the town of Konitz had become the site of major demonstrations and, with the accusations against Gustav Hoffmann in early

June, violent confrontations. The town now filled with reward seekers, private detectives, and still more journalists, many of whom helped carve out an anti-Semitic consensus. "The whole town is working to prove Moritz Lewy guilty of perjury," one of the journalists, Georg Zimmer, noted in late September.[67] These efforts paid off at the trials. At the Speisinger trial in October 1900, six people had come forward to proclaim that they had seen Lewy and Winter together; at the trial of Moritz Lewy the following February, witnesses numbered more than thirty. By this time, the consensus against the Jews—based on superstitions, rumors, false testimony, and biased reporting—had become an article of faith, and accusations an act of allegiance to a community that no longer included Jews. Denunciations were then not only safe but even dutiful, especially if they were directed against Jews whose lives already lay in shambles.

V I

If individual accusations in Konitz seemed disturbingly instrumental, it does not follow that they can be dismissed in all cases as conscious fabrications. It is, after all, still possible that the butcher believed his own tale, that Margarete Radtke really imagined her employer had hung himself from a hook, that Rosine Simanowski actually envisioned Jews chasing her with knives, and that Speisinger was convinced he had twice seen Moritz Lewy together with Ernst Winter. To raise this possibility does not make the tales true or the motives behind their telling less base; it merely keeps us from falling into "Descartes's error," that "thinking, and awareness of thinking, are the real substrates of being," and that the mind's operations of reason are neatly separable from the visceral reactions of emotion.[68] Accusations may rest on motive, and the accusatory heart may have its reasons, but this does not necessarily mean that it acts without the passion and feeling that comes only with believing in the validity of one's claims. In Konitz, some of the sightings may have been based on genuine, if distorted, memory.[69]

Contemporaries proved sensitive to this possibility. "The people make an image," we recall the wise Judge Brixus saying with respect to the sightings and accusations in the ritual-murder case in Xanten in 1892, "a few pieces of which they themselves experienced, then they gradually worked themselves into the image."[70] A similar theory of events was put forward in 1900 with respect to the Konitz case by a Berlin neurologist named Albert Eulenburg, who proposed that the sightings constituted a case of "retroactive hallucination," which he defined as "a falsification of memory . . . artificially brought about in susceptible persons or even in a larger unit of individuals."[71] People under this spell often confused their own observations with ideas planted by others, and they often believed that what they had been told, or what they had read, was something they had seen or heard themselves. Although Eulenburg's ideas were twisted with contemporary prejudices—he believed "primitive peoples," "less developed races," women, and uncultivated men to be especially susceptible to "retroactive hallucination"—his insights nevertheless point to a genuine problem. "Source misattribution"—one of the most ubiquitous and thoroughly documented causes of memory distortion—may well have tempered the soft substance of small-town rumor into the hard material of individual memory.[72]

To separate willed mendacities from accusations constructed upon fragments of memory, one must, in the words of Arthur Conan Doyle, "concentrate [oneself] upon the details." Within the welter of testimonies, the timing of the subject's recall, and the precise context of what psychologists call the "receiving environment," there may still be clues regarding the status of sightings reported.

As we would expect, given the imperfections of memory, many of the sightings in Konitz were reported as fragments, but not all. Major accusations came in the form of fully constructed, continuous narratives, the most comprehensive of which was that of Gustav Hoffmann, the Christian butcher. It seems extremely unlikely that the butcher's tale was a simply remembered one. Hoffmann's collusion with Wilhelm Bruhn, the precise coincidence of the story's release with

Hoffmann's interrogation, his later admissions that he "only wrote down what the people already knew," and the fact that there was no objective basis for his accusation—all of this evidence strongly suggests that the butcher's tale was a methodically constructed, willed falsehood. The same doubtless held true for the stories of Bernhard Masloff, lying in the alley listening as events transpired in Lewy's cellar, and the complicated tales invented by his mother-in-law, Anna Ross. The stories they told were too detailed, too motivated, too planned, too much the result of collusion, however botched, to be taken seriously as distinctive, individual memories. Perhaps it is possible that, having told their stories often enough, they came to believe them, but their utterances as they were carted off to prison suggest otherwise. Masloff punctured his mother-in-law's story by confessing that he himself was the mysterious farmhand from somewhere beyond Schlochau who had supposedly witnessed the torso being carried to the lake. And she in turn alleged, no doubt correctly, that his whole story was made up from the start.[73] The accusations of Joseph Laskowski seem similarly contrived. On the night of the murder, he "so ranted and raved against the Jews" that when he heard of Winter's murder, he immediately concluded that it "was none other than the old Lewy."[74] These accusations constituted the main charges directed against Adolph Lewy, and of these, only the sightings of Masloff, Ross, and Laskowski were purportedly based on direct experience. The evidence suggests they were based on willed untruths, not on distorted memory.

The secondary accusations, which appear more fragmented and illusory, seem more plausibly based on distorted memories. In the original butcher's tale, these focused on Wolf Israelski and Matthäus Meyer. The subaltern Fiedler was the first to see Wolf Israelski walking down the Schützenstrasse with a sack containing Winter's decapitated head. Israelski did in fact go on his rounds that morning, and he sometimes carried a sack; Fiedler's motivation for denouncing Israelski seems less than obvious, save that the skinner was a marginal, and harmless, figure. More decisive was the timing of the sighting, which occurred on Good Friday, a day not only of heightened symbolic awareness but also of a sharpened sense of unity for the Christian community. Furthermore, only a day earlier, the photographer Max Heyn had placed a picture of Ernst Winter in his storefront. The suggestive powers of the picture, the discussions it no doubt engendered, and the sense of community that the holidays inspired may well have made Fiedler more receptive to the familiar images of the ritual-murder charge in the form of one of its most persistent topoi—the marginal Jew carrying the head in a sack. Perhaps Fiedler had seen Israelski and from that simple glimpse—coupled with a historical narrative already familiar to him—had formed a memory. The final details of his vision were not complete until Easter Sunday, when Winter's head was found, and "the receiving environment" proved especially propitious. Fiedler then offered his testimony twice, consolidating the memory in his own mind, so that in the course of the spring it hardened into something he believed he had really seen.

The accusations against Matthäus Meyer may also have had their origins in memory and its distortions, and not just in the crude operation of willed falsehood. His is also the story of how readily Christians accused vulnerable Jews. A number of witnesses claimed to have seen a man come into Meyer's store with a list soliciting the support of the Jews of Konitz for the ritual slaughter of Ernst Winter. A conversation supposedly ensued, in which Meyer's daughter stated, "That's murder." The first accusation came from Mrs. Wiwjorra, the wife of a furniture maker and a woman who knew Ernst Winter well. Initially, she heard only the name Winter and the response of Meyer's daughter: "No, let that go, that's pure murder." Meyer's daughter often used the saying "That is worse than murder" to express amazement, and it seems entirely plausible that Mrs. Wiwjorra, who otherwise had no special animus against Meyer, actually heard this expression. Since the conversation took place in January, well before the murder, she had no reason to suspect anything nefarious. This may have changed after the murder of Winter, whom she knew well; it may also have changed around the time of the High Holidays, when she spoke with her neighbor Franz Arndt, a baker, at the edge of the Mönchsee. One may imagine that they spoke about the gruesome nature of the murder and that Wiwjorra might then have dimly recalled an old conversation. As it was recalled in this altogether different "receiving environment," the memory trace now emerged in a very different form. Wiwjorra rounded the picture out, more words accrued, a person with a list (perhaps an ordinary delivery man) became a messenger collecting signatures supporting the ritual murder. As she articulated the image and the overheard conversation, the memory consolidated, and, though we can only guess at this, it became something that she believed to be true, a genuine memory. A similar case might be made for Anton Hellwig, who along with his mother also heard the conversation in Meyer's store. He seems not to have been ill disposed toward the Meyers in any identifiable way, and anecdotal evidence even suggests that he had long been their trusted client. Moreover, he had misconstrued previous conversations. He had, for example, denounced Alexander Caminer for saying to Anton, "You look so fresh and red," and "Blood is very expensive this year." Caminer, who had never uttered these words, did subsequently admit to having said something like "You have such a red face, that the blood seems to be squirting out of you."[75] Perhaps the good-natured, but mentally limited, Hellwig similarly misconstrued Meyer's words and heaped new meanings upon otherwise harmless utterances. As he repeated them, and as his mother came to believe them as well, perhaps the statements solidified in his memory. Subsequent accusations against Meyer, inspired by the testimonies of Wiwjorra and Hellwig, seemed less likely to be based on direct experiences. These accusations either came significantly later or, like those of Mathilde Borchert, a Catholic woman from the village of Muskendorf, were based on a confessed lie.[76]

Whether based on memory or malice, the accusations against Matthäus Meyer struck at a time of tragedy. He had already been forced to give up his business, and, at the time of the imagined conversations, he was selling his last wares out of his living room on the second floor. He had also been diagnosed with liver disease. On March 4, a week before the murder, the family moved to Berlin, and shortly thereafter his eldest daughter, Jenny, died. The move, and the death of his daughter, only encouraged suspicions. As we know, the anti-Semitic newspapers accused him of poisoning his own daughter in order to hush her up, and officials in Konitz discussed exhuming her body to see whether this was true. Even more punitively, the chief prosecutor's office charged Matthäus Meyer with perjury, since he had denied all of the accusations against him. Although the Berlin courts did not admit the case, the pursuit of Meyer to the capital suggests the extremes to which these charges were officially carried.

VII

Ritual-murder charges, as Alan Macfarlane wrote of seventeenth-century witchcraft accusations, "were made between people who knew each other intimately."[77] To pursue these charges, to ferret out why one person denounced another, allows us to enter into the inner sanctum of a torn community. In Konitz, accusations between neighbors reflected the dynamics of personal power, with Christians typically asserting power over Jews they worked for, or had once been injured by, or, as in the case of Rosine Simanowski, had once been in love with. But this reversal of power relations does not cover all cases. The Hoffmanns' accusations of the Lewys constituted less a reversal of power than an attack on a vulnerable neighbor. The same may be said of the accusations directed against the Meyers and against Wolf Israelski. The unifying theme of all of them is their basis in human relationships, and that they target the weak points in the overall system of relations.

This is true for the specific case of ritual-murder accusations in Konitz in 1900, as it is for accusations involving witchcraft persecutions hundreds of years ago, or the more recent political denunciations in the totalitarian regimes of the past century.[78] "Witchcraft," the anthropologist Mary Douglas writes, "is not merely a brutal midwife delivering new forms to society, though it may be this; it is also an aggravator of all hostilities and fears, an obstacle to peaceful cooperation."[79]

Similarly, the historian Michael Geyer has written of the "antinomic consensus—to distrust each other—that despotism engenders" and has placed the breakdown of human solidarity at the center of a new understanding of the essence of the Third Reich.[80] "For it was the rejection of the possibility of human solidarity with strangers—the critical as well as moral presupposition of civil society—that the National Socialist regime made into the foundation for its existence."[81]

Such a breakdown in solidarity was also at the center of the events in Konitz. If specific accusations often had discrete and diverse individual functions, they nevertheless occurred within a communal context structured by social relations. By making accusations, people affirmed their allegiances, allied themselves with the powerful against the powerless, and severed whatever bonds they may have had with the Jews in their hometown. If the accusations in Konitz in 1900 foreshadowed the coming collapse of communal solidarity we associate with the Third Reich, they also tell a wider story about the fragility of individual human bonds.

This sixteenth-century woodcut suggests the symbolic reversal underlying what might be called the Christian performance of ritual murder.

CHAPTER FIVE

Performing Ritual Murder

There can be no society that does not feel the need of upholding and reaffirming at regular intervals the collective sentiments and collective ideas that make its unity and personality.

—EMILE DURKHEIM

The systematic looting of language can be recognized by the tendency of its users to forgo its nuanced, complex, mid-wifery properties, replacing them with menace and subjugation. Oppressive language does more than represent violence; it is violence; does more than represent the limits of knowledge; it limits knowledge.

—TONI MORRISON,
Nobel lecture in literature, 1993

I

A remarkable and horrific event occurred on July 10, 1941, in the Polish town of Jedwabne. The town, which had been under Soviet occupation, suddenly came under German control, and as part of the "final solution," the Germans ordered that the local Jews be killed. The Poles living in Jedwabne alongside their Jewish neighbors not only acquiesced but carried out the task themselves. Armed with axes and nail-studded clubs, they rounded up seventy-five Jews and, while beating them, forced them to carry a heavy monument of Lenin to a designated place. The Jews were then made to dig a large ditch in which to bury the monument; when they finished, the Poles butchered them with axes and tossed their mutilated corpses into the hole. Later that day, the Poles rounded up the rest of the Jews, beat them mercilessly, and herded them into a barn, which had been doused with kerosene. The Poles then set the barn on fire and burned to death all the Jews inside.[1]

The "ordinary Poles" of Jedwabne, as Jan T. Gross writes in *Neighbors*, had become "willing executioners" in a massacre that evoked a "deeper, more archaic layer" of anti-Semitic violence, recalling the primitive savagery of pogroms, as well as the horrible brutalities that followed the ritual-murder charges of earlier centuries.[2] Like the perpetrators in these earlier incidents, the Poles of Jedwabne murdered their Jewish neighbors: they tortured them in symbolically meaningful ways (reminiscent of the mockery of Christ carrying the cross) and ended the ordeal by burning all of them in a massive firestorm.

As an act of unspeakable violence, the massacre in Jedwabne also raises difficult questions for our examination of the riots in Konitz that followed the murder of Ernst Winter in the summer of 1900. These riots involved a great many people, more than a thousand in the major demonstrations in Konitz and hundreds of people in surrounding towns like Baldenburg and Hammerstein. The riots were no doubt terrifying, but they did not descend into a tempest of destruction. As enmity deepened and tempers flared, instead of wanton carnage, a familiar routine of ominous threats and symbolical gestures mediated the forces of hatred, animosity, and exclusion.

There are two simple answers, each inadequate in its own way, as to why, for the Germans of Konitz, it sufficed ritually to enact violence whereas the Poles of Jedwabne indulged in a bloody massacre.

First, one might view primitive anti-Semitic violence as the historical heritage of the east—the traditional landscape of pogroms—and locate a more ideologically driven anti-Semitism within German history, leading inexorably to the systematic extermination of the Holocaust. Yet this explanation disregards both the pervasiveness of ideologically driven anti-Semitism in Poland and Russia and the prevalence of pogrom-like, anti-Semitic violence in modern German and western European history.[3] The second, more convincing answer, centers on the position of the state. In 1900, imperial Germany safeguarded the rule of law and ensured the protection of its citizens, including Jews. Four decades later, the Third Reich attempted to annihilate the Jews and, as an occupying power in the Polish village of Jedwabne, encouraged violence. In this Hobbesian perspective, the state remains the only barrier between us and the hatchets of our neighbors, and, as a corollary, in 1900 only the Prussian army saved the Jews of Konitz from the clubs and axes of "ordinary Germans."

This explanation, aside from taking a dim view of human nature, slights the potentially civilizing influence of culture and history on humankind's propensity for violence. It also ignores the import of what actually happened in Konitz, where a symbolic ritual of violence, not an actual massacre, was the outlet for Christian animosity toward Jews, thus confirming Durkheim's insight that through ritual action communities reaffirm the collective sentiments that bind them together. Rather than reduce our explanation of the events in Konitz to a tough-minded platitude (they were all "willing executioners"), we can now interpret the actions of the crowd as we would a performance or a ritual. This act of interpretation does not exonerate the townspeople of Konitz. For even with respect to especially heinous historical events, the task of historians cannot simply be to assess damage, count dead bodies, and assign blame; they must also analyze meaning and, to borrow the anthropologist's metaphor, "strain to read over the shoulder" of the people who make history.[4]

I I

The crowds that filled the streets of Konitz and its neighboring towns in the twilight of the early summer were composed of different groups of people, some with central roles in the violent drama, others with cameo appearances. The human landscape was complex in this part of the German Empire, with prominent differences between Germans and Poles, Protestants and Catholics, rich and poor.

Contrary to what some German officials believed at the time, the main force behind anti-Semitic agitation was German, not Polish.[5] There were some exceptions, however. The anti-Semitic riots in Czersk, an industrial town with a predominantly Polish population, and the village jacqueries in the smaller agrarian communities of Bruss, Wielle, and Karschin drew their energy from angry Polish and Kashubian peasants. Throughout April and May, the Poles had eagerly consumed the anti-Semitic venom of the immensely popular *Gazetta Grudzionska*, whose articles on the murder case, though derived from the German press, no doubt inflamed the Polish population.[6]

The German population was itself divided between Protestants and Catholics, though the vast majority of uprisings occurred in predominantly Protestant towns, especially in eastern Pomerania and in the predominantly German counties of Schlochau, Flatow, and Deutsch Crone in West Prussia. Significantly, anti-Semitic violence had already erupted in these communities two decades earlier, following the Neustettin synagogue fire of 1881.[7]

In July 1881, hundreds of demonstrators marched through the streets of Neustettin chanting "hep-hep" and "out with the Jews," intoning as they ransacked houses and smashed the windows of stores that would beat the Jews to death.[8] From Neustettin, the riots spread throughout the region: in Hammerstein, locals attacked a Jewish judge and six mounted police proved unable to control the mob;[9] in Bärenwalde, eight miles northwest of Neustettin, small bands of artisans and apprentices shouted anti-Semitic epithets, hurled stones, and damaged the synagogue.[10] The worst riot of all occurred in

Schivelbein, nearly thirty miles west of Neustettin, where a crowd armed with crowbars and axes broke into stores, looted the wares, and tossed the furniture onto the street. Women participated as well, stealing fabric and mockingly wrapping the downtown lantern posts in cloth.[11] A dozen more riots flared up in the area, six of a more minor sort and six that involved large, angry, violent crowds. A number of these riots took place in towns in which violence would begin again in the summer of 1900: in Stolp, for example, and in Baldenburg, Rummelsburg, and Jastrow. Finally, there were riots in Konitz, which lasted eight days and consisted mainly of bands of youth shouting anti-Semitic slogans and hurling stones through windows.[12]

By contrast, the legacy of violence against the Jews was less pronounced in German Catholic towns, even though German Catholics read the *Westpreussisches Volksblatt*, a provincial Catholic newspaper that peddled a mixture of piety and prejudice—"sensational stories" and "unbelievable idiocies," as Baron von Zedlitz complained.[13] It is, of course, possible that Catholic peasants and townsmen, inspired by these "unbelievable idiocies," rode into Protestant towns to participate in the violence against the Jews—town air makes one free, a German proverb ominously reminds us.

In the large anti-Semitic gatherings, especially in Konitz itself, the crowd was diverse, readily crossing lines of nationality and religion. It also included women, who, if we believe Baron von Zedlitz, "had become the main proponents of a wild hatred of the Jews."[14] Certainly, the women emboldened the men of the crowd to take more vigorous action—to storm the synagogue and ransack its interior. The men who made up the violent core were mostly young, single, lower-class workers and artisans, some with previous arrests. "The smallest part [of the rioters] are to be found among the taxpayers," Zedlitz wrote. "Idlers, half-grown boys who have temporary jobs here, servants who are roaming around the streets without the permission of their masters, these," he believed, "are the elements that make up the rabble in Konitz."[15] But behind this core group, a wider crowd shared the evident anger of the rioters, tossing stones and desecrating holy sites.

Though perhaps biased, Zedlitz thought that only "a relatively small proportion" of the middle class joined this wider crowd.[16]

The realm of the middle classes proved not to be the streets but rather the meeting rooms of organizations like the Bürgerverein (Citizens Club), the Masonic lodge, and the patriotic leagues. Founded in 1874 as a liberal organization, the Bürgerverein had become increasingly conservative over the years; by 1900, it was dominated by men like Maximilian Meyer (a schoolteacher and the anti-Semitic foreman of the jury in the trials of Masloff and Ross), Julius Klotz, a city councillor and factory owner, and the anti-Semitic lawyers Gebauer and Vogel.[17] The Bürgerverein voiced its dismay at the violence in the street and took umbrage at the lack of loyalty shown to Prussian officials, yet, whether out of conviction or out of cowardice, the Bürgerverein failed to blunt the riots' specifically anti-Semitic edge.[18] The second major middle-class venue was the Masonic lodge, the St. Johannis Lodge, Friedrich of True Friendship, which belonged to the national-conservative branch of the Prussian mother lodge (Zu den drei Weltkugeln), an organization that had proved especially vigilant in excluding Jews since the 1880s.[19] The ubiquitous lawyer Max Vogel was the grandmaster (*Meister vom Stuhl*) of the lodge in Konitz, which counted among its longtime members local notables such as the county medical examiner, Dr. Gustav Müller; the school inspector, Heinrich Rhode (whose wife's handkerchief, as we shall soon see, was found near Winter's decapitated head); and the former mayor.[20] There were still other venues of sociability—patriotic associations, like the veterans' association and the shooting club (again with Vogel as its presiding official), various church groups, and various charity and professional organizations.[21]

The differences between the rioters in the streets and the leaders of the local establishment were differences in form but not substance. Mostly day laborers from the countryside, journeymen and apprentices, and industrial workers, the rioters expressed themselves in a rough and ready language of action: they threw rocks, beat houses with sticks, and threatened physical violence. Eschewing the chaos of the crowd, respectable middle-aged men preferred to pass orderly anti-Semitic resolutions.[22] For the rioters, actions spoke louder than words; for the men of the middle class, words, as Louis Althusser once said of concepts, cut like a knife.

I I I

While Konitz's respectable citizens may have been horror-struck by the mob at the front door of their Jewish neighbors, they tacitly supported the actions of the rioters. These actions offer clues as to the meaning of the riots, not least because, despite a profusion of reports, we have little evidence of what the crowd actually said. Without banners or manifestos or discernible slogans, save for "The Jews slaughter our children" and "Moritz, Moritz, give back his head," it is difficult to determine the message of the crowd.[23] Most reports simply refer to the call "hep-hep," the old and omnipresent slogan of anti-Semitic violence, which was introduced during the riots of 1819. Even at the time, commentators were unsure of the meaning of the slogan; explanations ranged from the acronym for "*Hierosolyma* [the Greek and Latin word for Jerusalem] *est perdita*" to an abbreviation of a German word for Jews, Hebräer.[24] Sometimes "hep-hep" was paired with "Jews out" or "beat the Jews to death," though these more violent threats appear less often in the reports. Partly, their absence in the historical record reflects the prejudices of county officials who no doubt thought the shouts of the mob unworthy of their elevated pen. Even so, there remained among the rioters a genuine poverty of expression, the effect of which was to place the burden of meaning almost solely onto the highly ritualized aggression that flared up throughout the night.[25] From the occupation of the marketplace to the smashing of windows, to the attempts to set the synagogue ablaze, to the threats to beat the last Jew to death, the rioters in the streets of Konitz reenacted a familiar drama whose historical resonances and tacit meanings, like those of a text, can be interpreted.

T he riots in Konitz unmistakably evoked the historical violence of Holy Week, which occurred throughout the Middle Ages, typically involving the stoning of houses and ghetto walls, sometimes as a prelude to bloody assaults. Beginning in the thirteenth century, this violence was overtly linked to theater—oftentimes literally following passion plays, in which local Christians staged the suffering of Christ, and integrated representations of Jews as killers of Christ into the performance. Suffused with religious meaning, the riots thus enacted a form of ritual vengeance. "Let his blood be on us and on our children," the crowd cries out in Matthew 27:25. The plays connected the Christian community of the present to its foundational moment in the past—a moment, moreover, that also marked the primal event of the Judeo-Christian encounter. In this sense, as the historian David Nirenberg has pointed out, Holy Week violence tied the two communities together through ritual. Only through staged violence against the Jews could Christians preserve the social memory of their origins.[26]

In contrast to this implicit connection, Holy Week was a time of sharpened social boundaries between Christians and Jews. According to the decrees of the Fourth Lateran Council in 1215, Jews were not allowed to show themselves "during the last three days before Easter . . . for the reason that some of them . . . are not afraid to mock the Christians who maintain the memory of the most holy Passion."[27] The violent actions of the crowd reinforced these boundaries. As the people threw rocks and beat Jewish houses with sticks, they symbolically marked off a ghetto behind whose walls Jews were forced to hover for protection.

In some cases of Holy Week violence, however, the people transgressed the symbolic restraints inherent in ritualized violence, and, to borrow an expression from E. Valentine Daniel, the "taming capacities of culture" failed.[28] This collapse was typically associated with ritual murder and host desecration charges, perilous alibis of exceedingly violent aggression. Thus the brutal Rintfleisch massacres commenced in the town of Röttingen a fortnight after Easter in 1298.[29] In Pulkau,

Austria, in 1338, they killed and burned the Jews at a time when Easter and Passover coincided.[30] In Upper Silesia in 1401, "the Jews were burnt outside of Glogau after Easter."[31] The tradition held in the modern era, too—during the Holy Week of 1881, pogroms began in Elisavetgrad in Ukraine. Well into the nineteenth century, the force and terror of Holy Week violence drew its power from the collective memory of these transgressions, from times when the barely controlled aggression of Christians washed over into unrestrained massacre.

These ruptures notwithstanding, the salient feature of Holy Week violence generally, and the ritualized aggression in Konitz specifically, was its boundedness: rioters stoned Jewish houses but did not enter them; the crowd threatened to kill the Jews but usually did not. In this sense, the Jews of Konitz well understood that they were safer in town, where the protocols of ritual held, than on the open road in the countryside.[32] The enhanced presence of the police in the towns also helped restrain physical violence, but until the army arrived, there was a disquieting discrepancy between the number of demonstrators and the forces of law. Equally unsettling was the aggression directed against symbols of authority seen as protecting the Jews: the attacks on the mayor, the brutalizing of the inspectors from Berlin, and the stoning of the Prussian army as it passed Tuchel by train. A sense of community was constructed against the Jews, but also, and just as significantly, against their perceived protectors. In this context, the crowd's anger was especially aroused when officials turned their suspicions on the Christian, not the Jewish, butcher. "We won't let him be arrested," they shouted, and "if you take him away, we're going too."[33] Even though the demonstrators did not directly challenge the government's legitimacy, they nevertheless criticized what they perceived as the government's attack on the Christian community and its failure to bring the Jews to justice. And if one takes the gestures of the crowd seriously, they must be seen as also usurping, at least in form, the government's role. For it was the demonstrators who now pursued, identified, and, by casting stones, judged and punished.[34]

The riots revealed a temporal structure that roughly corre-

sponded to the four stages—breach, crisis, redressive action, and reintegration—that, according to the anthropologist Victor Turner, constitute the nearly universal progression of ritual action. Like the
standardized plot lines of a familiar story, these stages framed not only
the unfolding of the riots but also their meaning.

Each of the riots started with a breach of the rules governing
everyday relations between Christians and Jews, which until the murder and the ensuing riots had by all accounts been stable.[35] This initial breach—whether the pummeling of houses with stones or
physical attacks on the streets—almost always occurred in the
evenings or on holy days, marking their status as events that occurred
outside the weave of the quotidian—in the selvage of the "liminal."
The space of the liminal is that of the margin: if structure and hierar-
chy mark our everyday life, the liminal is the place where order is
subverted, roles reversed, rules broken, and authority challenged.[36]
The first stage of the dramatic sequence also witnessed the slow
accumulation of exceedingly large crowds in concentric circles of
active participants, complicit supporters, and curious onlookers: the
actors, the chorus, and the audience. During the initial breach, when
nothing more than epithets and stones were tossed, these roles were
still differentiated, with only limited emotional bonds connecting the
three groups.

As the authorities attempted to disperse the crowd, threatening
even to open fire upon it, these bonds hardened, and, in this moment
of crisis, the larger crowd of onlookers chose sides. In the gathering
heat of the moment, the community that emerged included Germans
and Poles, Protestants and Catholics, peasants and workers, subalterns
and shopkeepers, artisans and their apprentices, women as well as
men, young and old. Emphatically, it did not include the authorities,
let alone the Jews. What linked the Christians in the crowd was more
than just a common antipathy toward authorities and Jews, however; it
was also lust for revenge. In this sense, the moment of crisis that gal-
vanized the community of demonstrators also served as the starting
point of more serious transgressions, including attempts to burn the

synagogue and threats to carry out "lynch justice." Symbolically significant, these ritual acts betray the deeper meanings of the riots.

The attempt to burn down the synagogue resonated with the biblical significance of fire, which, as we know from the Book of Deuteronomy, is one of humankind's oldest symbols of purification. From one direction, its flames envelop external enemies. "A consuming fire; / he [Yahweh] will destroy them, he will subjugate them before you, / so that you can dispossess them" (9:3). From another, it symbolically reduces internal deviants to blackened embers—"so you shall burn out the evil from your midst" (21:21). It is also the biblically prescribed means of eradicating the trace of religious difference, and in this sense the rioters in Konitz were following customs as ancient and timeless as ritual itself.

Rituals draw not only on symbolic archetypes but on histories of actual destruction as well. In anti-Semitic riots, the burning of the synagogue recalled earlier occasions when men, women, and children remained inside the blazing temple and whole Jewish communities were reduced to dust and ash. The towns and cities of central Europe were replete with markers harking back to this earlier time. In Deggendorf, where all the Jews had been burned, a plaque in the local church informed parishioners that in 1338 "the Jews were killed by the Christians out of a zeal for justice pleasing to God."[37] In Büren and in Pulkau, the ditch known as the "Jewish ditch" (*Judengrund* or *Judengrube*) marks the place where Christians had burned Jews in the fourteenth century.[38] The minster in Überlingen was constructed with the burial tablets of Jews who found their death on a pyre.[39] And in numerous places, Nuremberg most prominent among them, temples of Christian worship were erected upon the site of former synagogues and collapsed ghettos, remnants of a Jewish community destroyed, partly by massacre, partly by fire, in the wake of the Black Death.[40] In contrast to their forefathers in earlier centuries, the people of Konitz in the summer of 1900 did not intend actually to murder the Jews of their hometown, but as the intensity of their social drama deepened, they ignited a fire that called forth a history of purification, expulsion, and murder.

In the Konitz riots, lynching was another threat freighted with meaning and horrific associations. Baron von Zedlitz ceaselessly worried that the crowd armed with sticks and clubs would drag Adolph Lewy from his bed in order to satisfy its lust for "lynch justice." He had also heard that on May 28 the crowd intended to liberate Hoffmann, and, as Zedlitz wrote, "no one doubts that lynch justice against the Lewy family would have followed."[41] Although we primarily associate lynch justice with the postbellum American South, German crowds nearly lynched a number of people during the Revolution of 1848 and intermittently in the wake of ordinary crimes thereafter.[42] Admittedly, these instances bore none of the harrowing features of racially motivated torture, mutilation, and cruelty endemic to Euro-American lynching of African Americans. In Germany, the ritual did not culminate—as it did in roughly five thousand cases in the United States between the end of the American Civil War and 1968—in actual human sacrifice.[43]

Still, such a sacrifice was indeed intimated and remained a real danger, partly through the popular association with the American practice, partly because such deadly violence against Jews had occurred many times in the long history of ritual-murder accusations. The parallels between American lynching and German violence against Jews prove revealing. Like the accusations that led to lynching in the American South, ritual-murder accusations often focused on sexual defilement across lines of religion and race, and they almost always targeted a man, who was then tortured and murdered. But whereas American lynching involved a single human sacrifice, the violence of ritual-murder accusations often widened to include the whole community (since Jews allegedly acted in collusion). And whereas the burning cross often endowed American lynchings with an unmistakably sacral symbol, ritual-murder accusations had become increasingly secular, though not completely, and as late as 1892 in Neuss, following the Xanten case, "large blood red crosses" were painted on Jewish houses. Finally, whereas real human sacrifice continued to occur in the United States, the rituals on the streets of Germany remained, at least in Konitz in 1900, just that: rituals.

In Konitz, the rioters simulated the sacrifice of the Jews of their hometown. The events hastened to a climax in which the Christian community, believing itself aggrieved and sinned against, turned—and turned violent. In this "redressive" phase of the ritual, the Jews of Konitz barricaded themselves in their houses and huddled in corners, where—blinds down, lights out, their rage repressed—they prayed.[44] A demonstration of power and a spectacle of public degradation, the ritual imparted to the Jews of Konitz a sense of humiliation and powerlessness, which no doubt lingered for a very long time. When Rabbi Kellermann left Konitz to live in Berlin, he kept a stone on his writing desk; it was a stone, his son later recalled, that "had smashed his window during the anti-Semitic riots in Konitz, the little town in West Prussia where he had served as a rabbi."[45] The stone had cast him from a community of which he had once been a part, and it reminded him of why he was now in Berlin.

As the stone on Rabbi Kellermann's desk in Berlin suggests, the sacrifice of the Jews was symbolic in nature, not literal, for the stone was thrown in the midst of a performance. The theatrical link here is not purely metaphorical, but rather suggests the logic of the events. The imperatives of theater and its staging governed the movements and gestures of the people in the streets, including the use of resonant elements and themes, such as fire and stones, and the appropriation of a familiar ritual-murder script passed down through generations. The significance of the performance emerges only, though, when the script of the past is brought together with the improvisations of the present, and the actors and the audience lose themselves in the drama. In this sense, performance elicits real emotions—the anger of the crowd, its lust for vengeance—which have been rehearsed and learned.[46]

These emotions remain powerful, despite the fictive character of the performance. The Stanford prison experiment, conducted by Philip Zimbardo in 1972, demonstrated that role-playing can dramatically influence people's behavior and emotional state. In this experiment, college students were divided into two groups, prison guards and prisoners, each group outfitted with uniforms appropriate to their

roles and brought to the basement of the Stanford University psychol-
ogy building, remodeled to simulate the alienating conditions of an
actual prison. Within days, student guards began to humiliate student
prisoners, inflicting degrading and dehumanizing punishments on
them. And they did this, moreover, with all the seeming conviction of
real guards beating real prisoners, fists clenched, muscles taut, their
teeth grinding like stones.[47]

It remains to ask how such emotions are engendered and how the
beliefs that accompany them are instilled. With respect to the anti-
Semitic riots, a feature of the ritual, its lack of verbal expression, pro-
vides one answer. In ordinary language, statements lead to further
statements, sometimes in agreement, sometimes in contradiction; but
one does not argue with a song or contradict a chanting crowd. Slogans
are either repeated or there is silence.[48] In the streets, neither conversation nor argument, but only repetition occurred. "The first and most
obvious of the implications of abandoning linguistic choice," the
anthropologist Maurice Bloch writes, "is that an utterance instead of
being followed by an infinity of others can be followed by only a few
or possibly only one."[49] This narrowing effect is heightened in the context of ritual, which, according to Bloch, brings forth the emotional
assent that we associate with belief.

It is, then, the context of the words—the situation in which they
are uttered—that determines their salience and modulates their power.
The philosopher J. L. Austin was among the first to consider that for
certain classes of speech, context, rather than reference, determines
meaning.[50] The force of hate speech, for example, depends on who
utters the words and who is listening. When the farmhand Laskowski
"so ranted and raved against the Jews" in a country inn, he made
purely referential statements of little immediate importance, but when
he denounced Adolph Lewy, he initiated a chain of events for the
Jewish butcher.[51] What, then, resulted when he yelled, "Jews out" and
"Beat the Jews to death," as a member of a menacing crowd brandish-
ing sticks and torches?

That the force of words cannot be severed from context is now immediately apparent. The threatening pose gives the statement a perilous thrust; language is not just spoken—it is performed. "Speaking," to cite Judith Butler, "is a bodily act," and as such can slide into the juridically different domain of conduct—i.e., that of action.[52] Words, in this case, wound. "Oppressive language," to quote Toni Morrison, "does more than represent violence; it is violence."[53]

To imagine the stakes of Morrison's remark, consider the way in which the law traditionally argues the converse. Punishable conduct usually occurs when property is violated, when the flaming cross is burned on the black man's lawn, when the windows of Adolph Lewy are smashed. Compensation typically concerns the damage to the lawn or the windowpane and not, emphatically, the pain of the person violated.[54] And yet we know this pain exists; it sears because this is a ritual with a history, and a script known to both sides, and because it reinscribes a relation of domination and subjection. We know that this is an open wound. The real force of the speech act is to slice into it again.

The crowd's cry of "Jews out!" was not an exhortation to the authorities but an utterance that barred Jews from community, because community, as we have seen, is constructed by the stories told, the history invoked, and the accusations made by its members. A murder did not follow the call to "beat the Jews to death," though three years down the road in nearby Stegers, a Jewish man from Warsaw was mortally beaten by four men in an inn, his tormentors forcing him to kneel and recite the Lord's Prayer before striking him dead.[55] Still, one might argue that the riots brought about "social death," in the sense described by the sociologist Orlando Patterson. In his explication of slavery, Patterson has described the slave as living a kind of "social death": controlled without consent or contract, utterly bereft of autonomy, alienated from birth on, past and future erased, marginalized utterly, there but not there.[56] This does not describe the Jews in Konitz in 1900, though it comes close to characterizing the concentration camp universe forty years later.[57] Patterson's description suggests that social death was achieved, and then reinscribed, in ritual, in particular in rituals of degradation. And this, in turn, is what would give the words "beat the Jews to death" force: in referring to the devastations of the past, they elicited trauma in the encoded memory of the present. Spoken in the context of the riots, the words did not kill—but they enacted and performed, and what they performed was a murder: a ritual murder.

Not the Jews but their Christian accusers performed the ritual murder. This reversal, I would submit, is the key that gives us access to the meaning of the events in Konitz. Just as it unlocks the motivation behind the telling of the butcher's tale, it reveals the hidden script of the blood libel that bedeviled Christian relations with Jews for nearly a millennium.

I V

If rituals have a climax, they also have a denouement, what Victor Turner terms reintegration. In Konitz, this did not simply mean the reintegration of the Jews, though this occurred to some extent as well. More generally, it means the shift from the short-lived fever pitch of collective action to a community that existed, like all communities, in the dull gleam of the everyday. Rioting workers and artisans returned to their roles as ordinary Germans. Men who broke the law bent to its rules. There were arrests and prosecutions, ninety-two for Konitz and the area around it, with charges ranging from disturbing the peace and rebellion to property damage and assault and battery. Save for isolated cases in the town of Stolp, though, jail sentences never stretched beyond a year, and most were significantly shorter. Many of the rioters simply paid fines, and not a few remained too young to be prosecuted.[58] While twenty-nine-year-old Moritz Levy languished in prison, rioters had already returned to their families, jobs, and school.

As people resumed their everyday lives, they found that the events had changed the community. One could see this in the timidity with which local notables addressed what they, at some level, must have seen as the evident mendacity of the butcher's tale. Despite the private misgivings of some of its members, the town council, in a public meeting of July 26, 1900, provided Gustav Hoffmann with the public declaration of honor (*Ehrenerklärung*). Its members sat silently as the butcher reiterated his opinion that "the Jews wanted to destroy [him] by any means so that the Jewish murderer of Winter would remain unpunished."[59] The increasingly anti-Semitic consensus of the town fathers was further evident in the summons, dated November 24, 1900, to found a local organization, the Association to Solve the Konitz Murder, whose purpose was to "to help solve the murder and to ruthlessly pursue *every clue*."[60] The emphasis upon these last two words betrayed the real goal of the organization: to track down clues that incriminated the Jews, who the anti-Semitic lawyer Carl Gebauer and his associates believed were being let off the hook. "If one only put together a compendium of the clues brought forth and proved by the Christian population," one of the organization's declarations averred, "the murder as well as the perpetrators and accomplices would be as clear as day."[61] The summons was signed by the most important men in local affairs, by the pastor and the priest, by all the members of the town council, by important lords of manorial estates, and by the deputies to the provincial diet, the Prussian Landtag, and the German Reichstag.[62] By this time, in the wake of the riots, the center of power had shifted from the angry and capricious people in the crowd to the bourgeois men of Main Street, who once again became the principal organizers of the collective enmity directed against Berlin officials and the Jews next door.

Not everyone in Konitz and the surrounding area took part in the anti-Semitic consensus. Some resisted: the mayor, Georg Deditius, for example; the county official Baron von Zedlitz, who publicly declared "as superstition the idea that the Jewish religious community carried out a ritual murder"; the two non-Jewish liberals in the town council, the merchant Friedrich Paetzold and the high school teacher Dr. Ignaz Praetorius; and Dr. Paul Petras, a local publisher who founded a left-liberal newspaper intended to combat the infamies of the *Konitzer Zeitung* and who would pen an incisive critique of the events in Konitz.[63]

There may have been others whose protests went unrecorded, but the fate of Petras's newspaper suggests otherwise. In December 1900, he and other liberals attempted to publish a new local paper, the *Ostdeutsche Zeitung* (also known as the *Konitzer Anzeiger*), which promised "impartiality," to be "free of hatred," and to "dedicate ourselves to Kaiser and Reich."[64] Its editors insisted that "there are in fact many upstanding people (who are not anti-Semites) in our area." In the next sentence, however, the editors conceded, "Of course, they are silent now."[65]

This oppressive communal silence reflected the stillness of complicity and cowardice, the dead echo of a process that had started early on. "Respected members of the Jewish community, who had previously moved in different Christian social circles, were avoided like the plague," one paper reported in late April. "In the taverns one no longer speaks with them; their greetings are not returned."[66] Hofrichter, the schoolteacher, refused not only to speak with Jews but also to extend his hand to anyone he saw conversing with them.[67] Soon taverns and shops followed the ways of the street, where Jews "are constantly insulted."[68] The Golden Lion advertised itself as a place where you could get "good, home-cooked meals, refreshing drinks, comfortable beds and lodging free of Jews."[69] And Prussian soldiers, stationed in Konitz until the following year, had to safeguard the funeral of an old Jewish woman.[70]

Thus the divide deepened. It is difficult to gauge the breadth of the chasm that separated Christians and Jews: no questionnaires were distributed, no public opinion polls taken, and subsequent elections offer only mixed and indirect evidence. It is true, on the one hand, that the supporters of Mayor Deditius won a county election in 1903 against an explicitly anti-Semitic party.[71] Yet, in the same year, in a Reichstag election based on universal manhood suffrage in the neighboring and predominantly German district of Schlochau-Flatow, the anti-Semites received a third of the vote in the first round of the election. In the second round, after no single party received a majority, the anti-Semitic candidate ran against the Polish Party, and received a stunning two-thirds of the vote. This means that nearly all the Germans, except perhaps the Jews who were left, and the Catholics who followed the dictates of their party and supported the Poles, voted for the anti-Semites.[72]

Fewer and fewer Jews stayed in Konitz. The exodus had already been underway before the events of 1900, but since the murder and the riots that followed, the Jewish community had, according to the estimate of Mayor Deditius in 1902, declined by almost a third.[73] The Lewys had followed the Meyers to Berlin, and by 1905, according to the local address book, Wolf Israelski, Heinrich Friedländer, and Cantor David Nossek had left as well.[74] We also know that Rabbi Kellermann moved to Berlin and that, a bright moment in bleak time, Dumb Alex got his wish and with his family was able to emigrate to America.[75] As a result, the character of the Danzigerstrasse changed markedly, even as the street, and the downtown generally, remained marred by mutual incrimination.

Lawsuits, the most public manifestation of this mutual incrimination, abounded. Before the cantor left, Gustav Hoffmann charged David Nossek with slander, because the cantor had claimed that Hoffmann knew something about the murder.[76] He also sued a member of the synagogue council, the merchant Soldin, and brought suit against a Jewish butcher's apprentice, Jacob Heymann, who claimed that Hoffmann "carved up the body in order to better carry it away."[77] Never more than two steps behind her father, Martha Hoffmann (now Lehmann) sued the editor of a satirical magazine for suggesting that her anti-Semitic remarks placed her in the close company of the plebeian mob.[78] Mayor Deditius charged the schoolteacher Hofrichter with insulting a state official, and Hofrichter returned the favor and charged Deditius with the same for saying that he, Hofrichter, had pressured others to give false testimony.[79] Weichel, a teacher, also sued a number of journalists for defamatory remarks.[80] Inspector Block charged a conservative member of the town council, Hermann Stöckebrant, with perjury, and the town council member, in turn, brought suit against the police inspector for slander.[81] There was also a question whether or not to charge Martha Hoffmann, who had actively worked to condemn Moritz Lewy, with perjury. The authorities, though, were timid and desisted from another row with the butcher and his outspoken elder daughter.[82] Finally, an anti-Semitic lawyer in Berlin persuaded the bereaving father of Ernst Winter to sue Adolph Lewy in a civil suit for the murder of his son.[83]

It is no surprise, then, that some of the finest citizens of Konitz now looked elsewhere. Baron von Zedlitz left the shoals of his native West Prussia to become a county official in Linden, near Hanover.[84] Praetorius, the liberal-minded teacher, was transferred to a position in Graudenz.[85] And Mayor Deditius applied to become the mayor of a community in Upper Silesia but then stayed on in Konitz, where he would remain in his post until the outbreak of World War I.

"Grass will thrive," the poet Czeslaw Milosz tells us, but meanwhile the small world of Konitz became smaller, the streets narrower, and the pettiness of life stretched out that much longer.

Reward poster offering 20,000 marks for information about the murder of Ernst Winter. The A at the bottom right-hand corner is the letter embroidered into the hankerchief found near Winter's decapitated head.

CHAPTER SIX

The Killer

*Who used the words "ritual murder" to ignite
the masses? We do not know. Perhaps the killer
himself.*

—BRUNO BOROWKA,
author of a local chronicle

*We are doomed to be forever hailing someone who
has just gone around the corner and out of earshot.*

—SIMON SCHAMA,
Dead Certainties

The first month of the new year—which would be remembered in European history as the last days of the long reign of Queen Victoria, the grandmother of Kaiser Wilhelm II— began with a sensational find: Ernst Winter's clothes, missing for ten months, suddenly appeared. On Tuesday, January 8, some children found his vest and jacket along with the remains of a handkerchief in the city forest; then, on Sunday, January 13, a custodian discovered Winter's pants in the backyard of the Masonic lodge; and finally, on Tuesday, January 15, girls in school happened upon his black overcoat.[1] The clothes, especially the vest, revealed the discolored stains of coagulated blood.[2]

The discovery of Winter's bloodstained clothes set certain aspects of the case beyond reasonable dispute. The assumption, established by the county medical commissioner, Dr. Müller, in the first autopsy, that Winter had died from a cut to his throat could no longer be maintained, because the blood on his clothes, in this event, would not already have coagulated. As in the ritual-murder cases in Xanten and Polna, an erroneous initial autopsy had from the very beginning fueled the ritual-murder myth. That autopsy had also obfuscated the investigation, since the police wasted considerable time trying to establish whether the cut was made in the style of a kosher butcher (who slices the throat of animals in such a way that the vessels are quickly emptied).

But even before the clothes were found, there had been voices of dissent against what Inspector Braun called that "miserable" autopsy. In October, a professor of forensic medicine in Berlin, Dr. Puppe, had scrutinized the autopsy report and questioned its logic. Unlike Müller, Puppe placed considerable weight on the petechiae in the face and on the surface of the lungs as symptoms of suffocation. He also underlined the absence of blood suffusion on the skin in the area of the throat incision as an argument against a fatal cut to the throat. Like the other severences of the dismembered body, this cut had occurred postmortem. According to Puppe, suffocation, not fatal bleeding, was the probable cause of death. In a separate report, Müller's son, who was also a doctor, refused to accept Puppe's conclusions. Instead, he appealed to an old, if improbable, image of Jewish ritual murder: that the victims are hung by their feet as their throats are cut. "Petechiae are not necessarily symptoms of suffocation," Müller opined; "they can also be caused by gravity when the victim at the time of death is hung up by his feet with the head pointing down."[3] But now there was new evidence, and it did not allow room for such erroneous speculation.

Furthermore, the police found semen stains: on the vest (just below the left pocket), on the jacket, and on the outside of the pants close to the zipper.[4] The location of the stains revealed that Winter was killed, as a forensic report put it, "while attempting to have intercourse with his clothes on."[5]

I

This new evidence proved startling. Yet, even before Winter's clothes were discovered, some people had speculated about a sexual murder. From the start, and to the very end, Inspector Braun believed that Winter had been surprised by his killer while engaging in a sex act. Although Braun's peers did not share his suspicions of Gustav Hoffmann in this regard, there were other possibilities. Perhaps Winter lived a double life and found his death in the underworld of a small town, whether at the hands of a "pederast" or in the house of a prostitute.

The first possibility, involving "pederasty," centered on a rumor that a local tailor, Otto Plath, thirty-eight years of age, enjoyed the company of young boys and that he especially admired the tall and muscular Ernst Winter. Winter, for his part, spent considerable time at Plath's house, playing cards and trading stamps. Rudolf Plath, Otto's younger brother, also played with them.[6] According to one of Winter's best friends, the more intimate friendship was between the older tailor and the younger student.[7] But Otto Plath denied this and claimed that Winter came to his house mainly because of Rudolf, with whom Winter had taken dancing classes.[8] There was another reason for suspecting Plath, however. Winter's torso had been found neatly wrapped in packing paper and carefully bound with string. Both the paper and the string came from Plath's tailor shop.[9] Moreover, the knot was fastidiously tied, as if by a tailor.

The suspicions, though, rested mainly on speculation. There was little evidence that Plath had what Wilhelmine society considered "perverse sexual inclinations."[10] He also had no obvious motive, and he had an alibi that could be corroborated. On Sunday, March 11, Otto Plath had spent the afternoon with the teacher Weichel. Between 1:30 and 3:30 P.M., they were in the park and at the shooting club; thereafter they went to Hunzel's restaurant, where they stayed, having imbibed four bottles of apple wine, until sometime between 7:00 and 7:30, when, ill from the wine, Weichel walked home, accompanied by Plath. Plath then went to his own house for dinner and thereafter went out again, stopping for drinks in a number of pubs and not returning home until shortly after midnight.[11]

Other attempts to place Ernst Winter in the company of persons the police considered "perversely inclined" proved unsuccessful. One possible suspect was the cigar dealer Fischer. As students from the Gymnasium congregated in his store on the Danzigerstrasse, some people concluded that the middle-aged Fischer reveled in their company far too much. Yet, aside from the fact that Winter had been in the store on Sunday afternoon, there was no particular reason to suspect Fischer. Moreover, the rumors about Fischer remained unconfirmed, and when the police searched his house and store, they could find no incriminating evidence.[12] The same may be said of suspicions raised against Szymanski, a teacher who was employed in the girl's school. In his case, the police could not even connect him to Ernst Winter, though Szymanski had allegedly spent much time with Winter's younger roommate.[13]

Still, the second possibility seemed more likely: that, on the afternoon of Sunday, March 11, Winter had been with a prostitute. In the words of a high-level Prussian memorandum, "Ernst Winter could have been murdered in the apartment of a prostitute because he evidently had sexual relations with such women and was often seen in the company of people of the working class."[14] That Winter often visited local prostitutes was not just an invention of a constricted imagination: a close friend said as much and named "the black Dominika" as a possible example.[15] Winter talked often about his sexual exploits, sometimes bragging about them. When asked about his "back pain," he once replied, "You know, the women."[16] He often spoke about his "gallant adventures" and how he "tired the girls out."[17] He also told friends that he "masturbated often" and had already begun a few years ago to "masturbate almost every night."[18] At the end of the Victorian era, this was thought to be unnatural, and the police speculated that this practice weakened him and, in turn, helped explain how an otherwise strong and vital eighteen-year-old could be overcome in a struggle.[19]

The struggle, the police supposed, might have been with a local pimp, although "here in Konitz there are no pimps in the actual sense of the word."[20] Nevertheless, it was conceivable that Ernst Winter, "who allowed himself to be involved with women of the worst repute," fell into an argument with a male protector, who strangled or suffocated Winter and later dismembered his body.[21]

Such speculations were not as far-fetched as they nowadays might seem. In Wilhelmine Germany, middle-class sons who attended the Gymnasium typically turned to lower-class servants and prostitutes for premarital sex.[22] At the same time, sexual encounters with "well-to-do daughters" were not only strictly forbidden but sharply controlled. In Konitz, schoolteachers even attempted to discourage Gymnasium students from strolling up and down the Danzigerstrasse, because this only encouraged unsupervised contact between young men and women.[23] There still were, of course, ample opportunities for contact. Winter, for example, met with girls in dance class—though only under the watchful eyes of the dance instructor and the stern gaze of the mothers sitting in attendance. There was also ice skating on the Mönchsee, meetings in the cafés, visits to the theater, and occasionally clandestine moonlight promenades. All of this, however, rarely led to sexual encounters and, if so, only under the strictest secrecy.

In search of sexual adventures, German Gymnasium students routinely turned to prostitutes. Although rarely acknowledged, this had become part of a Janus-faced sexual economy that allowed, in the words of one contemporary author, "the young men to maintain their health and good humor, and the young women from better families to maintain their virtue."[24] Yet some young men feared going to prostitutes, partly because of the high incidence of venereal disease, but also because it opened the door to an often brutal and violent underworld. This is where the police imagined Winter's killer to be.

The police identified Wilhelmine Kammerov, a local prostitute with whom Winter had sexual relations, as a possible suspect and her lover, the mason Robert Zindler, as the man who might have murdered him. As a suspect, Kammerov seemed promising. In 1894, she had been implicated in the murder of Bluhm, an oarsman whose corpse, like that of Ernst Winter, had been dumped into the Mönchsee. Although witnesses claimed to have seen Kammerov with Bluhm near the railroad tracks on the day he was murdered, Kammerov was convicted neither of killing Bluhm nor of being an accomplice to murder. Yet, during the trial, she perjured herself when she swore under oath that she had not engaged in prostitution, and was sentenced to two and a half years in a local jail.[25]

On the day of Winter's murder, however, she seemed to have an alibi. On Sunday morning, March 11, she had attended church in Konitz and in the afternoon worked on the Fettke estate in the village of Briesen, three miles southwest of Konitz. Similarly, her lover Robert Zindler spent the day shepherding cattle in the village of Mossnitz, south of Konitz. In both cases, it seems difficult, though not impossible, to imagine that they could have slipped into Konitz without their employers' noticing their absence.[26]

Speculation about the possible role of a local prostitute also led the police to think that the scene of the crime might not have been the Mönchsee after all, but rather the "little red house" at the edge of town. Situated near the shooting club, and close to where Winter's decapitated head had been found, the "little red house" had previously been occupied by "loose women" and enjoyed a bad reputation among the polite classes.[27] Still, this house was not a particularly plausible location: it was more than a mile away from the basin of the Mönchsee—a long distance for the killer to carry the two halves of Winter's torso. The house was also quite small, with six families, including dozens of children, living within its four walls.[28] That no one noticed anything suspicious seems difficult to imagine. It was also unlikely that Winter had sought out a prostitute on the afternoon of Sunday, March 11: not only had he left his wallet at home, but, as Inspector Wehn determined by inquiring of local call girls, Gymnasium students who visited prostitutes almost always did so after dark.[29] Winter, one may recall, died before 7:00 P.M, when it was still light out.

Undeterred, the police clung tenaciously to the notion that

Winter may have fallen into the hands of a man from the Konitz underworld. From the perspective of good middle-class Wilhelmine citizens, this underworld was inhabited by the working-class proletariat—in their minds, dangerous people, anathema to the comfortable order of things. Not only was the working class viewed as politically unreliable, its members were seen as irreligious, sexually promiscuous, brutal, and often criminal.

Investigators entered this dangerous world when they followed another lead involving Ernst Winter's possible sexual encounters. A number of people had seen Winter on the afternoon of the murder walking with two men. For months the police had tried to trace their identity—to no avail. Then they offered a reward, and suddenly people began to remember. A beer distributor named Arthur Steffan came forward to claim that Winter had had a surreptitious meeting with Johann Gast and August Pikarski on March 11 at 2:00 P.M. on the Danzigerstrasse and that Winter had sexual relations with Marie Sawischewski, once the lover of Johann Gast and a sexual partner for Pikarski. Steffan, for his part, claimed to know Sawischewski well, for he too had sexual relations with her.

Yet Sawischewski denied ever having had sexual relations, voluntary or otherwise, with Ernst Winter. She did concede that "here and there she had sexual relations with various men in Konitz . . . mostly under the open sky . . ." She did not, however, "demand gifts from them" and instead gave herself satisfied with whatever her men gave."[30] An intimate relation with Winter, she reiterated, was out of the question. "I never knew boys from the Gymnasium," she said. "The men I had intimate relations with were mostly friends and acquaintances of Gast—mason apprentices and cobblers."[31]

Johann Gast was Sawischewski's fiancé. A twenty-two-year-old mason, he was one of the two men Steffan had allegedly seen walking with Ernst Winter on the afternoon of the murder. Sawischewski also had a child with Gast, but the child died on December 19, 1900, shortly before reaching its first birthday. Sawischewski could not say what caused the child's death or exactly when she broke off her engagement to Gast, though she placed the breakup in March 1900. "Gast was a drunkard," she told a police inspector. She also feared he would "bring about her condition again." To have another child with Gast was the last thing she wanted: he had done nothing for the child and, when drunk, often turned violent, even having publicly mistreated her at Schmeichel's dance bar.[32] Tellingly, the next man she met was a gentleman, a musketeer in the army and the son of a well-to-do businessman. He even wanted to marry her and wrote her many letters, but she turned him down. Someone of his station, she convinced herself, "would not marry someone like me, a poor girl."[33]

There was little doubt that Johann Gast was a violent man, but that he had killed Ernst Winter, or even that he knew him, was more difficult to establish. Though Sawischewski could not be sure, she did not think that Gast knew Winter, "since Gast spent time only with his own kind."[34] But the beer distributor Steffan had seen Gast together with Pikarski and Winter. Could Steffan have been mistaken?

August Pikarski, previously a mason, now a soldier, certainly claimed that this was so. But Pikarski nevertheless corroborated the view of Gast as a man capable of murder. "It did not come to a friendship between us," Pikarski said of Gast, "because I had a certain aversion to this extremely raw and brutal man, who reached for his knife at the slightest provocation."[35] Clearly, Gast was cut of the right cloth to commit a violent crime, and Pikarski would have "made no secret of anything he knew" about Gast's involvement in the death of Ernst Winter.[36] But he knew of no such involvement.

In his own deposition, Gast also said that he had never met Ernst Winter. "How could I have," he asked, "only workers and artisans go to the places I hang out. . . . Gymnasium students are not seen there."[37] Gast also denied other allegations against him. He denied that he was the father of Marie Sawischewski's child, claiming that, at the time of conception, they had not yet slept with each other. Sawischewski, moreover, never asked him for financial help or for any other kind of support for the child. "She obviously believed that I would someday marry her," he said, but added that she was at the same time intimate with a number of other workers from the local power plant.[38] Obviously, between Sawischewski and Gast, someone was not telling the whole truth.

An ex-convict, Gast had good reason to lie. For the afternoon of the murder, he had no alibi; when pressed, he said that he simply could not remember where he was that day. He did, though, remember that he was in Riedel's pub on the afternoon that the torso was found in the Mönchsee. When an apprentice came in and told Gast and his drinking buddies about the corpse, they immediately walked over to the basin of the Mönchsee to see the sight of Winter's dismembered body. Soon a crowd gathered, and people discussed nothing other than the question of who did it. Moreover, nearly everyone in Konitz stopped to consider where he or she was on Sunday afternoon, when Winter was last seen. Gast, however, had no recollection. Yet he was a mason, not a butcher, and Winter's body, one may recall, was neatly severed in several places, almost every cut skillfully executed. Could Gast, quick to reach for his knife, have cut the corpse so precisely? One piece of evidence points to this possibility. In January 1901, Gast was drafted into the army. In the course of evaluating new troops, his commanding captain asked the company who among them knew how to slaughter a cow. Eager to show off, Gast stepped forward. Perhaps he had nothing to hide. "I believe that I could kill an ox," he later deposed, "but to slaughter him in the correct way as a butcher would carve him, that would be difficult for me."[39]

Try as they might, the police could not place Ernst Winter in Gast's company, and Steffan's testimony, incorrect in a series of tangential details, proved too weak to support an arrest. An ex-soldier, Steffan was himself not beyond suspicion. In 1895, a military court had condemned him to six months in prison for falsification of documents, attempted fraud, abuse of office, and, in two instances, violence against subordinates.[40] In the Konitz case, he proved an opaque figure. Some people thought that the Jews had hired him, and he was even accused of trying to confuse witnesses against Moritz Lewy by hiring a doppelgänger, an Ernst Winter look-alike.[41] Yet the suspicions cut both ways. In one story, he claimed to have seen two men walking with Winter on the afternoon of the murder, and reported they were "not from here, and they were without doubt Jews."[42] With Steffan, one never knew. Perhaps he was after the reward. Perhaps he had been slighted by Sawischewski and was jealous of Gast.

Perhaps, too, the police were looking in the wrong milieu. Ernst Winter was, after all, a Gymnasium student and, as such, ostensibly a member of the middle class. The police, it is true, found it more difficult to imagine that a solid member of the German middle class could have committed such a brutal crime. Yet important clues pointed in this direction. In particular, they pointed to a pillar of Wilhelmine society: the schools.

I I

The first clue had already surfaced on Easter Sunday, 1900. In the ditch in which the head was found, there was a handkerchief, torn in four pieces, one embroidered with the letter A.[43] Upon examination of the handkerchief, the chemist Bischoff found traces of blood, on one piece "definitely," on another "with great probability."[44] Not knowing whose handkerchief it was, the police placed an announcement in the local newspaper imploring the owner of the handkerchief to report to the station. For two weeks, no one came forward. Then, fortuitously, Mayor Deditius found a very similar handkerchief in his own house. But it did not belong to him; rather, it belonged to Auguste Rhode, the wife of the superintendent of schools for Konitz County. She had been to Deditius's house for a soiree and had left it there unwittingly.[45] She was also a regular customer of the butcher Gustav Hoffmann, and, according to her former maid, Auguste Rhode often left her handkerchiefs lying around.[46] When confronted with the handkerchief, Rhode immediately recognized it as her own. When asked about the handkerchief in the ditch, she confessed that it, too, belonged to her.[47] Why had she not reported the handkerchief before? Inspector Wehn asked. "Because the Jews did it," she replied, and "she did not see the point of getting her handkerchief and her name and her person mixed up with the murder."[48] The murder, Rhode supposedly added, was a ritual murder. Confounded, Wehn shook his head: "this ridiculous tale."[49]

It was a tale that Auguste Rhode had helped to tell. She reported that she and her husband, along with the master mason Rudolf Hermann and his wife, Marie, had left the Masonic temple at eleven on the night of the murder. When they stepped onto the sidewalk of the Rähmestrasse (which led directly to the synagogue), Auguste Rhode allegedly said, "It smells here like burned woolen rags." She also noticed a light in the synagogue, about a hundred yards to their right.[50] Whether true or not (her husband and the Hermanns only partly corroborated her story), Auguste Rhode's observation about the flickering light in the synagogue and about the smell of burned rags made its way into popular lore and provided specious evidence for plot lines involving a Jewish cabal convening in the synagogue after the ritual slaughter of Ernst Winter.

The mystery of Auguste Rhode's handkerchief remained unsolved. She herself had no idea how it could have landed in the ditch close to Winter's decapitated head. She suggested that maybe her former maid (who had said that perhaps Mrs. Rhode left the handkerchief in Hoffmann's butcher shop) had stolen the handkerchief.[51] More plausibly, Rhode's son claimed that he had torn the handkerchief in four back in the fall of 1899 when he was in the woods and had to relieve himself. But like truth generally in the Rhode family, this recollection took its time to surface; the boy did not arrive at his epiphany until mid-January 1901, a full eight months after the handkerchief had been found.[52] Oddly, and despite the blood on the handkerchief, the police accepted his statement and closed the investigation. Indeed, they never took Auguste Rhode as a suspect seriously. "That she was involved in the murder," a ministerial memorandum stated, "seemed completely out of the question."[53] She was a woman and a member of the bourgeoisie, in every way an upstanding citizen.

A second set of clues pointed to Weichel, the teacher. A close friend of Otto Plath's, Weichel had corroborated Plath's alibi that on the afternoon of the murder they had walked in the park and visited the shooting club before going to dinner at Hunzel's restaurant. Sometime between seven and seven-thirty, Weichel fell ill and, accompanied by Plath, walked home.

Yet, when the murder became known, Weichel began to act strangely. On the morning after the torso was discovered in the Mönchsee, he boarded the 11:43 train for Berlin in order to inquire about a medical condition: a sore larynx, of all things. Unfortunately, the police did not ask why he needed to go to Berlin or when he had made the appointment. Moreover, despite a thorough medical examination, the throat specialist in Berlin could find nothing wrong with Weichel's larynx.[54]

When Weichel returned to Konitz, however, he pursued the details of the murder investigation with uncommon passion, quickly taking up company with every new journalist, private investigator, and reward seeker who came to town. He also proved a nuisance to the police. In late May, Chief Prosecutor Settegast complained, "For weeks Weichel passes his days in the pubs, ingratiating himself with every correspondent writing about the murder, talking ceaselessly about the deed, and calling the Jews the murderers."[55] That Weichel blamed the Jews was not in itself remarkable, but on the evening of May 29, the day that Gustav Hoffmann was apprehended and Bernhard Masloff interrogated by the unofficial citizens committee, Weichel had one too many drinks and began to brag that he, in fact, had killed Ernst Winter and that the people in the pub would one day remark that they had sat at the same table with the killer. He then tried to wrest a revolver away from one of the guests, ostensibly to commit suicide.[56]

The police hardly took Weichel seriously, for he had no evident motive for murder. Yet other circumstance rendered Weichel a more plausible suspect than the police supposed. When he was sixteen years old, he lived in Skurz, where the murder of fourteen-year-old Onofrius Czybulla had been turned into an alleged ritual murder. Weichel had seen the dismembered body of the young boy, and his father, a local teacher, had been involved in the murder trial. Weichel therefore learned the ritual-murder script firsthand, as a young man. Moreover, during military maneuvers he had been employed in a military hospital and therefore had at least some anatomical knowledge. Weichel himself confirmed this, bragging, soon after the murder, that he could carve up a body with ease.[57]

On the surface, the teacher seemed to lead an ordinary life. Married with three children, Weichel held a secure job and was, along with Superintendent Rhode, the chairman of the local veterans organization. He also served as the church organist. Once we peer behind the veneer of small-town satisfaction, however, we see a more startling picture. Not entirely stable, Weichel was a powerfully built man with a drinking problem and a violent streak. Constantly arguing with his wife, he had beaten her and had threatened her with a knife.[58] There were also rumors that he had pulled a gun on her and that she had filed for divorce. Weichel's wife denied both charges, conceding only that she had separated from him for a brief period when she suspected him of being unfaithful to her.[59] At the time of the murder, however, they were again living under the same roof, even though Weichel had not really changed. He spent much of his time hanging around with a shady character named Gustav Georg, who had been sentenced to twelve years in prison for breaking into people's houses and stealing from them.[60] Weichel was also chronically in debt, not least to his friend Otto Plath.

Yet Weichel had an alibi confirmed by independent witnesses. He and Otto Plath had been at Hunzel's restaurant from 3:30 P.M. to 7:00 P.M. He then came home to his wife shortly after 7:00 P.M. As his wife testified, Weichel was indeed ill from too much apple wine, and he stayed in his bed for the rest of the evening.[61] Weichel therefore had as a good an alibi as any for the afternoon and the evening of the murder. He also could not have distributed the body parts, for if he did indeed leave Konitz for Berlin with the 11:43 A.M. train on Thursday, March 14, he could not have thrown Ernst Winter's left arm over the gate of the Protestant cemetery that night or the next morning.[62]

Weichel may have been an "irascible," sometimes violent, if "lethargic," man "devoid of character" and "prone to drink."[63] That did not, however, make him a cold-blooded killer. More likely, it made him a person who screamed for attention; his drunken admission of guilt, his theatrical play at suicide, could be seen as pathetic attempts to place himself at the center of the whirlwind that hit this small town in the summer of 1900.

I I I

Still, the local police could not say who killed Ernst Winter, and for this reason a new chief investigator was appointed, the much celebrated Inspector von Kracht, a famous detective in the Rhineland, traditionally a fertile soil for the ritual-murder tale.[64] Unlike Inspector Braun from Berlin, Kracht, who came to Konitz in January 1901, entertained the blood libel charge and believed that in the past Jews might have slaughtered Christian children in order to use their blood. He had studied the material on the "ritual murders" in Skurz and Xanten, as well the "scholarly" literature on these cases. He "had no reason," he claimed, "to side with one or the other opinion." Nevertheless, he considered it his duty to look at the documentary material closely and impartially. "A very large part of the population of Konitz and of the German people do not consider a ritual murder or a murder for blood to be out of the question," Kracht opined.[65] "People high up in Konitz society," he added, "assume this to be the case."[66]

Inspector von Kracht wished to appease these people. He also genuinely suspected that the Jews were hiding something. "When the Jews are interrogated," he complained, "they assiduously deny everything."[67] He also believed in the real possibility of a Jewish conspiracy. Upon arriving in Konitz, he began his investigation by going back and tracing all the telegrams sent and received by the Jews of Konitz between March 1 and March 16.[68] Not surprisingly, he found nothing, except a lot of business communiqués.

Inspector von Kracht also fixed his attention on the Lewys.

Three clues, he believed, pointed to their complicity. The first involved the testimony of Bernard Masloff, which Kracht, following the trial jury, found credible. The second clue came from Moritz Lewy, who, in Kracht's eyes, had committed perjury by hiding his previous association with Ernst Winter. The very act of lying about this detail constituted "evidence of guilt," the inspector from the Rhineland reasoned. Finally, Kracht theorized that "with great probability" the sack in which the torso of the deceased Winter was found had made its way from the tailor Otto Platt via a since deceased Polish maid into the hands of Lewy's sister, the rag dealer, who then gave the sack to her brother Adolph.[69] Thus, Kracht thought, one of the central riddles of the murder—how the sack got into the hands of the killer— was solved.

Unfortunately, as Kracht himself had to admit, "this material was not sufficient for successfully indicting Lewy."[70] The same, he also had to admit, proved true of the other Jews he suspected: Lewinski, whose house on the Danzigerstrasse "seemed much better suited than Lewy's" for carrying out the deed; or the butcher Hamburger from Schlochau, who was denounced, nearly a full year after the deed, by a Christian meat inspector as the one who had probably cut Winter's throat; or Cantor Nossek, who on the evening of the murder had picked up six Jews at the train station and brought them to Lewinski's house. Kracht lacked concrete evidence for all of these suspects. "The suspicions raised against the Jews remain insufficient to proceed in any definite direction," he wrote.[71] The single-minded focus on the Jews did more than lead to a dead end; it damaged the investigation irreparably. Intelligent observers understood this well. In a memorandum dated November 11, 1900, the Prussian minister of the interior, Baron von Rheinbaben, and the Prussian minister of justice, Baron von Schudt, blamed "in no small measure" the "impassioned agitation" unleashed by the ritual-murder legend for the failure of the investigation.[72]

The police also failed to reconsider assumptions in the light of new evidence. Since the initial investigation, three important new facts had emerged: first, the petechiae found on the lungs of the deceased,

strongly suggesting that Ernst Winter died not of bleeding but of suffocation; second, the time of death, which forensic specialists now put
as late as 7:00 P.M.; third, the semen stains found on Winter's pants and
vest. Since evidence showed that Winter had suffocated, it was no
longer necessary to assume that the murder had been committed in
cold blood. Since the murder may have occurred as late as seven in the
evening, some alibis no longer held. Finally, since the murder certainly
involved a sexual motive, this aspect needed to be investigated with
renewed vigor.

Even without the semen stains, the evidence tentatively pointed to
an earlier suspect. On December 17, 1900, Chief Prosecutor Wulff of
the district of Marienwerder suggested that investigators consider the
case of Gustav Hoffmann anew. It was, on the one hand, "unthinkable"
that a man of Hoffmann's stature would commit such a crime, since he
was "universally admired" and led an "immaculate life."[73] On the other
hand, his alibi was not as airtight as it had first appeared. The time
between 6:00 P.M. and 7:00 P.M. remained unaccounted for. Perhaps the
investigation had been closed too hastily. "It is not entirely inconceivable that Hoffmann was the killer," Wulff cautiously speculated.[74]

Local inspectors, as well as Kracht, thought otherwise. Hoffmann
had been interrogated before, to no avail. An upstanding citizen,
Hoffmann did not appear to be someone capable of murder when
police had first interrogated him. He even made a good impression on
Inspector Braun. It is true that Hoffmann had denounced Adolph
Lewy without a shred of incriminating evidence. He also affixed his
signature to a printed pamphlet containing fanciful statements mas-
querading as facts. Yet the denunciations did not so much as dent his
reputation: as the citizens of Konitz so often maintained, Gustav
Hoffmann was a good man.

One official remained skeptical. In July 1901, District Attorney
Lautz, a prosecutor in Marienwerder, penned a detailed memorandum arguing that Hoffmann no longer had an alibi.[75] He also
thought it unusual that Hoffmann should know nothing about his
daughter's friendship with Ernst Winter, when in fact the two young

people had been seeing each other every Sunday for a long time. Anna Hoffmann also denied the relationship, yet at the trial, her older brother conceded that Winter "had been courting his sister."[76] Lautz also pointed to the suspicions voiced early on in the murder investigation by Ignaz Praetorius, the liberal-minded high school teacher. Praetorius recounted that when the sack that contained the torso was unraveled, Hoffmann had torn from the sack a scrap of paper that had pieces of meat stuck to it and thrown it back into the lake.[77] Praetorius also noticed that Hoffmann acted strangely that day. The killer stood before him, Praetorius thought for a moment.[78] The next day, both men, Hoffmann and Praetorius, looked through Hoffmann's ice cellar and sheds for clues, coming up empty.[79] The police took Hoffmann's vigilance as evidence that he could not have committed the crime. As Lautz pointed out, however, the evidence could cut the other way, and one could imagine a man anxious to make sure no incriminating evidence remained.

To be sure, such suspicions rested on weak conjectures. Yet, combined with an alibi that no longer held, Hoffmann's previous mendacity, and his choleric temper, it was at least conceivable that Hoffmann had killed Ernst Winter in the evening of March 11, 1900. According to Lautz, the following was the scenario.

Evidently waiting for someone, Ernst Winter had been promenading up and down the Danzigerstrasse in the late afternoon. Meanwhile, Anna Hoffmann was at the home of Wilhelm Ziebarth, the butcher, whom she and her family had visited that day. Anna Hoffmann left the Ziebarths around 5:45 P.M., and her father returned home fifteen minutes later. For some reason, he had cause to go to his shed near the lake, where he caught Winter with his daughter in flagrante delicto. She immediately fled and therefore had no idea of what happened next.

Given the ruined reputation that could result if her virtue had been damaged, her father was beside himself with rage. A large man, Gustav Hoffmann threw the boy to the ground and, in the heat of the tussle, strangled or suffocated him. Perhaps Hoffmann did not mean to kill Winter, but he quickly understood the gravity of what he had done. He must hide the body, he thought, and the obvious occurred to him. He would get rid of the body as he got rid of the rest of the meat in his shop: that meant cutting up the corpse, wrapping the parts in packing paper, and binding the packages with a string. The string had always constituted an important piece of evidence. It came from the shop of the tailor Plath, and this fact pointed to a killer who lived or worked in Konitz. Of equal importance, the packages were neatly wrapped and the knot elegantly tied. Hoffmann had many customers outside Konitz and sent meat to them, wrapped in packing paper and tied with a string.

The wrapping would take time, so Hoffmann first returned home, where he sat down with his family to a meal. At this point, Anna Hoffmann did not know what had happened to Ernst Winter. Hence she later that evening asked one of the apprentices to say hello to him in the theater. Filled with dread about his own deed, the father said nothing at the table. Instead, he sent the apprentices to bed early, ordered lights out earlier than usual, and, when the rest were asleep, left the house, fetched his tools, packing paper and string, and went to work.

Hoffmann carved up the body several hours after the murder, which explains the coagulation of the blood. Because the moon was full that evening, he could easily see where to cut. Still, this process took longer than he had expected, and at some point he panicked, changed plans, threw the larger pieces in the lake, and hid the others, taking them only later to the places where they were eventually found.

The killer, Lautz reasoned, must have been clever, and he must have had time to think. A mere ruffian would have thrown the body, clothes and all, into the lake. Moreover, the parts were cut as if by a butcher and packed as such. Hoffmann was a smart man. He had intended to disperse the body parts, each part neatly packaged, but time ran out.[80]

Time ran out for Lautz as well. In June 1901, he asked that the possibility that Gustav Hoffmann had killed Ernst Winter be considered anew. "Against the task of tracking down the circumstances of the murder," Lautz wrote, "the concern about possible unrest in the population must be put into the background." Lautz implored. The new chief prosecutor refused. His name was Schweigger ("silencer"). The case against Hoffmann, Schweigger replied, was closed, and he recounted the reasons why: the police had found nothing in Hoffmann's home; the interrogation had turned up no incriminating circumstances; the evidence of a sexual liaison between Anna Hoffmann and Ernst Winter was scant; Gustav Hoffmann did not even know of a liaison; and he was a good man, respected and revered by the community.[81] Lautz never responded to Schweigger's arguments, though he no doubt thought them threadbare, especially in light of new evidence. But exactly what he thought we will never know. Soon after he wrote the memorandum, Lautz passed away, a victim of a sudden and inexplicable aneurism. Schweigger continued with the investigation, and he "tended to the opinion that the killer is a person who had never been suspected before. . . ."[82]

I V

Did Lautz get it right? Looking back, it no longer surprises us that an eighteen-year-old boy might have seduced a fifteen-year-old girl from an upstanding family on a cold night in a shed. It is no longer inconceivable that a respectable man could commit a horrible deed. More confounding remains the charge of ritual murder itself, as if the charge were a blanket, concealing the truth about the killing of Ernst Winter, just as it pulled a cover of silence over the history of Christian violence against Jews. Although significant violence continued well into the modern period, in Konitz in 1900 it assumed the insidious character of a reenactment, of speech and act that did, in fact, perform its own version of ritual murder, stressing now the first word rather than the second.

Much as we would like to solve a crime now one hundred years old, we cannot interrogate Gustav Hoffmann again or return to the crime scene so hastily contaminated by the citizens of Konitz. In this sense, indeterminacy is the historian's lot. "We are doomed," as Simon Schama has written, "to be forever hailing someone who has just gone around the corner and out of earshot."[83] But even if we do not have the "dead certainty" to hang a man, we can see that in this West Prussian town, although there was only one corpse, there was more than one crime. And through the long forgotten story of Konitz, we can come closer to understanding the episodic recurrence of a crime that all too often has moved the bards of the Jewish community to lamentation. Less then forty years later, indeed not so far off the horizon, the virulent streams of anti-Semitic hatred would again rise, this time in a river of blood greater than the most pessimistic prophet had ever dared imagine.

"Greetings from Konitz in West Prussia." The Mönchsee
with a view of the town in the background.

Epilogue

Who today does not know the name Konitz?

—WÜRZBURGER GENERALANZEIGER,
25 October 1900

Death is a master from Germany his eyes are blue.

—PAUL CELAN

I

In March 1901, a full year after the murder of Ernst Winter, a local committee was busy erecting a monument to the deceased. "Here rests in God Ernst Winter, slaughtered [*geschlachtet*] by malicious hands," the epitaph read. Just beneath the cross were the words "Death has been transformed into victory" and on the pedestal "Make no mistake, God does not let himself be blasphemed."[1]

If the references on the monument were thinly veiled, the same cannot be said of the postcards distributed throughout the empire and beyond. One pictured the family Löwy (*sic*) as lions gnawing on the bones of Ernst Winter. Another showed a picture of the town along with Max Heyn's photograph of Winter, a copy of the reward poster, and a crying angel. There was even a postcard with a scene of the murder taking place in Lewy's cellar. "Remember the 11th of March 1900," the postcard admonished. "On this day the Gymnasium student Winter in Konitz was sacrificed to the knife of a kosher butcher."[2] The postcard not only showed the act itself, including the draining of Winter's blood, but featured Moritz Lewy as well, clearly identifiable, sporting a pince-nez, standing in the middle of the picture holding Winter's leg. The hunchbacked Wolf Israelski is holding a rope, and a man is walking toward the stairs, checking to make sure the coast is clear. "Watch over your siblings, those who are unmarried," the postcard also warned, and "protect your children."[3]

Despite these crude efforts at propaganda, the conviction among Germans that the Jews had murdered Ernst Winter began to ebb. In October 1903, Kaiser Wilhelm II even pardoned Moritz Lewy, who had already served two long years in prison. Whatever his personal opinion of Jews—the kaiser had made more than his share of anti-Semitic remarks—he nevertheless understood that Lewy had been the victim of a community in the throes of anti-Semitic passion.[4] When the recently released Lewy arrived at the train station in Berlin, there was no crowd, angry or otherwise, to greet him. The police thought it necessary to station guards at the home of his father, the Jewish butcher Adolph Lewy, who would now live out his days at Linienstrasse 11, not far from the splendor of Berlin's grand Reform Synagogue. But when Moritz arrived at his new home, no incident occurred.[5] Even in Konitz, where enmity was still pervasive, the belief that the Jews had killed Ernst Winter had begun to recede. "With few exceptions," a report of May 1904 stated, "the people are convinced that the suspicion of the Jews is unfounded."[6]

I I

Yet the notoriety of the case ensured a steady stream of continued speculation, much of it fanciful, about the identity of Winter's murderer. Among the many solutions to the crime advanced by journalists, reward seekers, and both amateur and professional detectives in the decade after its occurrence, one compels our attention and leads us back to the scene of the crime and the original actors in the drama. Leaked to a Berlin journalist in 1904, the solution stemmed, in all probability, from the wily and persistent Inspector Braun, who now believed Bernhard Masloff to have been the killer.[7]

By his own indiscretions, Masloff damaged his alibi. Originally, he claimed that he had been at home in his apartment in Hohe Höfe, a working-class street on the outskirts of the town, until 7:00 P.M. on the night of the murder. Masloff, it turned out, had actually been in town since 4:00 P.M., when he had coffee with his mother-in-law, Anna Ross, in her apartment at Postallstrasse 162.[8] The address is important. Ross lived in a dimly lit side street in a small two-bedroom apartment with a window looking onto the back of Hermann Lange's house, where Ernst Winter rented a room. Masloff and Ross knew Ernst Winter, and Winter knew their apartment because he had slept with the daughter of the previous occupant, a girl named Elisabeth Senske, who had since moved to Berlin. It is not clear that he knew the women who currently occupied the apartment. We do know, however, that Martha Masloff, Bernhard Masloff's young wife, came to the apartment sometime that afternoon, though exactly when is difficult to determine. We also know that she was very angry with her delinquent husband. Meanwhile, Anna Ross claimed to have gone to the Lewys at 7:00 P.M., but later evidence placed her at the Jewish butcher's house closer to 9:00 P.M. Why did Bernhard Masloff and Anna Ross lie about their whereabouts? And why was it so difficult to get the true story from Martha Masloff?

If one follows the corrected testimonies of Masloff and Ross, there was a window of opportunity to commit the crime sometime after 5:30 P.M. on Sunday. This is when, according to Braun's theory, Ernst Winter came to the apartment and seduced Masloff's frustrated, angry wife. When Bernhard Masloff and his brother-in-law, Johann Berg, unexpectedly returned from Sänger's pub, Masloff saw Winter with Martha. The men went after Winter, and one of them knocked him senseless with a blow to the head, then suffocated him, and later that evening cut up his body in the dark cellar beneath Postallstrasse 162.

Initially, this charge rested purely on speculation—no more or less convincing than similar suspicions brought against Gustav Hoffmann. In light of further evidence, however, a convincing case against Masloff began to take shape.

A scrap of a liberal newspaper, the *Tägliche Rundschau*, was found stuck to Winter's head in the ditch near the Dunkershagen farm. In the immediate vicinity of Konitz, only twelve people subscribed to the *Tägliche Rundschau*, and one of them was Borrmann, a farmer from the village of Paglau. Before coming to Konitz, Bernhard Masloff and his father had worked on Borrmann's farm, and they may well have had old newspaper wrapping left over from their previous employment. Masloff's work for Borrmann also helps explain the seemingly decisive issue of the butcher's cut. Clearly, a man who knew what he was doing had severed Winter's body parts, and the inspectors at first never believed someone like Masloff to have been capable of such precision. But other clues suggested a less than masterly exactitude. When trained butchers sever the intestinal cord of a cow, they usually cut it out whole, but in the original sack with the upper torso found in the Mönchsee, the authorities also discovered an intestinal sliver about ten centimeters in length. This was the kind of journeyman's mistake one expected of people who slaughter animals on occasion, as farmhands often did. When Masloff worked for Borrmann, he slaughtered sheep.

Two more unanswered questions of the investigation involved the sack from the store of the tailor Plath and the string, which was neatly tied. Naturally, the inspectors thought of butchers who both cut and pack their meat, as both Gustav Hoffmann and Adolph Lewy did. But here, too, evidence appeared that points to Masloff and his family, in particular his mother-in-law. Anna Ross not only sent her hired girls to clean at the tailor Plath's; she also washed and cleaned there herself. Furthermore, when she was in prison, a Berlin inspector asked her to sew a seam, and the knot she used closely resembled the knot with which the package containing the torso was fastened.

It was an article of faith to investigators that the crime had occurred on the banks of the Mönchsee, or very close to it. The police assumed this because they could not imagine a man carrying a torso across a busy town, but the upper and lower torso were wrapped, and why would one wrap body parts and bind them neatly with a string if only to throw them into the lake? More plausibly, those parts were carried, perhaps by more than one person, from Postallstrasse 162, a quiet, nearly windowless building in a dark street. Getting to the Mönchsee from there entailed walking only through dark alleys, save for a quick crossing of the Danzigerstrasse. The route to the Mönchsee was, then, no more precarious than it would have been for either Gustav Hoffmann or Adolph Lewy, and the cutting could more easily have been done in isolation, in the cellar.

In addition, the curious comings and goings of Bernhard Masloff and his wife in the days after the discovery of Winter's torso need to be explained. On Wednesday, they had taken their child in a carriage and walked back into town from their apartment in Hohe Höfe in order to stay the night with the Bergs and Anna Ross. "It was spooky," Masloff supposedly said, as if "a hand were twitching at the bed." The path from Hohe Höfe to the Postallstrasse led past the Protestant cemetery, where one witness apparently saw the Masloffs and where, we may recall, the left arm was found. There were footprints in the freshly fallen snow, a narrow gait—the footprints of Martha Masloff? On the Tuesday after Winter's death, Anna Ross and Martha Masloff, who had been sick on the day after the murder, walked to the village of Klein Konitz to pick up meat, and in order to carry the meat they took their baby carriage with them. The path to Klein Konitz led past the Hohe Höfe, the Jewish cemetery, the shooting club, and the Dunkershagen farm, where the head of Ernst Winter was buried.

With Masloff at the center of the story, the pieces interlock more forcefully than in previous scenarios, and the inspectors in Berlin believed that the material more than sufficed to go ahead with an indictment. Repeatedly, they wrote the district attorney in Konitz, urging him "to publicly and sharply proceed against the family of Masloff-

Berg-Ross."[9] But Chied Prosecutor Schweigger, who had refused to reopen the case against Hoffmann, stubbornly declined. Inspector Braun thought that Schweigger should be forced to act. Even people in Konitz did not "consider the suspicion unjustified."[10] If Schweigger was unwilling, Braun was unrelenting. Three years later, in 1907, he followed a lead in Halberstadt, the city in Saxony where Masloff and his family now lived. A neighbor had overheard the Masloffs incriminating each other in the heat of one of their many violent arguments. According to Inspector Braun, the grounds for an arrest were now "fundamentally more compelling."[11] Convinced of the plausibility of the charge, the authorities called in a district attorney from the nearby city of Halle. But rather than support Braun's suppositions, the district attorney argued that the neighbor who denounced Masloff was herself of ill repute, and the possibility that back in March 1900, Martha Masloff, a married woman, would have slept with a Gymnasium student in her own mother's apartment on a Sunday afternoon, when her husband was only a few blocks away at a local pub, remained absurd. The attorney who weighed in on the case had just been promoted to his new position in Halle from a provincial outpost in West Prussia, and he had prior knowledge of the case. The new prosecutor was none other than the erstwhile Schweigger.[12]

I I I

The town settled down in the years following the investigation, and even prospered to a degree. But because Konitz was located in the east, it stood exposed to the coming crosswinds of history. After World War I, Konitz fell just across the border into the so-called Polish Corridor and became the town of Chojnice. The German population, including Jews, declined precipitously, as the vast majority migrated westward to the cities and towns of the Weimar Republic. By 1921, only 3,500 Germans were left in a town of 10,500 people.[13] Both the majority of Poles and the minority of Germans rallied around their respective banners of nationality, with social and even religious life reduced to the cultivation of ethnic identity. "In the opinion of leading figures in the community, the value of the Protestant church essentially lies in its being a stronghold of Germandom," a church authority justifiably lamented.[14] In the course of this polarization, the Jews unmistakably sided with the Germans. This was already evident in 1919, when the Association of Jewish Communities in West Prussia issued a declaration against any measures "sacrificing their Germandom." "They would find it especially terrible," the Jewish communities of West Prussia declared, "to be at the mercy of Polish arbitrariness and intolerance."[15] Evidently, anti-Semitism remained ubiquitous throughout interwar Central Europe, and Jews perceived that it was worse among Poles than Germans. It also seems that their worst fears proved innocuous when compared with the murderous violence that rained down on the Jewish community just two decades later.

When German armies rolled across the Polish border on September 1, 1939, at the commencement of World War II, the Germans of Konitz, who were organized into "national self-protection societies," turned on their Polish and Jewish neighbors. According to the researches of Christian Jansen and Arno Weckbecker, the killing started on September 26, when 40 Poles and Jews were shot. On the next day, in the nearby village of Krojanke (Krojanty), at least 3 more people were killed, one of them a Polish priest from Konitz. Taking their lead from the Nazis, who were now planning to eliminate thousands of mentally ill Germans, members of the national self-protection societies massacred 208 patients in a psychiatric ward in Konitz on September 28. The river of blood began to overflow. Between September and January, local Germans, supported by the Gestapo and the Wehrmacht, massacred 900 Poles and Jews from Konitz and the outlying villages. In October and November, 200 more patients of a psychiatric ward in outlying Kamin (Kamien Pomorski) were also killed.[16]

The Holocaust arrived early in Konitz. The violence in that fatal fall of 1939 began before the Jews of Poland were packed into the first ghettos, waiting stations for worse to come. The local slaughters also preceded the more organized massacres of the mobile killing units, the *Einsatzgruppen*, which began systematic genocide in the summer of 1941. Given the opportunity, ordinary men, the Germans of Konitz, willingly murdered their neighbors.

Chojnice is now a quiet Polish town where the events of the wider world barely create a stir. It has grown in size. But there is no Jewish cemetery anymore, nor is there a Protestant graveyard. The synagogue near the Mönchsee and the Protestant church on the marketplace have disappeared as well, replaced by the drab contours that frame this all-but-forgotten town. Even the lake has been drained. Yet the house of Adolph Lewy still stands, three doors down from Hoffmann's, both in the shadows of the Catholic church, which for centuries nurtured the ritual-murder tale.

Notes

ABBREVIATIONS

AZJ   *Allgemeine Zeitung des Judentums*
BLHA   Brandenburgisches Landeshauptarchiv Potsdam
CVdSjG Central Verein deutscher Staatsbürger jüdischen Glaubens
DZ   *Danziger Zeitung*
GStAPK Geheimes Staatsarchiv Preussischer Kulturbesitz, Berlin-Dahlem
IdR   *Im deutschen Reich*
JP   *Jüdische Presse*
KB   *Der Konitzer Blutmord vor dem Berliner Gericht*
LA   Landratamt
ML   *Der Prozeß gegen Moritz Lewy*
MP   *Der Prozeß gegen Masloff und Genossen*
MVAA   *Mitteilungen aus dem Verein zur Abwehr des Antisemitismus*
SZ   *Staatsbürgerzeitung*
XK   *Der Xantener Knabenmord vor dem Schwurgericht zu Cleve*

PROLOGUE

1. *MVAA* 11,11 (13 March 1901), 102.
2. This is what his childhood friend Stanislaw in Samotschin, in the province of Posen, told him. Ernst Toller, *Eine Jugend in Deutschland* (Hamburg, 1963), 17.

3. GStAPK, Rep. 77, Tit. 500, no. 50, Bd. 2, 30, Advocate Appelbaum to CVdSjG, 10 June 1900; *IdR* 6,5 (1900), 259; *JP* 31,24 (1900), 243.

4. *DZ* 42, 271 (13 June 1900).

5. Peter Gay, *Freud, Jews, and Other Germans: Masters and Victims in Modernist Culture* (New York, 1978), 9.

6. Margaret Lavinia Anderson, *Practicing Democracy: Elections and Political Culture in Imperial Germany* (Princeton, 2000).

7. Burtin Feldman, *The Nobel Prize: A History of Genius, Controversy, and Prestige* (New York, 2000), 398–400.

8. Charlotte Schoell-Glass, *Aby Warburg und der Antisemitismus* (Frankfurt am Main, 1998), 17–18, 91–92, 94–101.

9. Daniel Jonah Goldhagen, *Hitler's Willing Executioners: Ordinary Germans and the Holocaust* (New York, 1996), 15.

10. Despite its prominence, the Konitz affair has until recently escaped the scrutiny of modern historians of anti-Semitism. But see now Christoph Nonn, "Zwischenfall in Konitz: Antisemitismus und Nationalismus im preußischen Osten um 1900," *Historische Zeitschrift* 266,2 (1998), 387–418, whose methods and conclusions are very different from my own. See also, for a narrative account of the events, Bernhard Vogt, "Die 'Atmosphäre eines Narrenhauses': Eine Ritualmordlegende um die Ermordung des Schülers Ernst Winter in Konitz," in *Zur Geschichte und Kultur der Juden in Ost- und Westpreußen*, ed. Michael Brocke, Margret Heitmann, and Harald Lordick (Hildesheim, 2000), 545–78.

11. Shulamit Volkov, "The Social and Political Foundations of Late 19th Century Anti-Semitism," in *Sozialgeschichte Heute*, ed. Hans-Ulrich Wehler (Göttingen, 1974), 427.

12. For the history of German anti-Semitism, this is a remarkable state of affairs, especially given the importance of community studies to understanding phenomena that are in some ways similar. For example, there is no work on communal anti-Semitism that can match Paul Boyer and Stephen Nissenbaum, *Salem Possessed: The Social Origins of Witchcraft* (Cambridge, Mass., 1974). But see now the essays in Werner Bergmann, Christhard Hoffmann, and Helmut Walser Smith, eds., *"Exclusionary Violence": Antisemitic Riots in Modern Germany* (Ann Arbor, 2002). For a remarkable local study on a different topic, but one in which many of the same communal pressures operate, see David Blackbourn, *Marpingen: Apparitions of the Virgin Mary in a Nineteenth-Century German Village* (New York, 1994).

13. To gauge the state of the field, see the introduction to Bergmann, Hoffmann, and Smith, eds., *"Exclusionary Violence,"* and the literature cited there.

14. On the methods of microhistory, see Giovanni Levi, "On Microhistory," in *New Perspectives on Historical Writing*, ed. Peter Burke (University Park, Pa., 1992), 93–113; Edward Muir, "Introduction: Observing Trifles," in *Microhistory and the Lost Peoples of Europe*, ed. Edward Muir and Guido Ruggiero (Baltimore, 1991), xxi; Jacques Revel, "Microanalysis and the Construction of the Social," in *Histories: French Constructions of the Past*, ed. Jacques Revel and Lynn Hunt (New York, 1995), 491–502; and, for a slightly different tradition, but with overlapping concerns, Alf Lüdtke, ed., *Alltagsgeschichte: Zur Rekonstruktion historischer Erfahrungen und Lebensweisen* (Frankfurt am Main, 1989).

15. Eva Hoffmann, *Shtetl: The Life and Death of a Small Town and the World of the Polish Jews* (London, 1988), 16.

CHAPTER ONE: MURDER AND RETRIBUTION

1. GStAPK, Rep. 77, Tit. 500, no. 50, Bd. 2, 46, Horn, 16 June 1900.

2. For temperature readings in March and April, as well as lunar position and snowfalls, see *Der Prozeß gegen Masloff und Genossen (Konitz, 25.10–10.11.1900) nach stenographischer Aufnahme* (Berlin, 1900), 127–30 (hereafter *MP*). For a sense of the state of vegetation, see also photographs in Kazimierza Lemanczyka and Hanny Rzaski, *Chojnice Miasto i Ludzie na Starej Fotografii* (Chojnice, 1998).

3. *SZ* 36, 423 (10 Sept. 1900).

4. GStAPK, Rep. I/84a (2.5.1), Nr. 16774, 13, Settegast, 31 March 1900.

5. See his statement in the Israelski trial, the stenographic record of which is reprinted in *MVAA* 10,37 (12 Sept. 1900), 290–92.

6. *MVAA* 10,14 (4 April 1900), 105; *Der Konitzer Blutmord vor dem Berliner Gericht: Die Verhandlungen des Pressprozesses gegen die "Staatsbürgerzeitung" vor der II. Strafkammer des Königl. Landgerichts I* (Berlin, 1902), 8 (hereafter *KB*).

7. GStAPK, Rep. I/84a (2.5.1), Nr. 16774, Settegast, 26 June 1900.

8. *MVAA* 10,14 (4 April 1900), 105; *KB*, 8.

9. Bruno Borowka, *Aus Sage und Geschichte von Konitz* (Konitz, 1919), 101–2.

10. GStAPK, Rep. I/84a (2.5.1), Nr. 16774, 14, Settegast, 31 March 1900.

11. GStAPK, Rep. 77, Tit. 500, no. 50, Bd. 2, 133, Konferenz zur Winterschen Mordsache, 24 May 1900.

12. *MVAA* 10,37 (12 Sept. 1900), 290–92. Pictures of Winter's family can be found in *Der Blutmord in Konitz*, with an intro. by Max Liebermann von Sonnenberg, 8th ed. (Berlin, 1901), 10.
13. *Der Prozeß gegen Moritz Lewy (Konitz, 13.–16. Februar 1901) nach stenographischer Aufnahme* (Berlin, 1901), 257 (hereafter *ML*).
14. *DZ*, 42,247 (20 May 1900).
15. GStAPK, Rep. 77, Tit. 500, no. 50, Bd. 2, 133, Konferenz zur Winterschen Mordsache, 24 May 1900.
16. *Die Gutachten der Sachverständigen über den Konitzer Mord*, ed. CVdSjG (Berlin, 1903), 9.
17. Ibid., 19–20.
18. Ibid., 6–9.
19. GStAPK, Rep. I/84a (2.5.1), Nr. 16774, 14, Settegast, 31 March 1900.
20. GStAPK, Rep. 77, Tit. 500, no. 50, Bd. 1, 8, Konitz, 31 March 1900.
21. Ibid.
22. Ibid.
23. Ibid.
24. Ibid.,12 *Konitzer Tageblatt*, 29 March 1900. (The warning was dated 27 March 1900.)
25. *SZ*, 36,144, Beilage (27 March 1900).
26. *MP*, 180. The photograph was developed at the end of March, and sales began on 12 April.
27. *DZ*, 42,179 (18 April 1900); *SZ*, 36,179 (18 April 1900).
28. GStAPK, Rep. 77, Tit. 500, no. 50, Bd. 2, 18, Settegast, 10 June 1900; GStAPK, Rep. I/84a (2.5.1), Nr. 16774, 45, Wulff, 2 May 1900.
29. GStAPK, Rep. 77, Tit. 500, no. 50, Bd. 1, 90, LA Konitz, 18 April 1900; *IdR* 6, 4 (1900), 214–15. The provincial court (*Landgericht*) found the evidence against Israelski insufficient. See GStAPK, I/84a (2.5.1) Nr. 16775, Staatsanwaltschaft Konitz, 10 Sept. 1900. A stenographic record of the Israelski trial is printed in *MVAA* 10,37 (12 Sept. 1900), 290–92.
30. *MVAA* 10,37 (12 Sept. 1900), 290–92.
31. *MVAA* 10,36 (5 Sept. 1900), 290.
32. *MVAA* 10,37 (12 Sept. 1900), 290–92; *MVAA* 10,17 (25 April 1900), 129.
33. GStAPK, Rep. 77, Tit. 500, no. 50, Bd. 2, 142, Kommittee zur Winterschen Mordsache, Konitz, 24 May 1900.
34. *IdR* 6,4 (1900), 214–15.
35. Cited in Michael A. Meyer, ed., *German-Jewish History in Modern Times*, 4 vols. (New York, 1996–98), 3:3, 153.

36. Ibid., 7.
37. Ibid., 11, 15.
38. Ibid., 15–16.
39. Steven Lowenstein estimates that at the end of World War I the majority of German Jews fell into one of these two categories. See his contribution in ibid., 153.
40. Ibid., 103.
41. GStAPK, Rep. 77, Tit. 500, no. 50, Bd. 1, 96, general secretary of the CVdSjG, Alphonse Lewy, to the Prussian minister of the interior, 21 April 1900.
42. Ibid., 31, telegram from Schlochau, 23 April 1900.
43. Ibid.
44. Ibid., 33, telegram from Schlochau, 24 April 1900.
45. *MVAA* 10,19 (9 May 1900), 145.
46. GStAPK, Rep. 77, Tit. 500, no. 50, Bd. 1, 25, *DZ*, 23 April 1900.
47. Ibid., 94, LA Flatow, 23 April 1900.
48. Ibid., 87, LA Konitz, 23 April 1900.
49. *MVAA* 10,18 (2 May 1900), 138.
50. *MVAA* 10,15 (11 April 1900), 115; *MVAA* 10,17 (25 April 1900), 130.
51. *DZ*, 42,157 (3 April 1900).
52. *DZ*, 42,217 (10 May 1900).
53. GStAPK, Rep. 77, Tit. 500, no. 50, Bd. 1, 69, Magistrat der Stadt Konitz, 27 April 1900.
54. GStAPK, Rep. I/84a (2.5.1), Nr. 16774, 50, Wulff, 2 May 1900.
55. *MVAA* 10,18 (2 May 1900), 137; *MVAA* 11,3 (16 Jan. 1901), 20.
56. *IdR* 16,5 (May 1900), 259.
57. *MVAA* 12,42 (15 Oct. 1902), 323.
58. *SZ*, 36,137 (22 March 1900); *SZ*, 36,198 (29 April 1900).
59. GStAPK, Rep. 14/181, Nr. 31519, 13; Oberregierungsrat Gyzicki, Konitz, 28 April 1900.
60. Moshe Zimmermann, *Wilhelm Marr: The Patriarch of Anti-Semitism* (New York, 1986), 92–93, 112–13.
61. Cited in *German-Jewish History in Modern Times*, 3: 206.
62. Ibid., 207.
63. Otto Pflanze, *Bismarck and the Development of Germany*, vol. 3 (Princeton, 1990), 50–51.
64. On the expulsions, see Helmut Neubach, *Die Ausweisung von Polen und Juden aus Preussen 1885/6* (Wiesbaden, 1967), esp. 120–39. For its context within anti-Jewish politics, see Jack Wertheimer, *Unwelcome*

Strangers: East European Jews in Imperial Germany (Oxford, 1987), 47–49.

65. BLHA, Rep. 30, Tit. 94, Nr. 8749, bl. 91, 108, 116, 129.

66. Richard S. Levy, *The Downfall of the Anti-Semitic Political Parties in Imperial Germany* (New Haven, 1975), 192–94.

67. Stephen Wilson, *Ideology and Experience: Antisemitism in France at the Time of the Dreyfus Affair* (East Brunswick, N.J., 1982), 106–24.

68. *MVAA* 10,36 (5 Sept. 1900), 282.

69. Cited in Hermann L. Strack, *The Jew and Human Sacrifice*, trans. Henry Blanchamp (New York, 1909), 230.

70. To this day, Leopold Hilsner has still not been cleared, despite a recent appeal to President Václav Havel of the Czech Republic.

71. On Polna, see the excellent essay by Georg R. Schroubek, "Der 'Ritualmord' von Polna: Traditioneller und moderner Wahnglaube," in *Antisemitismus und jüdische Geschichte: Studien zu Ehren von Herbert A. Strauss*, ed. Rainer Erb and Michael Schmidt (Berlin, 1987), 149–71.

72. GStAPK, Rep. 77, Tit. 500, no. 50, Bd. 1, 251, Regierungspräsident Marienwerder, 31 May 1900.

73. On Hammer, see *Die evangelischen General-Kirchen- und Schulvisitationen in Ost- und Westpreußen, 1853 bis 1944*, ed. Iselin Gundermann and Walther Hubatsch (Göttingen, 1970), 229. See also GStAPK, Rep. 77, Tit. 500, no. 50, Bd. 1, 148; *DZ*, 3 June 1900. The text of Hammer's oration is reprinted in *SZ* 36,245 (28 May 1900).

74. GStAPK, Rep. 77, Tit. 500, no. 50, Bd. 1, 159, chief of police in Berlin to Prussian minister of the interior, 18 May 1900.

75. He is not listed in *Das Bürgerbuch der Stadt Konitz von 1550–1850*, ed. Elisabeth Kloß (Danzig, 1927), 72–86. But, according to *ML*, 2, his son Moritz was born in Konitz on 9 Dec. 1871. Adolph Lewy is listed as a resident of the Danzigerstrasse in the 1885 census. See Archiv Panstwowe w Bydgoszcz/Akta Miasta Chojnice, 1675/161.

76. Dietz Bering, *Der Name als Stigma: Antisemitismus im Deutschen Alltag, 1812–1933* (Stuttgart, 1987), 55.

77. In 1812, the official gazette of the West Prussian district of Marienwerder published a list of some 2,300 Jewish names. See *General-Verzeichniß sämmtlicher in dem Departement der königlichen Regierung von Westpreußen vorhandenen Juden welchen das Staatsbürger-Recht ertheilt worden* (Marienwerder, 1812).

78. Peter Letkemann, "Zur Geschichte der Juden in Konitz im 19. Jahrhundert," *Beiträge zur Geschichte Westpreußens* 9 (1985), 108.

79. Ibid., 113. For an account emphasizing the poverty of the Jews in the early nineteenth century, see Kazimierez Wajda, "Die Juden im südlichen Westpreußen (Regierungsbezirk Marienwerder) im 19. Jahrhundert: Zahl und soziale Schichtung," in *Zur Geschichte und Kultur der Juden in Ost- und Westpreußen* (Hildesheim, 2000), 347.

80. *Das Bürgerbuch der Stadt Konitz von 1550–1850*, 72–86. For the period until 1850, we can say with certainty that the Jews of Konitz came from the surrounding area. Of the sixty Jewish men who moved to Konitz and, as heads of households, applied to be citizens of the town, only seven were not from the immediate area.

81. In 1843, there were 288 Jews in Konitz; in 1871, 497; in 1885, 563. See Letkemann, "Zur Geschichte der Juden in Konitz," 113.

82. Of 169 marriages between 1873 and 1876 in the town of Konitz, only one involved a Christian and a Jew. Church of Jesus Christ of Latter Day Saints, Family Library, film no. 1189050, Konitz, Standesamt, Zivilregister, 1877. In West Prussia between 1880 and 1900, 151 Jews converted to Protestantism. On migration, see Max Aschkewitz, *Zur Geschichte der Juden in Westpreussen* (Marburg, 1967), 178–80. Between 1885, at its height, and 1910, the Jewish population of Konitz County declined from 563 to 256, or 55 percent.

83. GStAPK, Rep. 77, Tit. 500, no. 50, Bd. 2, 18, Settegast, 10 June 1900.

84. Ibid., 18–19, Settegast, 10 June 1900.

85. *MP*, 331.

86. Gustav Sutor, *Der Konitzer Mord und seine Folgen* (Berlin, 1900), 14.

87. *SZ*, 229 (17 May 1900).

88. *KB*, 13.

89. *MVAA* 11,51 (18 Dec. 1901), 424.

90. GStAPK, Rep. 77, Tit. 500, no. 50, Bd. 1, 78, *Berliner Zeitung*, 30 May 1900. Borowka, *Aus Sage und Geschichte von Konitz*, 104.

91. *KB*, 9–10, 17, 21.

92. GStAPK, Rep. I/84a (2.5.1), Nr. 16777, 85, Schweigger, 17 July 1901; ibid., Nr. 16776, 291–92, von Kracht, 26 March 1901.

93. Ibid., Nr. 16776, 68, Lantz, 17 Dec. 1900.

94. Ibid., Nr. 16777, 91, Schweigger, 17 July 1901.

95. Ibid., 87, Schweigger, 17 July 1901.

96. Ibid., Nr. 16774, 107, Settegast, 30 May 1900.

97. Ibid., Inspector Wehn, 3 July 1900.

98. Ibid., 294, Settegast, 4 July 1900; ibid., Nr. 16777, 89, Schweigger, 17 July 1901.

99. Ibid., Nr. 16777, 85–86, Schweigger, 17 July 1901.
100. Ibid., Nr. 16774, 108, Settegast, 30 May 1900.
101. *MVAA* 12,42 (15 October 1902), 323.
102. GStAPK, Rep. 77, Tit. 500, no. 50, Bd. 1, 206, LA Konitz, 29 May 1900.
103. *IdR* 6,6–7 (1900), 399.
104. On the *Konitzer Tageblatt*, see *MVAA* 10,27 (4 April 1900), 212–13; *MVAA* 11,13 (27 March 1901), 115.
105. GStAPK, Rep. 77, Tit. 500, no. 50, Bd. 1, 206, LA Konitz, 29 May 1900; *MP*, 591–92.
106. Ibid., 210, LA Konitz, 30 May 1900.
107. Ibid., 191–93, LA Konitz, 31 May 1900.
108. Ibid., 222, LA Konitz, 4 June 1900.
109. Ibid. See also GStAPK, Rep. 77, Tit. 500, no. 50, Bd. 2, 30, Advocate Appelbaum to CVdSjG, 10 June 1900.
110. *MVAA* 10,23 (6 June 1900), 176.
111. GStAPK, Rep. 77, Tit. 500, no. 50, Bd. 1, 214, "An unsere Mitbürger," 1 June 1900.
112. Ibid., 216, Polizeiverwaltung Konitz, "Warnung," 1 June 1900.
113. GStAPK, Rep. I/84a (2.5.1), Nr. 16774, 134, Settegast, 10 June 1900.
114. GStAPK, Rep. 77, Tit. 500, no. 50, Bd. 1, 191–93, LA Konitz, 31 May 1900.
115. Ibid.
116. Ibid., Bd. 2, 30, Advocate Appelbaum to CVdSjG, 10 June 1900.
117. Ibid., 105, LA Konitz, 11 June 1900.
118. Ibid.
119. Ibid., Bd. 1, 254, LA Konitz, 8 June 1900.
120. Ibid., 270, LA Konitz, 9 June 1900.
121. Ibid.
122. Ibid., 254, LA Konitz, 8 June 1900.
123. GStAPK, Rep. I/84a (2.5.1), Nr. 16774, 139–40, Settegast, 10 June 1900.
124. *MVAA* 10,24 (13 June 1900), 186, citing *SZ*, 8 June 1900.
125. GStAPK, Rep. 77, Tit. 500, no. 50, Bd. 1, 261, Zedlitz, 6 June 1900. The parents had notified the police, however, and the boys were soon found wandering around in Tuchel and Frankenhagen. Ibid., 270, LA Konitz, 9 June 1900; ibid., 263, LA Konitz, 7 June 1900.
126. *DZ*, 42,271 (13 June 1900).

127. GStAPK, Rep. 77, Tit. 500, no. 50, Bd. 2, 2, report of LA Konitz, probably 10 June 1900.

128. Ibid.

129. Ibid., 1–6, report of LA Konitz, probably 10 June 1900.

130. Ibid., 30, Advocate Appelbaum to CVdSjG, 10 June 1900. GStAPK, Rep. I/81a, Nr. 16775. 136, 21 Aug. 1900.

131. GStAPK, Rep. 77, Tit. 500, no. 50, Bd. 2, 5, report LA Konitz, probably 10 June 1900.

132. Ibid., 30, Advocate Appelbaum to CVdSjG, 10 June 1900.

133. On the parallel demonstration, which also included the usual assaults on Jewish property, see ibid., 74, LA Tuchel, 11 June 1900.

134. *Berliner Neueste Nachrichten*, 12 June 1900.

135. *JP* 31,24 (1900), 243–44.

136. GStAPK, Rep. 77, Tit. 500, no. 50, Bd. 2, 116, LA Berent, 12 June 1900; ibid., 121, Regierungspräsident Bromberg, 18 June 1900.

137. On Hammerstein, see ibid., 63, Regierungspräsident Marienwerder, 12 June 1900, and *JP* 31,26 (1900), 264–65; on Janowitz, *JP* 31,25 (1900), 258.

138. *IdR* 6,9 (1900), 461, 471. Krajetski received four years in jail for assault.

139. *JP* 31,26 (1900), 265.

140. GStAPK, Rep. 77, Tit. 500, no. 50, Bd. 2, 42, LA Konitz, 14 June 1900. For the same statement a week later, see ibid., 150, LA Konitz, 22 June 1900.

CHAPTER TWO: THE BUTCHER'S TALE AND OTHER STORIES

1. Cited by Jan Romein, *The Watershed of Two Eras: Europe in 1900*, trans. Arnold J. Pomerans (Middletown, Conn., 1978), 111–12.

2. Peter Fritzsche, *Reading Berlin 1900* (Cambridge, Mass., 1996), 53–59.

3. *Wer ist's*, ed. Hermann A. L. Degener, 3rd ed. (Leipzig, 1908), 176.

4. For the classic distinction between "living for" and "living from" politics, see Max Weber, *Wirtschaft und Gesellschaft*, 5th ed., ed. Johannes Winckelmann (Tübingen, 1976), 829–30.

5. *IdR* 7,11 (1901), 78, 87.

6. *MP*, 590.

7. For train timetables to Konitz, see DZ, 42,451, Beilage (26 Sept. 1900).

8. Max Weber, *Die Lage der Landarbeiter im ostelbischen Deutschland: 1892*, ed. Martin Riesebrodt, vol. 1, pt. 3, of *Max Weber Gesammtausgabe*, ed. Horst Baier et al. (Tübingen, 1984), 324.

9. Ibid., 964–65.

10. Wilhelm Fuhrmann, *Statistik des Kreises Konitz* (Konitz, 1870), 18.

11. Leszek Belzyt, *Sprachliche Minderheiten im preußischen Staat, 1815–1914* (Marburg, 1998), 107.

12. Michael A. Meyer, ed., *German-Jewish History in Modern Times*, vol. 2, *Emancipation and Acculturation, 1780–1871*, ed. Michael Brenner, Stefi Jersch-Wenzel, and Michael Meyer (New York, 1997), 54–57.

13. These names are taken from an anti-Semitic postcard sent on 28 July 1900 and signed by seventeen "real German men," among them Paul Kühn, the hotel owner. It cannot be proven that they were guests at Kühn's hotel, though the likelihood is very high. *MVAA* 11,30 (24 July 1901), 254.

14. Iselin Gundermann and Walter Hubatsch, eds., *Die evangelischen General-Kirchen- und Schulvisitationen in Ost- und Westpreußen 1853 bis 1944* (Göttingen, 1970), 228.

15. *KB*, 9. We know that Bruhn sent free copies of the *Staatsbürgerzeitung* to citizens of Konitz, among them Mayor Deditius.

16. GStAPK, Rep. I/84a (2.5.1), Nr. 16777, 85, Schweigger, 17 July 1901; ibid., Nr. 16776, 291–92, report of Inspector von Kracht, 26 March 1901. On the character of Kühn's hotel, *ML*, 22–23.

17. See *SZ* 36,270 (13 June 1900). The "Defense" was also reprinted in its entirety in *Antisemitische Correspondenz* 15 (14 June 1900), 277–81.

18. For its distribution, see *MVAA* 11,3 (16 Jan. 2001), 20; and *Antisemitische Correspondenz* (21 June 1900), Beilage.

19. *MP*, 813–14; *KB*, 13. The testimony is from Inspector Braun, who, however, was not sure whether it was Bruhn or the dentist Meibauer who said this. In the trial against the *Staatsbürgerzeitung*, Police Commissioner Block testified that Bruhn was alone, leaving two possibilities: either Bruhn (and not Meibauer) did indeed say this or Braun's memory was not entirely accurate.

20. According to the testimony of the engineer Kuby, *MP*, 712.

21. Gustav Sutor, *Der Konitzer Mord und seine Folgen* (Berlin, 1900), 16.

22. *KB*, 31.

23. Ibid., 5.

24. Ibid.

25. *MP*, 946.

26. GStAPK, Rep. 77, Tit. 500, no. 50, Bd. 2, 48, LA Konitz, 17 June 1900.

27. Gérard Genette, *Narrative Discourse: An Essay in Method*, trans. Jane E. Lewin (Ithaca, 1980), 262.

28. Robert Darnton, *The Forbidden Best-Sellers of Pre-Revolutionary France* (New York, 1995), 191.
29. Barbara Meyerhoff, " 'Life Not Death in Venice': Its Second Life," in *The Anthropology of Experience*, ed. Victor Turner and Edward M. Bruner (Urbana and Chicago, 1986), 263.
30. *MP,* 460.
31. Ibid., 463. The interrogation took place on 25 April, the deposition given under oath on 2 May.
32. GStAPK, Rep. I/84a (2.5.1), Nr. 16774, 155–56, Masloff deposition, 8 June 1900. The last detail he added at his subsequent trial. See *MP,* 8.
33. The deposition is in GStAPK, Rep. I/84a (2.5.1), Nr. 16774, 143–47.
34. The deposition of 2 June is in ibid., 11–36.
35. *MP,* 59.
36. GStAPK, Rep. I/84a (2.5.1), Nr. 16774, Anna Ross deposition, 28 April 1900.
37. *MP,* 86.
38. Ibid., 60, 87.
39. On this incident, see also *KB,* 31. Block was temporarily stationed in Konitz from 1 April to 31 August.
40. *MP,* 178.
41. Ibid., 919.
42. Ibid., 485–87.
43. Ibid., 481.
44. Ibid., 500, 507.
45. Ibid., 500–501.
46. Ibid.
47. Ibid., 501.
48. Ibid., 584–85.
49. On Zimmer, see *ML,* 330; *MP,* 719.
50. Genette, *Narrative Discourse,* 262; *SZ,* 1 May 1900; *SZ* 2 May 1900.
51. *SZ,* 19 May 1900.
52. *SZ,* 29 May 1900.
53. SZ, 1 June 1900.
54. *MP,* 469.
55. *MVAA* 10,46 (14 Nov. 1900), 361.
56. GStAPK, Rep. 77, Tit. 500, no. 50, Bd. 3, 101, joint memorandum of the minister of justice and of the interior, 11 Nov. 1900.
57. *MP,* 1.

58. *IdR* 7,11 (1910), 596.
59. *MVAA* 10,45 (7 Nov. 1900), 354.
60. Ibid.
61. *ML*, 397.
62. *MP*, 1074.
63. *MVAA* 10,47 (21 Nov. 1900), 370.
64. *IdR* 6,6–7 1900), 331.
65. *JP* 31,19 (1900), 189.
66. *IdR* 6,6–7 (1900), 331.
67. GStAPK, Rep. I/84a (2.5.1), Nr. 16777, 104–5, Schweigger, 25 July 1901.
68. Ibid.
69. Ibid.
70. GStAPK, Rep. 77, Tit. 500, no. 50, Bd. 1, 140–1. Kommittee zur Winterchen Mordsache, 24 May 1900.
71. Ibid.; *MP*, 611–12.
72. For the story of Paul Orda, see GStAPK, Rep. I/84a (2.5.1), Nr. 16774, 213–20, Settegast, 6 June 1900.
73. *ML*, 118. On Lübke, see *MP*, 416–17.
74. *MP*, 423.
75. *KB*, 29.
76. GStAPK, Rep. I/84a (2.5.1), Nr. 16776, 224–29, deposition of Johann Winkelmann, 11 June 1900.
77. Ibid., 207–8, Anlage zu Settegast, 18 June 1900.
78. *MP*, 548–49.
79. Ibid., 646, 861. When he was younger, Hellwig supposedly believed in witches.
80. Ibid., 669–70.
81. Ibid., 678.
82. Ibid., 669ff.
83. Ibid., 861; *MVAA* 10,45 (7 Nov. 1900), 355–56.
84. *SZ*, Nr. 150 (30 March 1900). The word for Jewish girl is "Schicksel," which in more modern Yiddish has come to mean Christian girl, but in earlier times as often meant Jewish girls, especially those who were not pious and did not keep a kosher household. The unabridged *Muret-Sanders* of 1905 offers only "Jewish girl" as a translation. Moreover, given the stories about Winter and Selma Tuchler and Meta Caspari, this meaning can also be derived from the context.
85. *MVAA* 10,25 (20 June 1900), 196.

86. Henry Louis Gates, ed., *Race, Writing, and Difference* (Chicago, 1985), 5.
87. The story is recounted in *MP,* 910–11.
88. Ibid., 933.
89. Ibid., 920–21.
90. Ibid., 934.
91. Ibid., 372, 383.
92. Ibid., 382.
93. Ibid., 237; *IdR* 4 (1901), 230.
94. *MVAA* 12,42 (15 Oct. 1902), 321.
95. *KB,* 7–8.
96. Peter Brooks, *Reading for the Plot: Design and Intention in Narrative* (New York, 1984), 12.
97. See, in general, Toni Morrison, *Playing in the Dark: Whiteness and the Literary Imagination* (New York, 1992).
98. *The Riverside Chaucer,* ed. Larry D. Benson, 3rd ed. (Boston, 1987), 210.
99. Morrison, *Playing in the Dark,* xi.

CHAPTER THREE: HISTORY

1. Quoted in Christopher Ocker, "Ritual Murder and the Subjectivity of Christ: A Choice in Medieval Christianity," *Harvard Theological Review* 91,2 (1998), 175–76.
2. On the early period, see esp. Bernhard Blumenkranz, *Juifs et Chrétiens dans le monde occidental, 430–1096* (Paris, 1960), and, for substantial agreement, albeit with caveats, Robert Chazan, *European Jewry and the First Crusade* (Berkeley, 1987), 27–37.
3. Gavin Langmuir, *History, Religion, and Antisemitism* (Berkeley, 1990), 298–99. Among scholars of medieval history, one of the central points of contention is the role of Thomas of Monmouth in generating the myth. For the position that he was principally responsible, see Langmuir, *Toward a Definition of Antisemitism* (Berkeley, 1990), 209–36. For the argument that he was not, see John M. McCulloh, "Jewish Ritual Murder: William of Norwich, Thomas of Monmouth, and the Early Dissemination of the Myth," *Speculum* 72 (1997), 698–740.
4. *The Anglo-Saxon Chronicle,* trans. and ed. M. J. Swanton (London, 1996), 265–66. Erroneously, the scribe situated the murder among the events of 1137.
5. Robert Chazan, *Medieval Stereotypes and Modern Antisemitism* (Berkeley, 1997), 66.

6. Langmuir, *Toward a Definition of Antisemitism*, 216.
7. It is true that in the ancient world the idea that Jews engaged in ritual killing had surfaced before. The historian Posidonius related a case of cannibalism from the second century B.C.E. in which Jews fattened and ate a Greek soldier in order to express their antipathy. In the first century C.E., Apion in Alexandria recounted the tale, adding that the Jews did this every year. In the same century, Flavius Josephus, in *Against Apion*, also recounted the tale, if only to refute it. The other story that surfaced involved the Jews of Immenstar, in Syria, in the year 415 C.E. During the feast of Purim, some drunken Jews allegedly tied to a cross an effigy of Hamann (who in the Book of Esther unsuccessfully plots to kill all the Jews of the Persian Empire in the fifth century B.C.E.) and tortured the boy until he died. But the best evidence suggests that neither story—cannibalism in the second century, crucifixion in the fifth—had made its way to England by the middle of the twelfth century. For the argument, see Langmuir, *Toward a Definition of Antisemitism*, 211–16.
8. Charles Homer Haskins, *The Renaissance of the Twelfth Century* (Cambridge, 1928).
9. Chazan, *Medieval Stereotypes and Modern Antisemitism*, 11, 17, 21. For an excellent general overview, see also Michael Toch, *Die Juden im mittelalterlichen Reich* (Munich, 1998).
10. R. I. Moore, *The Formation of a Persecuting Society: Power and Deviance in Western Europe, 950–1250* (Oxford, 1987), 6–11.
11. Langmuir, *Toward a Definition of Antisemitism*, 264.
12. Cited in Hermann L. Strack, *The Jew and Human Sacrifice*, trans. Henry Blanchamp (New York, 1909), 179.
13. The texts, in Latin and German, are reproduced in *Dokumenten zur Aufklärung, vol. 2, Die Blutbeschuldigung gegen die Juden* (Vienna, 1900), 108–13.
14. Ibid., 114–17. See also, for commentaries on the text, Moritz Stern, ed., *Urkundliche Beiträge über die Stellung der Päpste zu den Juden* (Kiel, 1893), 63–69.
15. For a recent summary, see Robert Stacey, "From Ritual Crucifixion to Host Desecration: Jews and the Body of Christ," *Jewish History* 12,1 (Spring 1998), 12–13. For more detail, see Miri Rubin, *Corpus Christi* (Cambridge, 1991).
16. A translation of the decrees of the Fourth Lateran Council may be found in H. J. Schroeder, *Disciplinary Decrees of the General Councils: Text, Translation, and Commentary* (St. Louis, 1937), 236–96.

17. Quoted in Henry Osborn Taylor, *The Medieval Mind*, 4th ed., vol. 2 (Cambridge, Mass., 1949), 452. On the reception of Aristotle, and the timing of the translations, see Bernard G. Dod, "Aristotles latinus," in *The Cambridge History of Later Medieval Philosophy*, ed. Norman Kretzmann, Anthony Kenny, and Jan Pinborg (Cambridge, 1982), 45–79.

18. Cited in Rubin, *Corpus Christi*, 30.

19. Cited ibid., 14.

20. Beth A. Conklin, *Consuming Grief: Compassionate Cannibalism in an Amazonian Society* (Austin, 2001).

21. This insight I owe to Dr. Siegfried Weichlein of Humboldt University.

22. Langmuir, *Toward a Definition of Antisemitism*, 263–81. For this line of reasoning, see also Alan Dundes, *The Blood Libel Legend: A Casebook in Anti-Semitic Folklore* (Madison, Wis., 1991), 336–78.

23. Willi-Erich Peukert, "Ritualmord," *Handwörterbuch des deutschen Aberglaubens*, ed. Hanns Bächtold-Stäubli and E. Hoffmann-Krayer, 10 vols. (Berlin, 1927–42), 7:734.

24. Miri Rubin, *Gentile Tales: The Narrative Assault on Late Medieval Jews* (New Haven, 1999), 48. Friedrich Lotter, "Hostienfrevelvorwurf und Blutwundverfälschung bei den Judenverfolgungen von 1298 ('Rintfleisch') und 1336–1338 ('Armleder')," in *Fälschungen im Mittelalter*, ed. Monumenta Germaniae Historica (Hanover, 1988), 533–83.

25. Simon Dubnow, *Geschichte des jüdischen Volkes in Europa*, vol. 5 (Berlin, 1927), 298.

26. Quoted in Rubin, *Gentile Tales*, 50. According to Lotter, "Hostienfrevelvorwurf und Blutverfälschung," 553, the host desecration charge followed, rather than preceded, the massacres in Büren, Deggendorf, Würzburg, Weikersheim, Möckmühl, and Iphofen. See also ibid., 555, for the argument that Rintfleisch was more likely a butcher.

27. *Das Martyrologium des Nürnberger Memorbuches*, ed. Siegmund Saalfeld (Berlin, 1898), 346.

28. Rubin, *Gentile Tales*, 50.

29. To trace the Rintfleisch massacres, see the map appended to *Germania Judaica*, vol. 2, *Von 1238 bis zur Mitte des 14. Jahrhunderts*, ed. Zvi Avneri (Tübingen, 1968). For the fate of individual families, see the partial list of martyrs in *Das Martyrologium des Nürnberger Memorbuches*, 164–214.

30. Rubin, *Gentile Tales*, 50.

31. The reference is to Robert Conquest, *Reflections on a Ravaged Century* (New York, 2000).

32. Lotter, "Hostienfrevelvorwurf und Blutwundverfälschung," 564.
33. Ibid., 565–71.
34. Heinrich Graetz, *Volkstümliche Geschichte der Juden*, vol. 4 (Berlin and Vienna, 1923), 307.
35. Dubnow, *Weltgeschichte des jüdischen Volkes*, 300–309.
36. Alfred Haverkamp, "Die Judenverfolgung zur Zeit des Schwarzen Todes im Gesellschaftsgefüge deutscher Städte," in *Zur Geschichte der Juden im Deutschland des späten Mittelalters und der frühen Neuzeit*, ed. Alfred Haverkamp (Stuttgart, 1981), 27–93.
37. Dubnow, *Weltgeschichte des jüdischen Volkes*, 300–309; Haverkamp, "Die Judenverfolgung zur Zeit des Schwarzen Todes," 38.
38. For evidence that Job figures prominently in the Hebrew lamentations of the time, see *Das Martyrologium des Nürnberger Memorbuches*, 311–59.
39. *Germania Judaica*, 2:604. The stones of the staircase could be seen until 1917, when the staircase collapsed.
40. *Das Martyrologium des Nürnberger Memorbuches*, 180. See also Michael Toch, "Siedlungsstruktur der Juden Mitteleuropas im Wandel vom Mittelalter zur Neuzeit," in *Juden in der christlichen Umwelt während des späten Mittelalters*, ed. Alfred Haverkamp and Franz-Josef Ziwes (Berlin, 1992), 30.
41. Toch, "Siedlungsstruktur der Juden Mitteleuropas," 35–37.
42. For the view that Poland was not entirely hospitable, see Kacek Wijacka, "Die Einwanderung der Juden und antijüdische Exzesse im späten Mittelalter," in *Judenvertreibungen in Mittelalter und früher Neuzeit*, ed. Friedhelm Burgard, Alfred Haverkamp, and Gerd Mentgen (Hanover, 1999), 241–56.
43. On the trials, see Wolfgang Behringer, *Hexen: Glaube, Verfolgung, Vermarktung*, 2nd ed. (Munich, 2000), 35.
44. R. Po-chia Hsia, *The Myth of Ritual Murder: Jews and Magic in Reformation Germany* (New Haven, 1988), 42.
45. Wolfgang Treue, "Schlechte und gute Christen: Zur Rolle von Christen in antijüdischen Ritualmord- und Hostienschändungslegenden," *Ashkenaz* 2 (1992), 115.
46. Hsia, *The Myth of Ritual Murder*, 46–50.
47. Fritz Backhaus, "Die Vertreibung der Juden aus dem Erzbistum Magdeburg und angrenzenden Territorien im 15. und 16. Jahrhundert," in *Judenvertreibungen im Mittelalter*, 227, 239.
48. Moritz Stern, ed., *Andreas Osianders Schrift über die Blutbeschuldigung* (Kiel, 1893), 7–9.

49. Ibid.
50. Ludwig Geiger, *Das Studium der Hebräischen Sprache in Deutschland vom Ende des XIV. bis zur Mitte des XVI. Jahrhunderts* (Breslau, 1870). See also the brief comments in Ronnie Po-chia Hsia, "Witchcraft, Magic, and the Jews in Late Medieval and Early Modern Germany," in *From Witness to Witchcraft: Jews and Judaism in Medieval Christian Thought*, ed. Jeremy Cohen (Wiesbaden, 1996), 432–33.
51. Eisenmenger, *Entdecktes Judenthum*, vol. 2 (Königsberg, 1711), 227.
52. Hsia, *The Myth of Ritual Murder*, 217.
53. Ibid., 214.
54. Johann Jacob Schudt, *Jüdische Merkwürdigkeiten*, 4 vols. (Frankfurt am Main, 1714–17), 1:468, 3:328. The first story is taken from Christof Wagenseil.
55. Ibid., 3:329–30.
56. Ibid., 330.
57. Hsia, *The Myth of Ritual Murder*, 211–13; Johann Wolfgang Goethe, *Dichtung und Wahrheit*, in *Sämtliche Werke*, ser. 1, vol. 14 (Frankfurt am Main, 1986), 165.
58. Goethe, *Dichtung und Wahrheit*, 165. On Eisenmenger's *Entdecktes Judenthum* in the personal library of his father, see *German-Jewish History in Modern Times*, 1:157.
59. Rainer Erb and Albert Lichtblau, "'Es hat nie einen jüdischen Ritualmord gegeben.' Konflikte um die Abschaffung der Verehrung des Andreas von Rinn," *Oesterreichische Zeitschrift für Geschichtswissenschaft*, 17,3 (1989), 136–38.
60. Hsia, *The Myth of Ritual Murder*, 219–21. Indeed, the depiction in the nave of the church of Jews stabbing Andreas Oxner with knives remained there until well after World War II, when Simon Wiesenthal discovered it, and even then its removal awaited Vatican II. See Dundes, *The Blood Libel Legend*, 342–43. For the politics surrounding the removal of the anti-Semitic heritage of Rinn and Judenstein, see Bernhard Fresacher, *Anderl von Rinn: Ritualmordkult und Neuorientierung in Judenstein, 1945–1995* (Innsbruck, 1998).
61. R. Po-chia Hsia, *Trent 1475: Stories of a Ritual Murder Trial* (New Haven, 1992), 134.
62. Karl von Amira, ed., *Das Endinger Judenspiel* (Halle, 1883), 8.
63. Fr. Rohrbacher, *Ursula von Lienz: Ein von Juden gemartertes Christenkind* (Brixen, 1905), 13–14.
64. *Germania Judaica*, 2:666.

65. Ibid., 450.
66. Ludwig Steub, *Altbayrische Culturbilder* (Leipzig, 1869), 119.
67. The text of the song is printed ibid., 146–50. For the play, *Germania Judaica* 2:157.
68. Amira, ed., *Das Endinger Judenspiel*.
69. Hsia, *The Myth of Ritual Murder*, 40.
70. Stefan Rohrbacher and Michael Schmidt, *Judenbilder: Kulturgeschichte antijüdischer Mythen und antisemitischer Vorurteile* (Reinbeck-Hamburg, 1991), 287.
71. Zenon Gulden and Jacek Wijaczka, "The Accusation of Ritual Murder in Poland, 1500–1800," *Polin* 10 (1997), 139–40.
72. Zenon Gulden and Jacek Wijaczka, *Procesy o Mordy Rytulne w Polsce w XVI–XVIII* (Kielce, 1995), esp. 96–101.
73. Strack, *The Jew and Human Sacrifice*, 205.
74. Stephan Zuchowski, *Process kryminalny o niewinne dziecie Krasnowskiego juz to trzecie roku 1710 dnia 18 siepnia w Sendomirzu okrutinie od Zydow zamordowane* (n.p., 1713); On the Sandomierz case, see Gulden and Wijaczka, "The Accusation of Ritual Murder in Poland," 125–28.
75. For a summary and a refutation of this work, see Jacob Tugendhold, *Der alte Wahn vom Blutgebrauch der Israeliten am Osterfest* (Berlin, 1858). This pamphlet was originally published in Polish in 1836.
76. *Gutachten Ganganelli's in Angelegenheit der Blutbeschuldigung der Juden*, trans. A. Berliner (Berlin, 1888), 1.
77. Ibid., 41–43. See also Simon Dubnow, *History of the Jews in Russia and Poland*, trans. I. Friedlaender, 2 vols. (Philadelphia, 1916), 1:179–80. Cardinal Ganganelli was to become Pope Clement XIV.
78. In their inquisitorial methods, the Poles proved especially severe. See Dubnow, *History of the Jews in Russia and Poland*, 1:172–80.
79. Quoted in ibid., 175.
80. Cited in Stefan Rohrbacher, "Die 'Hep-Hep-Krawalle' und der 'Ritualmord' des Jahres 1819 zu Dormagen," in *Antisemitismus und jüdische Geschichte: Studien zu Ehren von Herbert A. Strauss*, ed. Rainer Erb and Michael Schmidt (Berlin, 1987), 137.
81. Rohrbacher and Schmidt, *Judenbilder*, 11–14.
82. Stefan Rohrbacher, "Ritualmord-Beschuldigungen am Niederrhein: Christlicher Aberglaube und antijudische Agitation im 19. Jahrhundert," *Menora* 1 (1990), 300. By the end of the nineteenth century, the Werner cult was, we may assume, still, or again, alive and well. In 1911, a new Werner

chapel was built, and a Catholic newsletter, *Pastor Bonus,* celebrated "the holy Werner" as the "last German martyr." See Stefan Rohrbacher, "Volksfrömmigkeit und Judenfeindschaft: Zur Vorgeschichte des politischen Antisemitismus im katholischen Rheinland," *Annalen des Historischen Vereins für den Niederrhein* 192–93 (1990), 131.

83. Rohrbacher, "Die 'Hep-Hep-Krawalle,' " 145.

84. See the map of Hep-Hep riots in Stefan Rohrbacher, *Gewalt im Biedermeier: Antijüdische Ausschreitungen in Vörmärz und Revolution (1815–1848/49)* (Frankfurt am Main, 1993), 127.

85. Jacob Katz, *Die Hep-Hep-Verfolgungen des Jahres 1819* (Berlin, 1994).

86. Rohrbacher, "Die 'Hep-Hep-Krawalle,' " 139.

87. *Elberfelder Zeitung,* 26 July 1834, cited in Strack, *The Jew and Human Sacrifice,* 206.

88. Rohrbacher, "Ritualmord-Beschuldigungen am Niederrhein," 304–6, 323, n. 62. The Jews were also accused, more than twenty years later, in Cologne in 1861.

89. Cited in Strack, *The Jew and Human Sacrifice,* 207.

90. Rolf Engelsing, "Die Perioden der Lesergeschichte in der Neuzeit," in Engelsing, *Zur Sozialgeschichte deutscher Mittel- und Unterschichten* (Göttingen, 1973), 140.

91. Johann Gustav Droysen, *Politische Schriften,* ed. Felix Gilbert (Munich, 1933), 3–4.

92. D. Chwolson, *Die Blutanklage und sonsterliche mittelalterliche Beschuldigungen der Juden* (Frankfurt am Main, 1901), 116–17.

93. Joseph S. Bloch, *My Reminiscences* (Vienna, 1923), 67.

94. Strack, *The Jew and Human Sacrifice,* 155–56. Eisenmenger's work was printed in 1700 but not published until 1710, because of efforts on the part of the Jewish community of Frankfurt am Main to halt its appearance. See Jacob Katz, *From Prejudice to Destruction: Anti-Semitism, 1700–1933* (Cambridge, Mass., 1980), 14.

95. Constantin Ritter Cholewa von Pawlikowski, *Der Talmud in der Theorie und in der Praxis,* 2nd ed. (Regensburg, 1881), 245–312.

96. Henri Desportes, *Le mystère du sang chez les juifs de tous les temps* (Paris, 1889), 53–250.

97. Bloch, *My Reminiscences,* 71.

98. *Das Martyrologium des Nürnberger Memorbuches,* 179–80.

99. On the violence in the early nineteenth century, see Rohrbacher, *Gewalt im Biedermeier.*

100. Irving Howe, *World of Our Fathers: The Journey of the East European*

Jews to America and the Life They Found and Made (New York, 1976), 5.

101. David Vital, *A People Apart: The Jews in Europe, 1789–1939* (Oxford, 1999), 282.

102. Disraeli cited in Howe, *World of Our Fathers*, 7.

103. Although only an estimate, the death toll may well have numbered in the hundreds. On the pogroms of 1881–84, see I. Michael Aronson, *Troubled Waters: The Origins of the 1881 Anti-Jewish Pogroms in Russia* (Pittsburgh, 1990). For pogroms in Russia generally, see John Klier and Shlomo Lambroza, eds., *Pogroms: Anti-Jewish Violence in Modern Russian History* (Cambridge, 1992).

104. The rough figures are from Zvi Gitelman, *A Century of Ambivalence: The Jews of Russia and the Soviet Union, 1881 to the Present*, 2nd ed. (Bloomington, 2001), 12. The quotation is from Howe, *World of Our Fathers*, 25.

105. Christhard Hoffmann, "Political Culture and Violence against Minorities: The Antisemitic Riots in Pomerania and West Prussia," in *"Exclusionary Violence": Antisemitic Riots in Modern German History*, ed. Werner Bergmann, Christhard Hoffmann, Helmut Walser Smith (Ann Arbor, 2002), 67–92.

106. Dubnow, *Weltgeschichte des jüdischen Volkes*, 10:106–7.

107. *MVAA* 11,51 (18 Dec. 1901), 424.

108. *JP*, 16,17 (23 April 1885), 166.

109. Ibid., 167; ibid., 15,20 (18 May 1884), 203.

110. *JP* 15,20 (15 May 1884), 203.

111. Otto Glagau, "Der Mord in Skurz vor Gericht," *Der Kulturkämpfer* (May 1885), 26.

112. *JP* 15,20 (15 May 1884), 204.

113. Simon Dubnow, *Weltgeschichte des jüdischen Volkes* (Berlin, 1929), 10: 50–51.

114. Glagau, "Der Mord in Skurz," 32.

115. *MVAA* 11,51 (18 Dec. 1901), 424.

116. Karl Mannheim, *Man and Society in an Age of Reconstruction* (New York, 1940), 279–81.

117. Strack, *The Jew and Human Sacrifice*, 222–23.

118. Ibid., 226–27.

119. *MVAA* 10,31 (1 Aug. 1900), 241–43.

120. *MVAA* 7,35 (28 Aug. 1897), 273–79.

121. *MVAA* 10,31 (1 Aug. 1900), 241–43.

122. *MVAA* 7,35 (28 Aug. 1897), 273–79.

123. *MVAA* 4,15 (15 April 15 1894), 241–43.
124. *MVAA* 10,31 (1 Aug. 1900), 241–43.
125. Judith R. Walkowitz, *City of Dreadful Delight: Narratives of Sexual Danger in Late-Victorian London* (Chicago, 1992), 204.
126. *Der Xantener Knabenmord vor dem Schwurgericht zu Cleve, 4.–14. Juli 1892; vollständiger Bericht* (Berlin, 1893), 17 (hereafter *XK*).
127. Ibid., 32.
128. Ibid., 16.
129. Ibid., 142.
130. Ibid., 408.
131. Ibid., 183.
132. Ibid., 407.
133. Ibid., 408.
134. Ibid., 327, cited in Schoeps, "Ritualmordbeschuldigung und Blutaberglaube," in *Köln und das rheinische Judentum*, ed. Jutta Bohnke-Kollwitz et al. (Cologne, 1984), 293.
135. *XK*, 327. For a comment on the *Landgerichtsrat's* observations, see *MVAA* 10,28 (11 Aug. 1900), 218.
136. *XK*, 268–69.
137. Ibid., 109.
138. Ibid., 162.
139. Bernd Kölling, "Blutige Illusionen: Ritualmorddiskurse und Antisemitismus im niederrheinischen Xanten am Ende des 19. Jahrhunderts," in *Agrarische Verfassung und politische Struktur: Studien zur Gesellschaftsgeschichte Preußens, 1700–1918*, ed. Wolfgang Neugebauer and Ralf Pröve (Berlin, 1998), 355–59.
140. Ibid., 358–59.
141. *XK*, 399.
142. For the role of the educated, see Kölling, "Blutige Illusionen," which argues convincingly that one cannot simply ascribe ritual-murder accusations to the uneducated or to the continuing vitality of superstition.
143. *XK*, 217.
144. Ibid., 18, 214–16.
145. See Bergmann, Hoffmann, and Smith, eds., *"Exclusionary Violence."*
146. Cited in *MVAA* 2,30 (24 July 1892), 253.
147. Cited in ibid.
148. Schoeps, "Ritualmordbeschuldigung und Blutaberglaube," 298.
149. *XK*, 473–75.
150. Ibid., 475.

151. Ibid.

152. Ibid., 386.

153. On the reaction of the press, see the illuminating work of Barnet P. Harston, "Judaism on Trial: Antisemitism in the German Courtroom (1870–1895)" (Ph.D. diss., University of San Diego, 1999), 235–38.

154. On the debate in the Prussian Landtag, see Harston, "Judaism on Trial," 238–39; Schoeps, "Ritualmordbeschuldigung und Blutaberglaube," 290–92.

155. *XK*, 388.

156. Ibid. 387–88.

157. Harston, "Judaism on Trial," 245–49.

158. *JP* 23,29 (22 Aug. 1892), 559.

159. Rohrbacher, "Volksfrömmigkeit und Judenfeindschaft," 139; MVAA 2,31 (31 Aug. 1892), 267.

160. Edward Muir, *Mad Blood Stirring: Vendetta in Renaissance Italy*, readers edition (Baltimore, 1993), xxiv.

161. Peter Gay, *The Cultivation of Hatred* (New York, 1993), 35–127.

162. Adolph Kohut, *Ritual-Mord Prozesse* (Berlin, 1913), 37.

163. Wolfgang Treue, "Schlechte und gute Christen," 109.

164. Ibid., 102–3; Hsia, *Trent 1475*, 31.

165. Treue, "Schlechte und gute Christen," 103; Hsia, *The Myth of Ritual Murder*, 70.

166. Treue, "Schlechte und gute Christen," 102.

167. GStAPK, Rep. 77, Tit. 500, no. 50, Bd. 1, 42, Appendix 2 to LA Konitz, 25 April 1900.

168. Kohut, *Ritual-Mord Prozesse*, 37.

CHAPTER FOUR: ACCUSATIONS

1. *SZ* 36,303 (2 July 1900).

2. *KB*, 16.

3. *IdR* 6,6–7 (1900), 331.

4. GStAPK, Rep. I/84a (2.5.1), Nr. 16774, 51, Wulff, 2 May 1900; MVAA 12,42 (15 Oct. 1902), 322.

5. A sense of this can be gleaned from marriage registers, extant for 169 marriages between the years 1874 and 1877. See Church of Jesus Christ of Latter Day Saints, Family History Library, film no. 1189050, Konitz, Standesamt, Zivilregister, 1874–77. Of the men to be married, only 22 percent were actually born in Konitz; the rest came from the villages in Konitz county and in neighboring counties, as well as from other towns

in the area. Of the women, 36 percent were born here. Both of these figures suggest a high level of in-migration. Although the differences in the
kinds of sources used preclude precise comparisons with studies based
on immigration and emigration data, the evidence from Konitz tends to
support two contentions advanced by Steve Hochstadt, *Mobility and
Modernity: Migration in Germany, 1820-1989* (Ann Arbor, 1999),
107-34, that towns, and not merely large cities, experienced considerable
migration and that the period of high migration antedates 1881, the con-
ventional starting point for considering the empire's migration history.

6. This insight is based on the geographical origins of marriage patterns.
See Church of Jesus Christ of Latter Day Saints, Family History
Library, film no. 1189050, Konitz, Standesamt, Zivilregister, 1874-77.
Very few people came to Konitz from the larger cities. From Danzig,
there is not one person in the marriage register; from Berlin, only two.
Moreover, very few people made their way from the western parts of
Germany to Konitz.

7. See GStAPK XIV, 226B, vol. 12. In order to calculate the number of
heads of households earning under 900 marks, I have subtracted the
"Censisten" from the total heads of households reported in the census
of 1905. This procedure may slightly inflate the number of people
below the threshold. Conditions were certainly better in Konitz than in
the surrounding countryside, where 92 percent did not meet the threshold for income tax, and they were even better than in some of the other
West Prussian towns. On the economic conditions of the latter, see Karl
Bessier, *Die Kriminalität der Provinz Westpreussen* (Halle, 1915), 189;
for regional differences in income more generally, see Gerhard A. Ritter
and Klaus Tenfelde, *Arbeiter im Deutschen Kaiserreich, 1871 bis 1914*
(Bonn, 1992), 477-81.

8. The quotation is from Gustav George, *Enthüllungen zur Konitzer
Mordaffäre* (Berlin, 1903), 23.

9. Here and in what follows, the social composition of the streets is drawn
from the street lists in *Addressbuch der Stadt Konitz* (Konitz, 1905), a
copy of which can be found in the library of the Chojnice Local History
and Ethnography Museum. It has been supplemented by the Archiv
Panstwowe w Bydgoszcz/Akta Miasta Chojnice, 1675/161 Kontrol-
liste für die Volkszählung am 1. Dezember 1885, and various pieces of
evidence that surfaced in the trials and other documents. On the
Rähmstrasse as a dumping ground, see Hermann Hamburger, *Der
Konitzer Mord: Ein Beitrag zur Klärung* (Breslau, 1900), 12.

10. GStAPK, Rep. 77, Tit. 500, no. 50, Bd. 2, 262, Magistrat der Stadt Konitz, 4 Aug. 1900.
11. Similarly, in East Germany, at the height of the power of the state security forces, men made up 90 percent of the unofficial informants (IM) of the so-called Stasi. See Alf Lüdtke and Gerhard Fürmetz, "Denunziation und Denunzianten: Politische Teilnahme oder Selbstüberwachung?" *Sozialwissenschaftliche Informationen* 27,2 (1998), 82.
12. *ML*, 32.
13. Regina Schulte, *Sperrbezirke: Tugendhaftigkeit und Prostitution in der bürgerlichen Welt*, 2nd ed. (Frankfurt am Main, 1984), and Dorothee Wierling, *Mädchen für alles: Arbeitsalltag und Lebensgeschichte städtischer Dienstmädchen um die Jahrhundertwende* (Berlin, 1987).
14. On the Rosenthal case, see also Mathias Niendorf, *Minderheiten an der Grenze: Deutsche und Polen in den Kreisen Flatow (Zlotów) und Zempelburg (Sepólno Krajenskie), 1900–1939* (Wiesbaden, 1997), 98–101.
15. *KB*, 20.
16. Ibid.
17. Ibid.
18. Her mother, who confounded the police by changing the details of the original testimony, supported Radtke's behavior. *KB*, 20.
19. GStAPK, Rep. I/84a (2.5.1), Nr. 16776, 48–51, Oeffentliche Sitzung des Schwurgerichts zu Konitz, 30 Oct. 1900.
20. Ibid.
21. Ibid.
22. Ibid.
23. Ibid.
24. *MP*, 227.
25. Ibid., 436–38.
26. *KB*, 35
27. *ML*, 87–92.
28. GStAPK, Rep. I/84a (2.5.1), Nr. 16775, 113, Speisinger Protokoll, 27 March 1900, in Settegast, 22 Aug. 1900.
29. *SZ* 36, 291 (25 June 1900).
30. *ML*, 96. This is not from Speisinger's account. In the trial against Moritz Lewy, Martha Lehmann, née Hoffmann, did not shy away from saying this outright.
31. GStAPK, Rep. I/84a (2.5.1), Nr. 16775, 341, Speisinger Protokoll, 27 March 1900, in Settegast, 22 Aug. 1900.

32. Ibid., 349.
33. *ML*, 95–97.
34. See the report on the Speisinger trial in *DZ* 42,468 (6 Oct. 1900).
35. *ML*, 189.
36. *MP*, 414.
37. *SZ* 36,289 (23 June 1900).
38. *SZ* 36,315 (7 July 1900).
39. GStAPK, Rep. I/84a (2.5.1), Nr. 16775, 58, Deposition Anna Lübke, 10 July 1900.
40. *ML*, 41.
41. Ibid., 385.
42. *SZ* 37,323 (13 July 1901)
43. Ibid.
44. *ML*, 32.
45. Ibid., 66.
46. Ibid., 78.
47. GStAPK, Rep. I/84a (2.5.1), Nr. 16776, 290, Kracht, 26 March 1901.
48. *SZ* 36,423 (10 Sept. 1900).
49. See the fascinating work of Kathy Stuart, *Defiled Trades and Social Outcasts: Honor and Ritual Pollution in Early Modern Germany* (Cambridge, 1999), 18, as well as the important work on which it is based: Mary Douglas, *Purity and Danger* (London, 1966).
50. *MP*, 545–46.
51. *SZ* 36,201 (1 May 1900).
52. *MP*, 297; *ML*, 267, 290.
53. *MP*, 569–70; *KB*, 29. Brueggemann referred to her as Helene Lewy. That, however, is the name of her daughter.
54. *MVAA* 10,36 (5 Sept. 1900), 291.
55. *JP* 31,37 (14 Sept. 1900), 384.
56. *ML*, 248.
57. *MP*, 281.
58. Ibid., 399.
59. Ibid., 332.
60. *MVAA* 12,42 (15 Oct. 1902), 325.
61. GStAPK, Rep. 77, Tit. 500, no. 50, Bd. 2, 130, Polizeikonferenz Konitz, 20 May 1900; *SZ* 36,260 (7 June 1900).
62. *MP*, 946–47.
63. Ibid.
64. Ibid., 226.

65. For other early, though unspecific, accusations, see *SZ* 36,144, Beilage (27 March 1900).
66. *SZ* 36,177 (17 April 1900).
67. *ML*, 317.
68. The quotation is from Antonio R. Damasio, *Descartes' Error: Emotion, Reason, and the Human Brain* (New York, 1994), 248.
69. On individual memory, see Daniel L. Schacter, *Searching for Memory: The Brain, the Mind, and the Past* (New York, 1996), and Endel Tulving and Fergus I. M. Craik, *The Oxford Handbook of Memory* (Oxford, 2000).
70. *XK*, 327.
71. A. Eulenburg, "'Retroaktive' Suggestion und Hallucination bei Zeugen," *Nation* (Oct. 20), reprinted in *MVAA* 10,43 (24 Oct. 1900), 340.
72. Elizabeth F. Loftus, Julie Feldman, and Richard Dashiell, "The Reality of Illusory Memories," in *Memory Distortion: How Minds, Brains, and Societies Reconstruct the Past*, ed. Daniel Schacter (Cambridge, Mass., 1995), 65.
73. GStAPK, Rep. I/84a, Nr. 16776, 314–15, Kracht, 26 March 1901.
74. *MP*, 429, 434.
75. *MP*, 349; GStAPK, Rep. I/84a, Nr. 16775, 324, Lautz, 21 Nov. 1900.
76. GStAPK, Rep. I/84a (2.5.1), Nr. 16774, 300–23, Wehn, 3 July 1900.
77. Alan Macfarlane, *Witchcraft in Tudor and Stuart England* (New York, 1970), 168.
78. Keith Thomas, "Anthropology and the Study of English Witchcraft," in Mary Douglas, ed., *Witchcraft Confessions and Accusations* (London, 1970), 68. With respect to twentieth-century accusations, see the pathbreaking work of Robert Gellately, *The Gestapo and German Society: Enforcing Racial Policy, 1933-1945* (Oxford, 1990); Eric A. Johnson, *Nazi Terror: The Gestapo, Jews and Ordinary Germans* (New York, 1999); and the special issue of the *Journal of Modern History* 68,4 (Dec. 1996), entitled "Practices of Denunciation in Modern European History, 1789-1989," ed. Sheila Fitzpatrick and Robert Gellately.
79. Quoted in John Putnam Demos, *Entertaining Satan: Witchcraft and the Culture of Early New England* (New York, 1982), 277. For the argument that large-scale cases of witchcraft accusations are usually dysfunctional, see H. C. Erik Midelfort, *Witch Hunting in Southwestern Germany, 1562–1684: The Social and Intellectual Foundations* (Stanford, 1972), 4.

80. Michael Geyer, "Resistance as an Ongoing Project: Visions of Order, Obligations to Strangers, and Struggles for Civil Society, 1933–1990," in *Resistance against the Third Reich, 1933–1990*, ed. John Boyer and Michael Geyer (Chicago, 1994), 326.

81. Ibid., 341.

CHAPTER FIVE: PERFORMING RITUAL MURDER

1. Jan T. Gross, *Neighbors: The Destruction of the Jewish Community in Jedwabne, Poland* (Princeton, 2001), 19.

2. Ibid., 120–21, 124.

3. For a more detailed treatment, see Werner Bergmann, Christhard Hoffmann, and Helmut Walser Smith, *"Exclusionary Violence": Antisemitic Riots in Modern German History* (Ann Arbor, 2002), 1–4.

4. Clifford Geertz, "Notes on the Balinese Cockfight," in Geertz, *The Interpretation of Cultures* (New York, 1973), 452.

5. *KB*, 9. Mayor Deditius speculated that the anti-Semitic movement got its start because of anger in the Polish Party and the Center Party that Jewish delegates gave decisive votes to the candidate of the German Conservative Party, Arnold Osiander, in the runoff race of the supplementary Landtag election of 4 May 1900. For the results, see Thomas Kühne, *Handbuch der Wahlen zum Preussischen Abgeordnetenhaus, 1867–1918* (Düsseldorf, 1994), 27.

6. GStAPK, Rep. 77, Tit. 500, no. 50, Bd. 1, 87, LA Konitz, 23 April 1900. See, e.g., the story in *Gazetta Grudzionska* 7,83 (12 July 1900), which is based on an article in the *Danziger Allgemeine Zeitung*. A copy of the *Gazetta* can be found in the main library of the University of Torun. For its circulation, see Fritz Schultz, *Die politische Tagespresse Westpreußens* (Deutsch Krone, 1913), 27.

7. On the Neustettin uprisings, see the excellent article by Christhard Hoffmann, "Political Culture and Violence against Minorities: The Antisemitic Riots in Pomerania and West Prussia," in Bergmann, Hoffmann, and Smith, eds., *"Exclusionary Violence,"* 67–92.

8. *JP* 12,31 (4 Aug. 1881), Beilage; *AZJ* 45,31 (2 Aug. 1881), 509.

9. *JP* 12,32 (11 Aug. 1881), 344.

10. Ibid., 343–44.

11. *JP* 12,33 (18 Aug. 1881), 350–51; *AZJ* 45,35 (30 Aug. 1881), 570.

12. *AZJ* 45,35 (30 Aug. 1881), 575.

13. GStAPK, Rep. 77, Tit. 500, no. 50, Bd. 1, 42, LA Konitz, 25 April 1900.

14. Ibid., 105.

15. Ibid.

16. Ibid.

17. Archiv Panstwowe w Bydgoszcz/Akta Starostwo Powiatowe w Chojnicach, 1773–1919, Landratsamt 960 (den Bürgerverein Konitz), Jahresbericht 1902; GStAPK, Rep. 77, Tit. 500, no. 50, Bd. 2, 261, *DZ*, 27 June 1900. See also ibid.,163, Zedlitz, 30 June 1900.

18. *DZ*, 97,28 (June 1900); GStAPK, Rep. 77, Tit. 500, no. 50, Bd. 2, 163, Zedlitz, 30 June 1900.

19. Stefan-Ludwig Hoffmann, "Brothers or Strangers? Jews and Freemasons in Nineteenth-Century Germany," *German History* 18,2 (2000), 152, 157–59.

20. *Mitglieder-Verzeichniss der . . . St. Johannis-Loge . . . im Orient zu Konitz für das Maurerjahr 1899/1900* (Konitz, 1900). A copy of this document can be found in the Staatsbibliothek Berlin (West).

21. For a list of local organizations, see *Addressbuch der Stadt Konitz* (Konitz, 1908), 30–32.

22. On the public sphere, and the argument for a wider conception of it, see Geoff Eley, "Nations, Publics, and Political Cultures: Placing Habermas in the Nineteenth Century," in *Culture/Power/History: A Reader in Contemporary Social Theory*, ed. Nicholas B. Dirks, Geoff Eley, and Sherry B. Ortner (Princeton, 1994), 297–335.

23. Bruno Borowka, *Aus Sage und Geschichte von Konitz* (Konitz, 1919), 106; *SZ*, 23 May 1900.

24. Richard S. Levy, "Continuities and Discontinuities of Anti-Jewish Violence in Modern Germany, 1819–1938," in Bergmann, Hoffmann, and Smith, eds., *"Exclusionary Violence,"* 199.

25. On this poverty and its place in violent ritual, see Thomas Lindenberger and Alf Lüdtke, "Physische Gewalt—eine Kontinuität der Moderne," *Physische Gewalt: Studien zur Geschichte der Neuzeit*, ed. Thomas Lindenberger and Alf Lüdtke (Frankfurt am Main, 1995), 22–27.

26. David Nirenberg, *Communities of Violence: Persecution of Minorities in the Middle Ages* (Princeton, 1996), 201.

27. The text is translated in H. J. Schroeder, *Disciplinary Decrees of the General Councils: Text, Translation, and Commentary* (St. Louis, 1937), 236–96.

28. E. Valentine Daniel, "The Limits of Culture," in *In Near Ruins: Cultural Theory at the End of the Century*, ed. Nicholas B. Dirks (Minneapolis, 1998), 69.

29. Miri Rubin, *Gentile Tales: The Narrative Assault on Late Medieval Jews* (New Haven, 1999), 50.

30. *Germania Judaica*, vol. 2, *Von 1238 bis zur Mitte des 14. Jahrhunderts,* ed. Zvi Averni (Tübingen, 1968), 665–66.

31. Rubin, *Gentile Tales*, 72.

32. *JP* 25 (2 June 1900), 258.

33. GStAPK, Rep. 77, Tit. 500, no. 50, Bd. 1, 194, *Konitzer Tageblatt*, 31 May 1900.

34. In this sense, they showed a family resemblance to the grain rioters famously described by E. P. Thompson, "The Moral Economy of the English Crowd in the Eighteenth-Century," *Past and Present,* no. 50 (1971): 76–136.

35. Victor Turner, "Social Dramas and Ritual Metaphors," in Turner, *Dramas, Fields, and Metaphors: Symbolic Action in Human Society* (Ithaca, 1974), 23-59. Another model for this temporal structure derives from Arnold van Gennep's analysis of rites of passage and is subdivided into separation rites, transition rites, and rites of incorporation. Arnold van Gennep, *The Rites of Passage*, trans. Monika B. Vizedom and Gabrielle L. Caffe (Chicago, 1960), 10–11. For the argument that these ritual structures, and in particular van Gennep's, underlie all theater performance, see Richard Schechner, *Between Theater and Anthropology* (Philadelphia, 1985), 20.

36. Turner, "Social Dramas and Ritual Metaphors," 23–59.

37. On Deggendorf, see Friedrich Lotter, "Hostienfrevelvorwurf und Blutverfälschung bei den Judenverfolgungen von 1298 ('Rintfleisch') und 1336–1338 ('Armleder')," in *Fälschungen im Mittelalter*, ed. Monumenta Germaniae Historica (Hanover, 1988), 533–83.

38. *Germania Judaica*, 2:144, n. 4; 2:144, n. 4, 666.

39. Ibid., 840.

40. Ibid., 604.

41. GStAPK, Rep. 77, Tit. 500, no. 50, Bd. 1, 222, LA Konitz, 4 June 1900. See also ibid., Bd. 2, 30, Advocate Appelbaum to CVdSjG, 10 June 1900.

42. Manfred Gailus, *Strasse und Brot: Sozialer Protest in den deutschen Staaten unter besonderer Berücksichtigung Preußens, 1847–1849* (Göttingen, 1990), 114; Thomas Lindenberger, "Die 'verdiente Tracht Prügel': Ein kurzes Kapitel über das Lynchen im wilhelminischen Berlin," in Lindenberger and Lüdtke, eds., *Physische Gewalt*, 197-98, n. 25.

43. On the ritual of lynching, and especially its sacrificial content, see Orlando Patterson, *Rituals of Blood: Consequences of Slavery in Two American Centuries* (New York, 1999), 169–232; and Grace Elizabeth Hale, *Making Whiteness: The Culture of Segregation in the South* (New York, 1999), 199–240. For the differences between small- and large-scale lynching, see W. Fitzhugh Brundage, *Lynching in the New South: Georgia and Virginia, 1880–1930* (Urbana, 1993).

44. Anton Blok, "The Enigma of Senseless Violence," in *Meanings of Violence*, ed. Göran Aijmer and Jon Abbink (Oxford, 2000), 31.

45. Henry J. Kellermann, "From Imperial to National-Socialist Germany: Recollections of a German-Jewish Youth Leader," *Leo Baeck Institute Yearbook* 39 (1994), 310.

46. See now William M. Reddy, *The Navigation of Feeling: A Framework for the History of Emotions* (Cambridge, 2001).

47. Philip G. Zimbardo et al., "Reflections on the Stanford Prison Experiment: Genesis, Transformations, Consequences," in *Obedience to Authority: Current Perspectives on the Milgram Paradigm*, ed. Thomas Blass (Mahwah, N.J., 2000), 193–238.

48. Here I follow Maurice Bloch, "Symbols, Song, Dance and Features of Articulation: Is Religion an Extreme Form of Traditional Authority," in Bloch, *Ritual, History and Power: Selected Papers in Anthropology* (London, 1989), 19–45.

49. Ibid., 27.

50. J. L. Austin, *How to Do Things with Words* (New York, 1965), 108. Austin famously divided the use of speech, or more precisely speech acts, into three categories: locutionary acts, where words refer to things; illocutionary acts, where words bring about an immediate and specific effect; and perlocutionary acts, where words initiate a set of possible consequences.

51. *MP*, 429.

52. Judith Butler, *Excitable Speech: A Politics of the Performative* (New York, 1997), 9.

53. Toni Morrison, *Lecture and Speech of Acceptance, upon the Award of the Nobel Prize for Literature* (New York, 1994), 16.

54. Butler, *Excitable Speech*, 52–65.

55. *MVAA* 13,41 (19 Oct. 1903), 324.

56. Orlando Patterson, *Slavery and Social Death: A Comparative Study* (Cambridge, Mass., 1982), 38–51.

57. Ibid.

58. The distribution of these cases, as well as the range of sentences, was as follows:

Town	Number	Minimum	Maximum
Stolp	33	4 weeks	3 years
Bütow	10	fine	10 months
Konitz	24	fine	1 year
Czersk	10	fine	8 months
Berent	9	fine	12 months
Rummelsburg	4	4 weeks	1 year
Hammerstein	2	1 month	2 months

The statistics are from M. Horwitz, "Konitz," *Im deutschen Reich* 7, 1 (1901), 571–605.

59. *MVAA* 10,31 (1 Aug. 1900), 245; *SZ* 347 (27 July 1900); *DZ* 349 (28 July 1900).

60. *MVAA* 10,50 (12 Dec. 1900), 393–94.

61. GStAPK, Rep. I/84a (2.5.1), Nr. 16777, 111–14, Verein zur Aufklärung des Konitzer Mordes, 4 March 1901.

62. Ibid., Nr. 16776, 37–48, Konitz, 20 Dec. 1900. Significantly, the signature of the Polish delegate to the Reichstag, Wladislaus von Wolzlegier, is absent.

63. Zedlitz's statement in GStAPK, Rep. 77, Tit. 500, no. 50, Bd. 1, 216, *DZ* 29 June 1900. On members of the town council and on a meeting on June 27 of "citizens who enjoy general trust in our town," see ibid., Bd. 2, 163, LA Konitz, 30 June 1900. On Dr. Praetorius, *MVAA* 40 (1900), 316.

64. GStAPK, Rep. 77, Tit. 500, no. 50, Bd. 3, 161, *Konitzer Anzeiger*, 5 Dec. 1900.

65. The passage from the *Ostdeutsche Zeitung* is quoted in *IdR* 7,5 (1901), 286.

66. GStAPK, Rep. 77, Tit. 500, no. 50, Bd. 1, 70, Magistrat der Stadt Konitz, 27 April 1900. See also *SZ*, 182 (20 April 1900), citing *Danziger neueste Nachrichten*.

67. *MVAA* 10,26 (27 June 1900), 202.

68. *SZ*, 182 (20 April 1900), citing *Danziger neueste Nachrichten*.

69. GStAPK, Rep. 77, Tit. 500, no. 50, Bd. 3, 157, *Konitzer Tageblatt*, 7 Dec. 1900.

70. *SZ* 297 (28 June 1900).

71. *MVAA* 13,10 (4 March 1903), 70.

72. The election returns are in *Vierteljahrshefte zur Statistik des deutschen*

Reichs 12,1 (1903), 3:44–45. The anti-Semitic parties did not put up a candidate in the electoral district of Konitz for the Reichstag elections of 1903; but this was because the district's religious and electoral composition always ensured a Polish victory. In the first ballot in the district of Schlochau-Flatow, the anti-Semites ran against candidates from the National Liberal Party, the Center Party, the Polish Party, and the Agrarian League. In this round, the anti-Semites received 33 percent of the vote and were forced to a runoff with the Polish party, which captured 25 percent of the ballots. In the second election, the anti-Semites won 64 percent and the Polish Party 36. It is difficult to gauge precisely what the second round meant, since even the Jews faced a difficult dilemma when confronted with a Polish and an anti-Semitic candidate. See *MVAA* 13,25 (24 June 1903).

73. *KB*, 9. As a result of the anti-Semitic agitation, the population in other towns declined as well. See *Jeschrun* 1,46 (17 May 1901).

74. *Addressbuch der Stadt Konitz* (Konitz, 1906).

75. *Jeschrun* 35 (23 Aug. 1901); Kellermann, "From Imperial to National-Socialist Germany," 310.

76. *Jeschrun* 27 (28 June 1901), 779. According to the *MVAA* 10,36 (5 Sept. 1900), 294, Hoffmann had also accused two Jewish women of slander, but the report does not name them.

77. *SZ* 421 (8 Sept. 1900); *DZ* 474 (10 Oct. 1900).

78. *MVAA* 11,27 (3 July 1901), 232.

79. GStAPK, Rep. I/84a (2.5.1), Nr. 16774, 192–93, Settegast, 6 June 1900; *MVAA* 10,44 (31 Oct. 1900), 345.

80. *MVAA* 11,27 (3 July 1901), 232.

81. *MVAA* 12,15 (9 April 1902), 54.

82. GStAPK, Rep. I/84a (2.5.1), Nr. 16774, 331, Ministry of Justice to Settegast, 15 July 1900.

83. Ibid., Nr. 16777, 333, Schweigger, 18 June 1902. The case, initiated in November 1900, was dismissed.

84. *MVAA* 11, 26 (26 June 1901), 222

85. GStAPK, Rep. I/84a (2.5.1), Nr. 16777, 87–88, Schweigger, 17 July 1901; *MVAA* 10,38 (19 Sept. 1900), 299–300; *MVAA* 10,40 (3 Oct. 1900), 316. The anti-Semitic Hofrichter was transferred as well. See GStAPK, Rep. 77, Tit. 500, no. 50, Bd. 2, 191, Studt, 13 July 1900.

CHAPTER 6: THE KILLER

1. *Die Gutachten der Sachverständigen über den Konitzer Mord*, ed. CVdSjG (Berlin, 1903), 55.

2. Ibid.
3. Ibid., 39.
4. Ibid., 56.
5. Ibid, 65.
6. GStAPK, Rep. I/84a (2.5.1), Nr. 16774, 300–323, Wehn, 3 July 1900.
7. *ML,* 91.
8. *MP,* 550.
9. GStAPK, Rep. 77, Tit. 500, no.50, Bd. 2, 137, Kommission zur winter-schen Mordsache, 24 May 1900.
10. Ibid.
11. GStAPK, Rep. I/84a (2.5.1), Nr. 16774, 300–323, Wehn, 3 July 1900
12. Ibid.
13. Ibid.
14. GStAPK, Rep. 77, Tit. 500, no. 50, Bd. 3, 94, Denkschrift, 11 Nov. 1900.
15. *ML,* 90.
16. GStAPK, Rep. I/84a (2.5.1), Nr. 16774, 300–323, Wehn, 3 July 1900.
17. *MVAA* 10,48 (28 Nov. 1900), 378.
18. GStAPK, Rep. I/84a (2.5.1), Nr. 16774, 300–323, Wehn, 3 July 1900.
19. Ibid.
20. Ibid., Nr. 16776, 296, Kracht, 26 Mar. 1901.
21. Ibid.; ibid., 67, Oberste Staatsanwalt Marienwerder, 17 Dec. 1900.
22. Ulrich Linse, "'Geschlechtsnot der Jugend': Ueber Jugendbewegung und Sexualität," in *"Mit uns zieht die neue Zeit": Der Mythos der Jugend,* ed. Thomas Koebner, Rolf-Peter Jenz, and Frank Trommler (Frankfurt am Main, 1985), 245–309.
23. *ML,* 89.
24. Hjalmar Söderberg, *Martin Bricks Jugend* (Leipzig, 1904), 136, cited by Regina Schulte, *Sperrbezirke: Tugendhaftigkeit und Prostitution in der bürgerlichen Welt,* 2nd ed. (Frankfurt am Main, 1984), 151.
25. GStAPK, Rep. I/84a (2.5.1), Nr. 16776, 296, Kracht, 26 March 1901.
26. Ibid.
27. Ibid., Nr. 16774, 279, Settegast, 26 June 1900.
28. Ibid., Nr. 16776, 298, Kracht, 26 March 1901.
29. Ibid., Nr. 16774, 300-323, Wehn, 3 July 1900 (310–12).
30. Ibid., Nr. 16776, 211–15, deposition Marie Sawischewski, 11 Jan. 1901.
31. Ibid.
32. Ibid.
33. Ibid.
34. Ibid.

35. Ibid., 217–18, deposition August Johann Pikarski, 17 Jan. 1901.
36. Ibid., 220–21.
37. Ibid., 224, deposition Johann Gast, 16 Jan. 1901.
38. Ibid., 227.
39. Ibid., 229–30.
40. Ibid., 153–54, Schweigger, 23 Jan. 1901.
41. Ibid., 290, Kracht, 26 March 1901.
42. Ibid., 281.
43. GStAPK, Rep. 77, Tit. 500, no. 50, Bd. 2, 140, Kommittee zur winter-schen Mordsache, 24 May 1900.
44. GStAPK, Rep. I/84a (2.5.1), Nr. 16776, 71, Oberste Staatsanwalt Marienwerder, 17. Dec. 1900.
45. *MVAA* 10,19 (5 May 1900), 145.
46. GStAPK, Rep. 77, Tit. 500, no. 50, Bd. 2, 57, Gustav Schiller, 19 May 1900.
47. *MVAA* 10,19 (9 May 1900), 145.
48. *MP,* 329; *MVAA* 12,42 (15 Oct. 1902), 325.
49. *MP,* 329.
50. Ibid., 327–28.
51. GStAPK, Rep. I/84a (2.5.1), Nr. 16776, Oberste Staatsanwalt Marienwerder, 17 Dec. 1900.
52. Ibid., 151–52, Schweigger, 23 Jan. 1901.
53. GStAPK, Rep. 77, Tit. 500, no. 50, Bd. 3, 94, Denkschrift, 11 Nov. 1900.
54. GStAPK, Rep. I/84a (2.5.1), Nr. 16774, 109–11, Settegast, 30 May 1900; ibid., 300–323, Wehn, 3 July 1900.
55. Ibid., 109–10, Settegast, 30 May 1900.
56. Ibid.
57. GStAPK, Rep. I/84a (2.5.1), Nr. 16776, 152–53, Schweigger, 23 Jan. 1901.
58. Ibid.
59. Ibid., 210, Schweigger, 27 Feb. 1901.
60. Ibid., Nr. 16774, 300–323, Wehn, 3 July 1900.
61. Ibid., Nr. 16776, 114, Schweigger, 27 Feb. 1901.
62. Ibid., 289, Kracht, 26 Mar. 1901.
63. Ibid., 209, Schweigger, 27 Feb. 1901.
64. *MVAA* 11,7 (13 Feb. 1901),58.
65. GStAPK, Rep. I/84a (2.5.1), Nr. 16776, 303, Kracht, 26 Mar. 1901.
66. Ibid.

67. Ibid., 312.
68. Ibid., 310–11.
69. Ibid., 312–15.
70. Ibid., 315.
71. Ibid., 316.
72. GStAPK, Rep. 77, Tit. 50, Bd. 3, 102, joint memorandum of the minister of justice and the interior, 11 Nov. 1900.
73. GStAPK, Rep. I/84a (2.5.1), Nr. 16776, 68, chief prosecutor Marienwerder, 17 Dec. 1900.
74. Ibid.
75. Ibid., Nr. 16777, 93–100, Lautz, 25 June 1901. The following discussion, unless otherwise noted, is based on this memorandum.
76. *ML,* 216.
77. GStAPK, Rep. 77, Tit. 500, no. 50, Bd. 2, 56, Schiller, 19 May 1900.
78. GStAPK, Rep. I/84a (2.5.1), Nr. 16777, 88, Schweigger, 17 July 1901.
79. Ibid.
80. Ibid., 93–100, Lautz, 25 June 1901.
81. Ibid., 88, Schweigger, Konitz, 17 July 1901.
82. Ibid., 90.
83. Simon Schama, *Dead Certainties* (New York, 1991), 320.

EPILOGUE

1. *Jeschrun* 3,22 (29 May 1903), 282. Earlier information, before the monument was erected in May, reported the inscription as follows: "The murderers shall be warned. The Christians shall protect their dearest possessions." *MVAA* 11,16 (17 April 1901), 144.
2. Stefan Rohrbacher and Michael Schmidt, *Judenbilder: Kulturgeschichte antijüdischer Mythen und antisemitischer Vorurteile* (Reinbeck-Hamburg, 1991), 352. The postcard appeared in March 1901. See *MVAA* 11,13 (1901), 113. The earliest reference to an anti-Semitic postcard that I have been able to find is to a postcard announcing the 20,000-mark reward. See *SZ* 293 (26 June 1900).
3. Rohrbacher and Schmidt, *Judenbilder,* 352. See also Helmut Gold and Georg Heuberger, eds., *Abgestempelt: Judenfeindliche Postkarten* (Frankfurt am Main, 1999), 162-64.
4. GStAPK, Rep. I/84a, Nr. 16785, Berlin, 16 Oct. 1903.
5. Ibid., *Deutsche Zeitung,* 16 Oct. 1903.
6. GStAPK, Rep. I/84a, Nr. 16778, 35, Schweigger, 20 May 1904.
7. Ibid., 37–38.

8. The following discussion, unless otherwise noted, is based on GStAPK, Rep. I/84a, Nr. 16778, 39–49, Schweigger, 19 May 1904.

9. Ibid., 33–48, Schweigger, 20 May 1904.

10. Ibid., 35, Schweigger, 20 May 1904.

11. According to a summary of his views in ibid., Otto Kröhnke, 23 May 1907.

12. Ibid., 101–7, Schweigger, 4 June 1907

13. *Der Große Brockhaus*, 15th ed. (Leipzig, 1931), 10:389.

14. *Die evangelischen General-Kirchenvisitationen in den von Ost- und Westpreußen sowie Posen 1920 abgetrennten Kirchenkreisen*, ed. Walther Hubatsch (Göttingen, 1971), 154. On nationality conflicts in the region, see Mieczyslaw Wojciechowski, "Nationalitätenverhältnisse in Westpreußen zu Beginn des 20. Jahrhunderts (1900–1920)," *Historische Grenzlandschaften Ostmitteleuropas*, ed. Mieczyslaw Wojciechowski and Ralph Shattkowsky (Torun, 1996), 75–96. On the 1920s and 1930s, see Mieczyslaw Wojciechowski, *Miasta Pomorza Nadwislanskiego i Kujaw w okreisie I wojny swiatowej oraz w miedzywojennym dwudziestoleciu, 1914–1939* (Torun, 2000).

15. Quoted in Wojciechowski, "Nationalitätenverhältnisse in Westpreußen," 94.

16. Christian Jansen and Arno Weckbecker, *Der "Volksdeutsche Selbstschutz" in Polen 1939/40* (Munich, 1992), 214.

Bibliography

I have divided this bibliography into three sections: the first for archival collections; the second for printed documents, including contemporary works pertaining to the Konitz case; and the third for secondary works that have influenced the writing of this book in matters of more than just detail. Except for the listing of archives, the bibliography makes no claim to completeness and does not include all the sources cited in the notes. Rather, it is meant to give the reader a sense of the main sources and to offer suggestions for further exploration. To this end, I have briefly annotated the final section.

I. Archives

Archiv Panstwowe w Bydgoszcz
    Akta Miasta Chojnice, 1801–1937
    Akta Starostwo Powiatowe w Chojnicach, 1773–1919

Brandenburgisches Landeshauptarchiv Potsdam
    30 Berlin C Polizeipräsidium Berlin

The Church of Jesus Christ of Latter-Day Saints, Family History Library, Salt Lake City
    Konitz, Standesamt, Zivilregister, 1874–1877
    Katholische Kirche Konitz, Kirchenbuch, 1651–1890
    Evangelische Kirche Konitz, Kirchenbuch, 1632–1917

Geheimes Staatsarchiv Preussischer Kulturbesitz, Berlin-Dahlem

Rep. 77 Ministerium des Innerns
Rep. 81 Justizministeriums

II. PRINTED DOCUMENTS

A. NEWSPAPERS

Allgemeine Zeitung des Judentums
Antisemitische Correspondenz
Danziger Zeitung
Gazetta Grudzionska
Im deutschen Reich
Jeschrun
Jüdische Presse
Konitzer Tageblatt
Mitteilungen aus dem Verein zur Abwehr des Antisemitismus
Staatsbürgerzeitung

B. STENOGRAPHIC COURT RECORDS

Der Konitzer Blutmord vor dem Berliner Gericht: Die Verhandlungen des Pressprozesses gegen die "Staatsbürgerzeitung" vor der II. Strafkammer des Königl. Landgerichts I. Berlin: Verlag der Staatsbürgerzeitung, 1902.

Der Prozeß gegen Masloff und Genossen (Konitz, 25.10–10.11.1900) nach stenographischer Aufnahme. Berlin: H. G. Hermann, 1900.

Der Prozeß gegen Moritz Lewy (Konitz, 13.–16. Februar 1901) nach stenographischer Aufnahme. Berlin: H. G. Hermann, 1901

Der Xantener Knabenmord vor dem Schwurgericht zu Cleve, 4.–14. Juli 1892; vollständiger Bericht. Berlin: Verlag Siegfried Cronbach, 1893.

C. CONTEMPORARY ACCOUNTS OF THE KONITZ CASE

Der Blutmord in Konitz. Introduction by Max Liebermann von Sonnenberg. 8th ed. Berlin: Deutschnationale Buchhandlung, 1901.

Borowka, Bruno. *Aus Sage und Geschichte von Konitz.* Konitz: Johannes Schmolke, 1919.

George, Gustav. *Enthüllungen zur Konitzer Mordaffäre.* Berlin: G. Koenig, 1903.

Die Gutachten der Sachverständigen über den Konitzer Mord. Edited by Centralverein deutscher Staatsbürger jüdischen Glaubens. Berlin: Centralverein, 1903.

Hamburger, Hermann. *Der Konitzer Mord: Ein Beitrag zur Klärung.* Breslau: Preuss and Jünger, 1900.

Nathan, Sally. *Motivia: Die Trägödie von Konitz.* Berlin: W. Schroeder, 1901.

Sutor, Gustav. *Der Konitzer Mord und seine Folgen.* Berlin: Hugo Schilderer, 1900.

Zelle, W. *Wer hat Ernst Winter ermordert? Eine psychologische Studie.* Braunschweig: R. Sattler, 1904.

III. SECONDARY WORKS

Anderson, Margaret Lavinia. *Practicing Democracy: Elections and Political Culture in Imperial Germany.* Princeton: Princeton University Press, 2000. Major revisionist work arguing that in the imperial period Germans were practicing democracy and getting better at it. This work is also important for emphasizing communal pressures over hierarchical structures in German political culture.

Austin, J. L. *How to Do Things with Words.* 2nd ed. Cambridge, Mass.: Harvard University Press, 1975. Groundbreaking argument about how context determines the meaning of speech.

Avneri, Zvi, ed. *Germania Judaica,* 2 vols. *Von 1238 bis zur Mitte des 14. Jahrhunderts.* Tübingen: J. C. B. Mohr, 1968. Indispensable reference work on Jewish communities and anti-Semitism in the medieval period.

Bergmann, Werner, Christhard Hoffmann, and Helmut Walser Smith, eds. *"Exclusionary Violence": Antisemitic Riots in Modern German History.* Ann Arbor: University of Michigan Press, 2002. A collection of essays that highlights anti-Semitic violence in the German tradition of anti-Semitism.

Blackbourn, David. *Marpingen: Apparitions of the Virgin Mary in a Nineteenth-Century German Village.* New York: Alfred E. Knopf, 1994. Important microhistory, focusing on the Catholics and the impact of the state.

Bloch, Maurice. *Ritual, History and Power: Selected Papers in Anthropology.* London: Athlone Press, 1989. On the relation between ritual and belief.

Blok, Anton. *Honour and Violence.* Cambridge: Polity, 2001. Insightful essays on the meanings of violence.

Browning, Christopher R. *Ordinary Men: Reserve Police Battalion 101 and the Final Solution* in Poland. New York: HarperCollins, 1992. Exemplary social and psychological study of a battalion of men who massacred Jews during the Holocaust.

Butler, Judith. *Excitable Speech: A Politics of the Performative*. New York: Routledge, 1997. On hate speech.

Chazan, Robert. *Medieval Stereotypes and Modern Antisemitism*. Berkeley: University of California Press, 1997. Astute essays insisting on the continuous legacy of anti-Semitism amid changing circumstances.

Davis, Natalie Zemon. "The Rites of Violence." In Davis, *Society and Culture in Early Modern France*, 152–87. Stanford: Stanford University Press, 1975. Early, seminal essay on the ritualistic aspects of collective violence.

Demos, John Putnam. *Entertaining Satan: Witchcraft and the Culture of Early New England*. New York: Oxford University Press, 1982. Especially good on the community pressures that engendered witchcraft accusations, this book is also a model of a multidisciplinary approach to the study of a community.

Frankel, Jonathan. *The Damascus Affair: "Ritual Murder," Politics, and the Jews in 1840*. Cambridge: Cambridge University Press, 1997. Thorough account of a famous ritual-murder case and its repercussions throughout Europe.

Gay, Peter. *The Cultivation of Hatred*. Vol. 2 of *The Bourgeois Experience Victoria to Freud*. New York: W. W. Norton, 1993. On the manifold manifestations of aggression.

———. *Freud, Jews, and Other Germans: Masters and Victims in Modernist Culture*. Oxford: Oxford University Press, 1978. Compelling for the larger framework of German-Jewish history.

Gellately, Robert. *The Gestapo and German Society: Enforcing Racial Policy, 1933–1945*. Oxford: Oxford University Press, 1990. On how the Gestapo depended on neighborhood informants.

Genette, Gérard. *Narrative Discourse: An Essay in Method*. Translated by Jane E. Lewin. Ithaca: Cornell University Press, 1980. A theory about the shifting perspectives of the storyteller.

Geyer, Michael. "Resistance as an Ongoing Project: Visions of Order, Obligations to Strangers, and Struggles for Civil Society, 1933–1990." In *Resistance against the Third Reich*, 1933–1990, ed. John Boyer and Michael Geyer, 325–50. Chicago: University of Chicago Press, 1994. Interprets central themes in the Third Reich as a breakdown in human solidarity.

Goldhagen, Daniel Jonah. *Hitler's Willing Executioners: Ordinary Germans and the Holocaust*. New York: Alfred A. Knopf, 1996. Monocausal thesis about the origins of the Holocaust: Germans, at least since the nineteenth century, harbored "eliminationist anti-Semitism."

Gross, Jan T. *Neighbors: The Destruction of the Jewish Community in Jedwabne, Poland*. Princeton: Princeton University Press, 2001. The recently discovered story of how the Poles of a small town massacred their Jewish neighbors in the midst of the Holocaust.

Harris, James F. *The People Speak!: Anti-Semitism and Emancipation in Nineteenth-Century Bavaria*. Ann Arbor: University of Michigan Press, 1994. Important for gauging the depth of rural anti-Semitism in Germany.

Hsia, R. Po-chia. *The Myth of Ritual Murder: Jews and Magic in Reformation Germany*. New Haven: Yale University Press, 1988. A series of case studies.

Kertzer, David I. *The Kidnapping of Edgardo Mortara*. New York: Vintage Books, 1998. A brilliantly told social history of the most celebrated case of Catholic anti-Semitism in the nineteenth century.

Klier, John D., and Schlomo Lambroza, eds. *Pogroms: Anti-Jewish Violence in Modern Russian History*. Cambridge: Cambridge University Press, 1992. Collection of essays arguing that the czarist government did not initiate the pogroms, as is commonly thought; rather, the pogroms were a consequence of grassroots agitation.

Langmuir, Gavin I. *Toward a Definition of Antisemitism*. Berkeley: University of California Press, 1990. Controversial essays on the local origins of the first ritual-murder accusations.

Levy, Richard S. *The Downfall of the Anti-Semitic Political Parties in Imperial Germany*. New Haven: Yale University Press, 1975. Shows how party squabbles and infighting led to the early demise of political anti-Semitism.

Lotter, Friedrich. "Hostienfrevelvorwurf und Blutwundverfälschung bei den Judenverfolgungen von 1298 ('Rintfleisch') und 1336–1338 ('Armleder')." In *Fälschungen im Mittelalter*. Edited by Monumenta Germaniae Historica, 533–84. Hanover: Hahnsche Buchhandlung, 1988. Careful, detailed study of medieval host desecrations.

Malamud, Bernard. *The Fixer*. New York: Dell, 1966. Arresting fictional account of a Jewish man falsely accused of committing ritual murder.

Meyer, Michael A., ed., with the assistance of Michael Brenner. *German-Jewish History in Modern Times*. Vols 1–4. New York: Columbia University Press, 1996–98. These volumes constitute both the definitive account representing the current state of knowledge and the starting place for further reading in this field.

Moore, R. I. *The Formation of a Persecuting Society: Power and Deviance in Western Europe, 950–1250*. Oxford: Basil Blackwell, 1987. Important, if dated, synthesis.

Morrison, Toni. *Playing in the Dark: Whiteness and the Literary Imagination*. New York: Vintage Books, 1993. On the ways in which race influences literature.

Muir, Edward, and Guido Ruggiero. *Microhistory and the Lost Peoples of Europe*. Baltimore: Johns Hopkins University Press, 1991. Concise statement of microhistory as a method. See especially Muir's introduction and the essay, "The Name of the Game," by Carlo Ginzburg and Carlo Poni.

Nirenberg, David. *Communities of Violence: Persecution of Minorities in the Middle Ages*. Princeton: Princeton University Press, 1996. Powerfully argues that anti-Semitic violence must be understood in its precise historical context and not as a timeless malady of Western history.

Nonn, Christoph. "Zwischenfall in Konitz: Antisemitismus und Nationalismus im preußischen Osten um 1900." *Historische Zeitschrift* 266,2 (1998), 387–418. Important article on the Konitz case that argues, mistakenly, I believe, for the importance of economic crisis in causing the eruption of anti-Semitic violence.

Patterson, Orlando. *Rituals of Blood: Consequences of Slavery in Two American Centuries*. New York: Basic Civitas, 1999. The second chapter brilliantly reveals the ritual qualities of Euro-American lynching practices, which in some ways paralleled the violence accompanying ritual murder charges.

Rohrbacher, Stefan. *Gewalt im Biedermeier: Antijüdische Ausschreitungen in Vormärz und Revolution (1815–1848/49).* Frankfurt am Main: Campus, 1993. Comprehensive work on anti-Semitic violence in Germany in the first half of the nineteenth century.

Rohrbacher, Stefan, and Michael Schmidt. *Judenbilder: Kulturgeschichte antijüdischer Mythen und antisemitischer Vorurteile.* Reinbeck-Hamburg: Rowohlt, 1991. Includes material on the cultural history of the ritual-murder charge.

Rubin, Miri. *Gentile Tales: The Narrative Assault on Late Medieval Jews.* New Haven: Yale University Press, 1999. On the narrative construction of host desecration charges.

Schacter, Daniel L. *Searching for Memory: The Brain, the Mind, and the Past.* New York: Basic Books, 1996. Excellent introduction to current research on individual memory and its distortions.

Schechner, Richard. *Between Theater and Anthropology.* Philadelphia: University of Pennsylvania Press, 1985. Argues that theatrical performance follows logic akin to ritual.

Schroubek, Georg R. "Der 'Ritualmord' von Polna: Traditioneller und moderner Wahnglaube." In *Antisemitismus und jüdische Geschichte: Studien zu Ehren von Herbert A. Strauss,* ed. Rainer Erb and Michael Schmidt, 149–171. Berlin: Wissenschaftlicher Autorenverlag, 1987. Concise, expert treatment of the Polna case.

Strack, Hermann L. *The Jew and Human Sacrifice.* Translated by Henry Blanchamp. New York: Bloch, 1909. Still the best general introduction to the ritual-murder charge in Western history.

Toch, Michael. *Die Juden im mittelalterlichen Reich.* Munich: Oldenbourg, 1998. Best short introduction to the current state of research concerning Jews in the Middle Ages.

Turner, Victor. *Dramas, Fields, and Metaphors: Symbolic Action in Human Society.* Ithaca: Cornell University Press, 1974. Fundamental for understanding ritual process.

Vital, David. *A People Apart: The Jews in Europe, 1789–1939.* Oxford:

Oxford University Press, 1999. Mainly about anti-Semitism and the Jewish reaction to it.

Vogt, Bernhard. "Die 'Atmosphäre eines Narrenhauses': Eine Ritual-mordlegende um die Ermordung des Schülers Ernst Winter in Konitz." In *Zur Geschichte und Kultur der Juden in Ost- und Westpreußen*, ed. Michael Brocke, Margret Heitmann, and Harald Lordick, 545–78. Hildesheim: Georg Olms Verlag, 2000. Short, accurate, narrative account of the Konitz case.

Index

Page number in *italics* refer to illustrations.

DATE DUE
